CW00349730

Rowntree's: The Early History

For Anne, Rachael and Rebecca –
on the front line in 2020

By the same author

Cadbury & Fry Through Time
A History of Chocolate in York
Old Bournville
Confectionery in Yorkshire
Tea: A Very British Beverage
Coffee: A Drink for the Devil
The Rowntree Family of York
The Rowntrees: Tales from a Chocolate Family
Old York
A History of Sweets

Rowntree's

The Early History

Paul Chrystal

First published in Great Britain in 2021 by
Pen & Sword History
An imprint of
Pen & Sword Books Ltd
Yorkshire – Philadelphia

Copyright © Paul Chrystal 2021

ISBN 978 1 52677 889 5

The right of Paul Chrystal to be identified as Author of this work has
been asserted by him in accordance with the Copyright, Designs and
Patents Act 1988.

A CIP catalogue record for this book is
available from the British Library.

All rights reserved. No part of this book may be reproduced or
transmitted in any form or by any means, electronic or mechanical
including photocopying, recording or by any information storage and
retrieval system, without permission from the Publisher in writing.

Typeset by Mac Style
Printed and bound by CPI Group (UK) Ltd,
Croydon, CR0 4YY

Pen & Sword Books Limited incorporates the imprints of Atlas,
Archaeology, Aviation, Discovery, Family History, Fiction, History,
Maritime, Military, Military Classics, Politics, Select, Transport,
True Crime, Air World, Frontline Publishing, Leo Cooper, Remember
When, Seaforth Publishing, The Praetorian Press, Wharncliffe
Local History, Wharncliffe Transport, Wharncliffe True Crime
and White Owl.

For a complete list of Pen & Sword titles please contact

PEN & SWORD BOOKS LIMITED
47 Church Street, Barnsley, South Yorkshire, S70 2AS, England
E-mail: enquiries@pen-and-sword.co.uk
Website: www.pen-and-sword.co.uk

Or

PEN AND SWORD BOOKS
1950 Lawrence Rd, Havertown, PA 19083, USA
E-mail: Uspen-and-sword@casematepublishers.com
Website: www.penandswordbooks.com

Contents

About the Author

Paul Chrystal has classics degrees from the universities of Hull and Southampton and is the author of 100 or so published books, a number of which are about confectionery and beverages. He has written features on aspects of the history of food and drink for the *Daily Express* and for a number of history magazines; he has appeared on the BBC World Service, Radio 4's *PM* programme and various BBC local radio stations talking on a wide range of subjects, but notably confectionery. Paul has also contributed to a six-part series for BBC2 'celebrating the history of some of Britain's most iconic craft industries' – in this case chocolate in York, which aired in 2019. He has been history advisor for a number of York tourist attractions relating to chocolate including 'York's Chocolate Experience'. He is also editor of *York Historian*, the journal of the Yorkshire Architectural and York Archaeological Society. In 2019, he was guest speaker for the Vassar College (New York) London Programme with Goldsmiths University speaking to US social history students on the history of chocolate.

paul.chrystal@btinternet.com
www.paulchrystal.com

Acknowledgements

No book is the work of one person alone. This book certainly is not and that is why I must thank the following for their assistance and generosity: without them it would be a much diminished work. Thanks to, in no particular order, Mark Sessions and W. K. Sessions for permission to use images published in *The Tukes of York*: Nicholas Melia at the Borthwick Institute for Archives, University of York, for the Joseph Rowntree Foundation photographs and allowing access to numerous other primary sources; Raoul Guise and his excellent website; Dr Catherine Oakley, executive secretary at The Rowntree Society; Michael and Ian Collinson for permission to quote from the Pavement shop ledger book; Laura Yeoman, archivist (access and engagement) at Explore York Libraries and Archives, York Explore Library Learning Centre. Thanks too to John Lazenby, grandson of Percy Lazenby, for filling a gap in our industrial history which few knew even existed when he provided information on the elusive Lazenby & Son (York) Ltd. I am also grateful to Sue Major, John Stevens and Mavis Morris of Clements Hall Historical Society for permission to use their research on York Confectionery Company and H. Backhouse & Co.

Introduction

T he Rowntree family, especially Henry and the younger Joseph Rowntree, are, along with the Frys, Cadburys, Mars and Terrys, synonymous with the birth and growth of the chocolate industry in Britain. Between them, they *were* the chocolate industry in Britain for many years.

This book charts the fascinating story behind the creation and development of the chocolate empire that was Rowntree's. It is, however, important to place this in the context of the industrial and commercial landscape of York at the time of Rowntree's foundation, and of the confectionery industry in York, England and continental Europe. Background information to the early history of Rowntree's, therefore, comes by way of chapters on the early history of the Rowntree family, contemporary York, the chocolate industry in York, in the UK, and in Europe, the relationship between Quakers and chocolate, and the Tuke family business – without whom there would have been no Rowntree's.

Henry, it is usually forgotten, was the founder of Rowntree's. He made the momentous decision to sign the deal with the Tukes and we join him in those early days of the fledgling company and watch how he helped it through some very dark and occasionally humorous times in what was then a very shambolic set-up – cash-strapped and making it up as the company lurched from crisis to crisis. Henry made the pivotal decision to take the Rowntree family into the manufacturing of chocolate but he was an easily distracted man, and he also took it to the brink of disaster. Paradoxically, his fervent pursuit of Quaker orthodoxies took his mind off the day job to such a degree that he had to call in his elder brother to save the company.

It was Joseph, his elder brother, who became the driving force to eventual global success, mixing his hectic business life with acts of philanthropy and enlightened, ahead-of-its-time industrial management, all of which paved the way for decent wages, pensions, insurance and mutual respect in the workplace at large. Charity work extended beyond the factory to lift many of his workers and others out of the slums of York and relocate them to a healthy garden village where comfortable, sanitary housing awaited them as well as a rewarding social life. His philanthropy extended beyond New Earswick – one of the UK's most successful industrial housing projects – to York residents generally by the provision of an extensive park, public swimming pool and education for children and adults by way of two schools and a progressive programme of adult education. As stated above, context is given with chapters on the commercial environment the Rowntree's start-up found itself in during nineteenth-century York. This includes the advancements in chocolate production and marketing, early twentieth-century rivals in the domestic and overseas markets, and mergers and acquisitions in an increasingly competitive and brutal industry and marketplace. The dark side of confectionery is covered too. Unlike some other titles on Rowntree's, this book does not shy away from the issues relating to slavery, industrial espionage and cartels, all of which were part of the Rowntree story.

The company's role in the First World War is covered, along with Joseph's long-standing struggle to accept the need to advertise and brand his products, to penetrate export markets and to install cutting-edge technology.

Altogether this book provides a refreshing and accessible history of a great York company through these two fascinating biographies of two exceptional and driven brothers, who worked together to form one of the world's greatest companies – producing some of our best-loved confectionery products while at the same time laying the foundations of vital and enduring social reform and industrial relations. It is, of course, impossible to separate the non-commercial from the commercial actions of either Henry or the younger Joseph: for both brothers one so clearly informed the other. Joseph's philanthropy defined the man: the good work he did outside the factory was reflected on how he ran his business and how he treated and rewarded his staff. The two major strands of his life are inextricable. His Quaker-driven humanity is evident in his championing of pioneering industrial relations, in his tireless work in adult education, in his wrestling with social injustice, in his construction of a decent place to work in Haxby Road, in his establishment of a sanitary and healthy place to live in New Earswick, and in his founding of the Rowntree trusts, which to this day testify to his humanity and generosity in all sorts of ways. The work of Joseph, and of Henry, outside the boardroom greatly defined their work within the factory gates, and vice versa.

Another key influence on Joseph and Henry was their father, Joseph Rowntree senior. The strict but at the same time liberal way in which he and his wife, Sarah, brought their children up was to have a huge impact, particularly on the boys. Joseph senior was a first class and highly respected role model: the religious, social, occupational, political and economic impact he had on his family was inestimable. For that reason, it is important that we place the lives of Henry and the younger Joseph into further context by describing their father and his actions where relevant.

In the end, it was Henry's devotion to the tenets of Quakerism imbued by his father, and the time he spent pursuing these which distracted him so much from building and strengthening the nascent cocoa business in Tanner's Moat, and which led to the full-time involvement of his elder brother who gave up the work he clearly loved in the Pavement grocery shop to bail out Henry and his ailing cocoa works.

The contribution of both brothers to the city of York is immense. Joseph gave this vibrant market city, noted most for its sublime ecclesiastical history, a viable industrial base. York had avoided the worst the Industrial Revolution could inflict on a community in terms of pollution and downtrodden workforces. He propelled and transformed famously historic but economically insignificant York into a place with a globally successful commercial reputation which, albeit indirectly, endures today. In doing so, he made it a relatively prosperous and decent city in which to live. For a man and a family so devoted to eradicating the causes of poverty this must have been extremely gratifying, leading him to found the famous three Rowntree trusts which, like the chocolate, endure today and which have helped and supported millions of people, not just in York but all over the world.

The contribution of Joseph to the economic and social well-being of York is, then, incalculable. However, it might surprise many a reader of this book that there is still no statue here to the man who has done, and continues to do, so much for the city.

Chapter 1

Henry Rowntree and That Decision

T he night of Sunday 1 June, or thereabouts, in 1862, may well have been troubled for Henry Isaac Rowntree. He had arranged a meeting the following day with the Tukes, owners of a cocoa, chicory and chocolate firm in York's Castlegate.

Throughout November and December of 1861, and in the early part of January 1862, Henry had been indecisive, procrastinating over whether or not to purchase the Tukes' business. When Samuel Tuke died in 1857 his sons engaged John Casson as a partner. The Tukes then moved the tea dealership part of their business to London – Tukes & Co, 20 Fenchurch Street near Mincing Lane, the epicentre of the London tea market – and eventually, in June 1862, sold it to Casson leaving the York-based cocoa and chicory business somewhat up in the air. In the early twentieth century, the London firm presumably thrived and became Tuke Mennell & Co, Wholesale Tea and Coffee Dealers, at Great Tower Street, London.

Back in York, chicory was big business but the Tuke business was not listed in the trade directories as 'Chicory Manufacturers' – the sole entry under this heading was for Thomas Smith & Son of Orchard Street, Phoenix House, Castle Mills Bridge and Jewbury. They remained the only entry in *Kelly's* for many a year but were joined by H. Wilberforce & Son at 124 Walmgate in the *1861 Post Office Directory* and thereafter, both are listed under 'Chicory Grinders'. Mr Wilberforce knew what he was doing – Walmgate was home to many Irish immigrants who had a long tradition of chicory cultivation in and around York, even before the mass immigration caused by the potato famine.

During 1861, all three Rowntree brothers – John Stephenson, Joseph and Henry – all declared an interest in the cocoa side of the Tuke firm, but blew hot and cold. John's letter to Joseph dated 30 September 1861 indicates that they were contemplating renting the property for manufacturing – '£80 is quite as high a rent as we should pay' – although the Tuke family rated it £30 higher at £110. John concluded: 'I think I can quietly settle down in the belief it is best for us not to take the concern.' He apparently felt that Joseph might be interested in acquiring it for himself: 'In considering it lately I have felt rather apprehensive. I should feel very closely bound to the Pavement business if thou were withdrawn.' Joseph, for his part, in a 24 November 1861 letter, perhaps looking to the long term, kept his fiancée Julia in the loop: 'Nothing has yet transpired about the Castlegate business, the question remains unsettled as ever'; then on 29 December: 'John Casson comes next 5th day and a good deal may hang upon his visit', and finally in January 1862: 'I have almost fixed not to take Tuke's old place on Castlegate but what the other brothers will do in a business way is not known.'

Henry's appetite for the business had been whetted by work experience in his family's grocery shops first in Scarborough (established by his grandfather, John Rowntree, on Bland's Cliff) and then in York's Pavement. His experience as acting manager of the Tuke & Casson company enthused him as he enjoyed free rein in a world of machinery and professionals, immersed in weighing, counting, measuring – all requiring exactitude and meticulous procedures for which the Quakers in business were famous. The younger Tukes, meanwhile, focused on their banking interests, building up a business with their relatives the Barclays. They had no interest in the humble York shop, originally leaving it to a Henry Hipsley to run. Henry Rowntree succeeded Henry Hipsley in November 1859 when Joseph, his father, died of cancer.

We know that Henry was enthusiastic about the cocoa trade from a story about a chance meeting with a relative, William S. Rowntree, in the early 1860s when he was a pupil at Bootham School. Henry dragged him along to see a new cocoa grinding machine installed in a small room in his works near the corner of Coppergate and Castlegate. Henry explained to William that his objective in life was to make something that would be an essential commodity, a must-have item, in every home.

And so it was in early June 1862 that Henry Isaac Rowntree left that pivotal meeting having bought, as sole owner with a £1,000 legacy from his father's will, the Tukes' cocoa, chocolate and chicory business, which was based in a workshop at the back of the Tuke premises in Castlegate, re-branding it the 'Cocoa, Chocolate and Chicory Works'. Henry's letter to Julia Seebohm, dated 4 June 1862, reveals that he cannot attend her wedding to his brother Joseph on 15 August as the 'striking event' when he 'begins business' was scheduled for 1 July 1862.

The notice of sale posted by William Tuke read as follows:

We have to inform you that we have relinquished the manufacture of cocoa, chocolate and chicory in favour of our friend, H. I. Rowntree, who has been for some time practically engaged on the concern, and whose knowledge of the business in its several departments enables us with confidence to recommend him to the notice of our connections.

Henry, in turn, circulated the following sales letter to his customers:

The genuine Rock Cocoa introduced by my predecessors, and which from its superiority commands an exclusive sale [*sic*]. I shall continue to supply in its integrity and purity my special attention will be directed to this branch of the business with a view to the introduction of such improvements in the manufacture as may present themselves. My representative Richard Wilson expects to have the pleasure of waiting upon you about the usual time your orders will at all oblige and receive my careful and prompt attention.

Chicory

Chicory (*Cichorium intybus*) is a perennial herbaceous plant of the dandelion family Asteraceae, used in salads, and as a coffee substitute and food additive. A coffee additive, it is mixed in filter coffee in India, parts of Southeast Asia, South Africa, and the southern United States, particularly New Orleans. Prussia lays claim to opening the first chicory factory to powder the root in 1770. In France, a mixture of sixty per cent chicory and forty per cent coffee is sold as Ricoré. It was widely used during the Great Depression in the 1930s and the Second World War. In Napoleonic France, chicory was an adulterant in coffee, or a coffee substitute. Chicory was adopted as a coffee substitute first by the Dutch around 1750. It was consumed by Confederate soldiers during the American Civil War, and is still common in the United States. Chicory root has long been used as a substitute for coffee in US prisons. By the 1840s, New Orleans was the second largest importer of coffee after New York because Louisianans began to add chicory root to their coffee when Union naval blockades during the American Civil War cut off the port of New Orleans. It was also used in the UK during the Second World War, where Camp Coffee, a coffee and chicory essence, had been on sale since 1885. Chicory, with sugar beet and rye, was used as an ingredient of the East German Mischkaffee introduced during the 'East German coffee crisis' of 1976–79.

In York, chicory allowed cultivation and employment opportunities for women as well as men, and in 1851 about a third of the women in the Irish community were employed in chicory.

Why did he do it?

The stimulus for Henry to buy the Tuke business may have come from the fact that his father's, Joseph Rowntree's, existing business in Pavement was already well established and capably run by Henry's brothers, John Stephenson (1834–1907) and Joseph who were, to the exclusion of Henry, made partners on reaching their majority. Henry, accordingly, could see little room for himself in Pavement; the business would survive without him. It may have been triggered by a desire to offer the public a non-alcoholic beverage consonant with Quaker temperance convictions as pioneered by Joseph Fry in Bristol and then George Cadbury in Bournville.

George Cadbury was himself apprenticed at the Pavement shop for three years, and would have no doubt been a persuasive influence on his colleagues. Lewis Fry was another apprentice although he was not, as is often thought, a member of the Bristol chocolate family. The Lewis Fry working at Pavement was the son of a Devon corn merchant while the chocolate family Lewis Fry is in the census as a solicitor who trained in Bristol. Henry will also have been seduced by the prospect of manufacturing as opposed to simply retail and wholesale. We know that he loved the practical and mechanical – working with cocoa and chocolate machines would have delighted him. Whatever the reason for the purchase, Henry had benefitted financially from his father's will and perhaps he chose the Tuke option for the independence it offered, as opposed to a future in the Pavement business with its attendant and inevitable family-driven constraints. Looking at Fry and Cadbury and further afield towards European chocolatiers, Menier and Cailler, he may even, presciently, have identified not just a growing market, but an incipient mass market. In 1820, cocoa consumption in Britain was 267,000 lbs or 0.01 lb per head of population; this had grown to 4,583,000 lbs or 0.16lb per head by 1860, and by 1900 to 43,680,000 lb or 1.06 lb per head.

Who knows? Joseph senior's will was published four years before his death and it shows how far the Pavement grocery business, worth £13,400 – equivalent to more than £1 million today – had developed since 1822 around the Lady Peckett's Yard part of Pavement. Crucially, as noted, Joseph Rowntree senior left the business to first sons John Stephenson and Joseph. Henry may have been insulted and sidelined not just by this but also when his father, obviously not envisaging the Pavement business being run by all three sons, left £1,000 to each of his children with instructions to his trustees John and Joseph to advance to Henry a further sum of money 'for the purpose of enabling him to engage in business'. This was a discretionary advance out of the estate 'on security of his promissory notes bearing interest at 5% per annum such sums as they may think suitable not exceeding £2000'. His father probably intended this as a well-intentioned helping hand to get Henry started in business, but not in the family business. Joseph senior must have believed that young Henry did not possess the required commercial acumen, the attention to detail and a facility with figures – qualities which his brothers John and Joseph exhibited in spades. Henry took this as a slight and resolved to show father and brothers that he too was going to be a successful businessman.

John Stephenson Rowntree, Joseph's first son, had left Bootham School in the autumn of 1850 and went straight to work in his father's grocer's shop; when he was 21 he was made partner in the business and moved into rooms above the shop to live alongside the apprentices.

Henry's pivotal decision would have far-reaching consequences for the Rowntree family, for the emerging European confectionery industry and for the social and industrial welfare of the British people. His decision was, in effect, the first step in the inexorable rise of Rowntree's as a powerful force in the global confectionery industry.

Chapter 2

The Tuke Business

The firm had been established in 1725 as a grocery shop, first in Walmgate, then Castlegate, by the redoubtable Mary Tuke, (1695–1752), a Quaker whose grandfather, William Tuke I (c. 1600–1669), a contemporary of George Fox and a blacksmith working near St Denys Church, was jailed twice as a recusant (along with 4,000 other Quakers nationally) in the 1660s.

Burdened by the twin facts that she was a woman and a Quaker woman at that, Mary predictably became embroiled in a series of tortuous commercial legal wrangles with the Company of Merchant Adventurers of York. To trade in York, it was necessary to be a freeman of the city and to achieve such a status it was necessary to pay £25, to serve an apprenticeship, or else to be related to an existing freeman. Mary was accorded the status of freeman by patrimony, citing her father as a deceased member. The inscription on the Freeman's Roll of the City of York reads, in a curious mixture of English and Latin: 'Maria Tewk, spinster Fil Willelmi Tuke, blacksmith'.

But Mary was still not permitted to trade. Now she was required to be a member of the Company of Merchant Adventurers, or else be granted a licence by them; but she had no means of achieving either. After flouting what was essentially a pointless and outmoded law, Mary was prosecuted for trading without a licence at the Midsummer Court in June 1725 ('Merchandising and following Trade without being free of this Fellowship'). She then went on to defy the company (the court had offered leniency if she mended her ways) for a further two years when she was allowed six months to dispose of her stock. She was later permitted to trade until the next Lady Day Court was in session, at which time she would be liable for a fine or prosecution. In July 1728, the Merchant Adventurers finally relented (on grounds of cost alone, presumably) and allowed her to trade at the pleasure of the court, on payment of 5 shillings every six months, and on condition she bought all her goods locally and took on no apprentices. In 1732, Mary was finally allowed the concession to trade in perpetuity after a one-off payment of £10. The significance of Mary's achievement against all odds in a conservative male world against a powerful, exclusive monopoly should not be underestimated. Her tenacity, patience and courage served as a profound example and symbol of hope to the Tukes, and others – not least the Rowntrees – who followed her.

In 1733 Mary married Henry Frankland, a local Quaker stuff weaver, and moved the shop to Castlegate – then one of York's busiest streets. It lay en route to the market around Pavement, the prison, the castle, the gallows and, crucially, it was conveniently close to the Friends' Meeting House and other non-conformist places of worship for Wesleyans and Unitarians, and the patronage that such a location would have brought. Henry gave up stuff weaving for groceries in 1736, after another protracted and unseemly battle with the Merchant Adventurers and a £25 fee. Mary was left on her own in 1739 when Henry died.

The business was continued by her nephew William, William Tuke III, or 'Old William' (1732–1822) in 1746, who had started off as a 14-year-old apprentice. He inherited the business on Mary's death in 1752 when he was 20 with two years to run on his apprenticeship. He graduated as a freeman grocer and, in 1754, a member of the difficult Merchant Adventurers. The Castlegate shop now specialised in the sale of tea, coffee, chicory and the making of drinking chocolate. William's son Henry (1755–1814), at that time hoping to become a doctor, joined the firm in 1770, having renounced his 'taste for the physic' and in 1785, in a typically Quakerish act, committed himself to the business as a partner.

As well as co-founding, with his father, York's The Retreat, the world's first humane asylum for the mentally ill based on revolutionary Quaker principles, Henry was also a subscriber to the African Institution, a body which set out to create a viable, civilised refuge for freed slaves in Sierra Leone. By now he was also a prominent tea dealer with a solid reputation, particularly in the north of England. Henry Tuke was eager to dramatically expand his product base: possibly with an eye on Fry's success in Bristol and the French, Swiss and Dutch imports flooding the market. He brought to market brands such as Tuke's Rich Cocoa, Tuke's Plain Chocolate, British Cocoa Coffee (mocha chocolate), Tuke's Superior Rock Cocoa and Tuke's Milk Chocolate (not milk chocolate as we know it but chocolate used for mixing with milk). There was now a warehouse in Coppergate to support the shop. A 1785 price list shows 'best congou leaf tea, fine souchongs, good common green teas, good coffee, good chocolate, milk chocolate, Churchman's Patent Chocolate, fine cocoa shells and cocoa nibs'.

His son Samuel Tuke (1784–1857), also a Quaker, social and mental health reformer of some repute and philanthropist, joined the firm in 1795, became a partner in 1805 and managed the business until 1852. Henry died in 1814 and William retired in 1818; their places filled by Robert Waller and Favill Copsie to form Tuke, Waller & Copsie.

The Articles of Company Partnerships report that Tuke, Waller and Copsie had formed their partnership on 2 February 1818. It was:

> between Samuel Tuke of the City of York Merchant and Teadealer of the first part Robert Waller of the same City Merchant and Teadealer of the second part James Favill Copsie of the same City Merchant and Teadealer of the third part and William Tuke of the same City Merchant and Teadealer of the fourth part.

The capital and stock was valued at £20,000 'and upwards'; Waller and Copsie paid Samuel Tuke £3,000. That partnership was dissolved on 1 October 1838.

The East India Company's monopoly on tea ended in 1834 and meant that tea traders could now unload in northern ports and not just London. To take advantage of this, Tuke, Waller and Copsie opened a Henry Tuke & Co office in Liverpool with warehousing in Bristol and Hull. This shrewd move streamlined importation and enabled them to sell and transport manufactured goods to their customers more economically and direct from all parts of the country.

Another partner was appointed, John Casson, to join Samuel Tuke, James Hack Tuke and William Murray Tuke and the firm was renamed Tuke & Casson: 'carrying on business as Wholesale Tea and Coffee Dealers, in the city of London and also in the city of York'. This, in turn, was dissolved on 22 May 1851. Samuel retired in 1852 due to ill health and in 1857, James Hack moved on to bankers Sharples & Co in Hitchin. As mentioned above William Tuke then relocated the tea dealership part of his business to London and eventually, in June 1862, sold it to John Casson. In the early 1900s it became Tuke, Mennell & Co, Wholesale Tea and Coffee Dealers, at St Dunstan's Buildings, Great Tower Street, London. Tuke and Mennell separated in 1923.

Samuel Tuke was a close friend of Joseph Rowntree senior; they had much in common. As well as being related to each other through marriage, Samuel and Joseph shared their Quaker faith: they campaigned for the return of William Wilberforce as local MP, supported The Retreat, set up the Friends' Provident Association in 1832 and established schools which would later become the prestigious Bootham for boys and The Mount for girls.

The ever-perceptive Joseph could read the writing on the wall. His friend's business was likely to be left rudderless because he knew that Samuel's ambitious sons had no interest in involving themselves in the York business; small potatoes to them as they eyed the lucrative world of high street banking. Joseph almost certainly smoothed the way for Henry and arranged that meeting with Samuel Tuke.

Chapter 3

Joseph Rowntree (1801–1859):
A Profound Influence

The elder Joseph Rowntree was born 10 June 1801 in Scarborough of Quaker stock. He was the third son of John Rowntree (1757–1827) and Elizabeth Lotherington (1764–1835) – brothers William and John were born before him in 1786 and 1788 and there were four sisters. The life and achievements of Joseph Rowntree have, to a large degree, been overshadowed by subsequent generations of notable Rowntrees, particularly his sons, Henry and Joseph (1836–1925) and his grandson Benjamin Seebohm (1871–1954). However, his contribution to the achievements of all three and to their siblings, his profound influence on them and his contribution to the work of others in the family, is inestimable.

From when he was about 11, Joseph worked in the shop at Bland's Cliff on the corner of Cross Street, later Eastborough, in Scarborough, receiving over time a grounding in all aspects of the grocery business. We can assume that he enjoyed the work because in 1822, around the time of his twenty-first birthday, he headed west from Scarborough to York, intent on setting up his own business and building on the ten years' experience he already had under his belt. Joseph Rowntree bought the shop at 28 Pavement at auction at The Elephant & Castle Inn in Skeldergate. The auctioneer was so drunk that Joseph, aided by his friend James Backhouse, was forced to plunge the man's head into a barrel of sobering cold water so that he could conclude the sale. Joseph then set about refurbishing the somewhat dilapidated but elegant Georgian building with its bow windows and fanlight. He transformed it into a grocer's, tea merchant and coffee-roasting establishment: his mahogany counters, iron grilles, full-length curtains upstairs and elaborate fire guards were considered somewhat 'fancy' by Quaker standards. Elizabeth, his unmarried sister, had come with him from Scarborough to manage the busy household which always included the two shop apprentices. Elizabeth remained in the post until 1832 when she left to marry Henry Bewley of Dublin.

It is interesting to note that in 1828 there were twelve other tea and coffee dealers in the city of York, six of them in High Ousegate and New

Bridge Street, rising to forty-nine in 1851, so competition for Joseph would have been intense.

However, Joseph, like Mary Tuke long before him, was obliged to satisfy York's strict commercial regulations before he could start trading. It was necessary to become a fully paid up member of the Merchant Adventurers and thereby a freeman of the city: he was admitted to the former on 15 July 1822, having paid his £60 fee, and was finally registered a freeman on 12 November 1823. The custom was for the Adventurers to initiate new members with a wine party; Joseph's was duly held, with the usual inebriation of the Adventurers but it so appalled him that he left early. This, and probably the earlier experience with the auctioneer, imbued in Joseph 'a distrust of alcohol in all its forms'.

Life on the Pavement

What was life like around the Rowntree shop? Pavement was a veritable menagerie and a hive of frenzied activity; all life was there. *Ye Old Streete of Pavement*, written by W. Camidge in 1893 and published by *The Yorkshire Gazette*, provides a colourful, vivid picture of life there over the years, much of which would have been familiar to Joseph and his staff. We read of the Goose Flags – the path in front of St Crux signifying the goose market there; boots and shoes on sale 'in Whip-ma-whop-ma-gate, where members of the "Worshipful Company of Translators" sold these commodities, old and new' and 'the basket market ... at the bottom of Colliergate', plus the pleasure fairs 'at Whitsuntide and Martinmas'. The shows which accompanied them were very popular too. There were dog and lion fights 'and other shows with fat women, deformed men, giants and dwarfs, reptiles, waxworks, mechanical inventions, fortune tellers, circuses, boxing booths' along with swing boats and hobby horses. Peep shows were particularly popular – 'their incidents stirring, and their pictures very striking ... chiefly battles ... Waterloo and the crossing of the Alps by Napoleon ... described by the showman in measured and monotonous tones in which fact and fancy were mixed up in most bewildering confusion.'

On most Saturdays, there were auction sales in Pavement:

Not the least interesting was the sale of a woman [in 1839]. She had left her husband through his drunken habits and ill-treatment, and in one of his mad freaks he had brought her into the Market-place ... with a halter round her neck. She was mounted on a table beside the auctioneer, who descanted on her virtues and spoke of her as a clean, industrious, quiet and careful woman, attractive in appearance and well mannered.

She went for 7s 6d, bought as seen, halter included, and proceeded to live with her purchaser near to Pavement. Twenty years later her husband died and she married her saviour; she herself died in the 1880s 'at a great age, respectable and respected'.

Election times were especially riotous. Camidge gives a graphic account of the near anarchy and corruption which attended these dubious expressions of democracy:

> It was not unusual during the progress of an election to roll into the Pavement large barrels of ale, one end of which was speedily knocked in, and then a scene of indescribable confusion and contention ensued. Men, women and children rushed for the beer barrel, and with every description of kitchen and other utensils they sought to drink their fill, and carry off what unsteady legs, and intense excitement would allow them to get away with. It was no uncommon thing as the beer neared the bottom for someone to fall, or be pushed into the barrel.

Pavement and Minster Yard were 'proverbial for fights' – the latter because of the ready supply of staves as:

> the Minster was at that time encircled with wood palisades ... one man ... dyed his whiskers and hair to the colour he had voted, but found himself minus of much of his hair before he escaped from the crowd.

Camidge also records that 'public-houses were also opened as "free houses" where an elector on producing a ticket could have a free drink'; this cost one candidate in 1830 around £1,200.

Given his own way, Joseph Rowntree senior would have avoided standing for election at all costs, but he was anxious to improve things, particularly those things relating to public health in York where the improvement commissioners were often impotent. Although he served thirteen years as a Liberal councillor, the pursuit and tenure of office in local government presented Joseph, as a Quaker, with a dilemma or two. First, as noted, he was reluctant to seek election but knew that he had to be elected before he could tackle the problems; second, he was opposed to the bribery and 'treating' described above which was accepted practice and prevalent at elections. Nevertheless, Joseph became York's first Quaker alderman in November 1853. The 1848 Public Health Act facilitated and accelerated much badly needed work in York from the early 1850s. Rules relating to the drainage of buildings came into force; housing plans were approved; the Walmgate ward report of 1852 led to twenty-two areas of improvement, mainly in the state of lodging houses, many of which were now inhabited by Irish immigrants. By 1854 a further report could claim a marked improvement in the state of 254 lodging houses.

A few examples of the improvement work Joseph was involved in gives an idea of the range of issues besetting the city: drainage in Goodramgate (April 1832); projecting window in Stonegate (February 1833); street widening at Garden Place, Hungate (March 1833); Ousegate widening (August 1834); alterations at The Punch Bowl Inn, Stonegate (October 1835); widening Petergate (February 1836); lighting in Dalton Terrace (December 1836); widening Lendal (October 1839); new road between Micklegate and the station (October 1841); flagging New Street (August 1844); lighting Lady Peckett's Yard (October 1844); River Foss survey (April 1847); widening Monk Bar (August 1847); repairs to Castle Mills Bridge (May 1848) and widening North Street (April 1850).

Most significantly, the chronic problems relating to the flood-prone rivers, especially the disgusting, insanitary, disease-ridden Foss, were finally resolved between 1852 and 1859. No one could fault or question the man's industry in office, his determination to do something about the parlous state of public health in his city and its effects on his fellow residents. But fault and question they did. Criticism came thick and fast with allegations of mismanagement and favouritism towards the wealthier areas of the city; much of which would have been politically motivated, delivered as it was through the pages of the Tory *York Gazette* between April and August 1857. From around 1838 the Tories dominated York politics and 'the Railway King' George Hudson dominated the Tories. As became evident later, Hudson lacked the moral rectitude which characterised Joseph Rowntree.

Life on the Pavement shop floor

So Pavement was an ideal site for a progressive and top end grocer's shop. It was at the centre of things commercially, benefitting from the crowds flocking to the market outside and close to the city centre around

Parliament Street. Pavement and the Rowntree shop were part of a veritable north country entrepôt.

Now that he was able to, Joseph senior soon got on with the business of running his shop. Training was obviously high on his list of priorities and apprentices figured large in the programme. For example, the close-knit Quaker community enabled the likes of George Cadbury to train there. Cadbury served a three-year apprenticeship with Rowntree at the Pavement shop before he joined his family firm in Bournville in 1857. He would have quickly become familiar with the regime there: the rules of the Pavement shop were rigorous and uncompromising, as set out in Joseph's 1852 *Memoranda of Business and Household Arrangements*:

> The object of the Pavement establishment is business. The young men who enter it ... are expected to contribute ... in making it successful ... it affords a full opportunity for any painstaking, intelligent young man to obtain a good practical acquaintance with the tea and grocery trades ... the place is not suitable for the indolent and wayward.

Not unusually for the times, hours were long: 7 or 7.30 am to 8 pm six days a week with late night opening on market days until 10 pm; two days' holiday – Good Friday and Christmas Day. It is worth quoting more from Mr Rowntree's fearsome *Memorandum*:

> Punctuality in the time of rising etc is important in each member otherwise the thoughtless or ease-loving individual wastes the time of the others ... without neglecting business much may be done ... to prevent the needless extension of meal-taking ... a gratuity of 26 shillings per year is allowed to the punctual.

So the relaxed timekeeping which, as we will see, prevailed at Tanner's Moat was replaced by a rigorous system where all employees were obliged to note in a book their precise time of arrival as given by the office clock.

The following extracts from the Pavement ledger give a flavour of the very business-like regime there and the duties of the apprentices, including Henry:

> Edwin Appleton (T): Dusts office, counters, desks, reflectors etc. Has charge of the Office. Washes the tea-things & is responsible for the various articles of Office furniture being in good order &

in their places [E.G. rulers, ink stands, indigo-rubber, pen-holders, pencils, writing paper. Inkstands to be washed out on Mondays & filled with clean ink.] Gets ready for instruction on tasting samples which come by post. Posts letters twice a day. Fills Cocoa-holes. Brings down supplies of dry soap black lead etc. for Saturdays' sale. Hangs up brown paper on Fridays. Counts copper in the evenings.

The Bell-man is to remain in the shop or office every evening till he has permission to go. He must always ascertain whether any palers or errand boys have to return, & whether carts are out. When persons are working in the shop or warehouse, the Bell-man must remain upon the premises, & visit the workers at least once an hour.

Note on the taking & setting up of Orders [Important to all.]
In taking orders be explicit in stating the particular kind of article wanted: e.g. if Coffee is ordered, state on order, whether whole, ground, mixed or genuine is wanted. – if Tea, – Black, Mixed, Assam, or whole-leaf: if Sugar, Lump, Raw or Moist. Orders are as far as possible to be examined by the persons who take them. The person who gets them up is to mark each article, & the examiner as he sees each article to cross the mark [tick crossed through] & then to sign the order. The person sending out goods, is to enter them in the book, & to put down in the same book jars to which have to be returned – also enter the name of the paler who delivers the goods. Goods like Baking-powder liable to burst should be double wrapped, & strong paper should be used to divide soap or other goods that may flavour articles of food. The printed forms for taking down orders are very useful in reminding both servers & customers of goods. Every efficient server will try & make his orders as large and profitable as he can. Acquaint yourselves with the profits of goods – & sell the most profitable you can but always with tact, not attempting to force on a customer that which is not wanted. N.B. Errors in orders have occurred thro' the examiner signing before he had seen every article – never do this. And when examined let the parcel be wrapped up, or the goods be put in a basket at once. If these directions are intelligently carried out few errors in orders will occur.

Regulations for the Receipting of Bills
When a bill or book is brought for payment it is to be receipted by the Book-keeper or assistant book-keeper to whom the money

is to be paid. Persons coming to settle accounts must be dealt with according to circumstances. Sometimes the Book-keeper must go to speak to them, sometimes they may be taken to his desk. Very frequently they will want to give another order. In that case the server should hand the bill to the Book-keeper, and at once return to the customer & take down the order, or talk so that they do not think they are being neglected. The bookkeeper is responsible for the money received agreeing with the receipts. Every evening he is to add up his receipts & give a memorandum with the cash to Thomas Hills or John Simpson. The Book-keeper & his assistant should never be absent from their desk at the same time.

Miscellaneous Memoranda

The Saturday market trade is a valuable part of the business, tho' much smaller than formerly. It is particularly desired that the Market customers may be well & quickly served. To promote this the mid-day meal on Saturday is a lunch – for partaking of which twenty minutes absence from the shop is the maximum time allowed.

1888 Jan 13th

Henry Darby to have the general care of the Electric Light and the new Engine in the Soap Cellar. The Engine to be cleaned once a fortnight on Wednesday morning – or other convenient time. H. D. to bring his tea, and take it at 28 the Pavement – stopping the engine and putting out the Electric Light at 9 o'clock in the evening excepting on Saturday when H. D. should remain till 10. H. D. is to put up the grates in front of the Creamery Windows every night and to see that the grating is locked and to leave everything safe.

Wilfred M. Brown dusts the whole of the centre of the shop, has charge of the biscuit cases, keeping them replenished and bringing forward the stock so as to prevent stale goods. Collects orders at Fulford on Wednesdays. Has charge of cases in connexion with the provision side – must see that Green fruit as onions, grapes, oranges is constantly on view in the centre of the shop.

John was charged by his father to take over the running of the living quarters there and to look after the apprentices. In 1858 he married Elizabeth Hotham, daughter of Sarah and James Hotham, a successful Leeds draper; she took on the role vacated by her mother-in-law, looking after the household and catering for the family and the apprentices. The paternalistic advice she received from her father-in-law was 'not to spare trouble, or even cost, in thy arrangements for the comfort of the young men.' The Hothams are said to have been active in the establishment of the Band of Hope Union in Leeds around 1847 – the temperance group set up for children under 16 to teach them about Christianity and drink-associated problems, and to encourage them to live a healthy, alcohol-free lifestyle. By 1897, the year Queen Victoria became patron, the membership was 3,238,323.

Life in the family rooms above the shop can only be described as hectic; an almost commune-style domestic set-up where family lived alongside up to twelve apprentices – their numbers swelled yet further by a constant stream of visits by family and Quaker friends. Luther Worstenholm, a family friend, describes games which involved kicking apprentices' hats as far as possible down the stairs. Somewhat more adventurous was the time when the boys slipped out unnoticed into the dark streets with a candle which extinguished itself in Ousegate; they were returned home in a cab after asking for a re-light, serendipitously at Caleb Williams' house, the family doctor.

The family cook, a Mary Tasker, had a hard time of it. She fought an endless battle against rodent infestation in her kitchen, and the dining room was, most inconveniently, on a different level to the kitchen. Stock for the shop was delivered to, and equally inconveniently stored in, the living quarters. Son Joseph's bedroom was converted from a corner of the drawing room. Meals were taken with the apprentices – often exciting and interesting companions for the young Rowntree boys. Schooling was at home on the third floor in the early years. The fact that there was no garden may explain some of the boisterousness; attempts to curb it came in woodworking and encouragement to collect plants, butterflies and the like; a treasured, but decomposing, lark had to be removed from the kitchen at one point. Chemistry experiments, electrotypes produced from plaster of Paris and gelatine coin impressions were other popular and happy diversions.

Even when the family moved out to a more suitable family house in Blossom Street in 1845 – which boasted that all-important garden – the apprentices remained at Pavement where Joseph's father continued to eat with them and read to them from the Bible.

To Joseph, the straight and narrow quite simply lay in Bible-based education. To equip his assistants better – namely his sons John, Joseph, Henry and various apprentices – for teaching at the day schools and adult school, he held two-hour Bible lessons for them every Sunday night for over twenty years. Over time a number of alumni associations of former apprentices were established: one such was the York Bond of Brothers formed in March 1849 'to keep alive the friendship and interest which existed among the members during their tarriance with Joseph Rowntree.'

In short, Joseph was a powerful and influential role model for his sons and grandsons. Little that they achieved in their lives, and they achieved an awful lot, did not have its origins in Joseph's work and fatherly guidance. His meticulous running of the grocery business at 28 Pavement, his paternalistic care for his staff; his forensic use of statistical methods in carefully argued research, his public works for the betterment of peoples' lives; his fascination with, and cultivation of, education for all; his charitable and philanthropic work for the groundbreaking medical institutions, The Retreat and The Dispensary (serving the sick and penniless); his devotion to Quakerism; his compassion for the urban poor – all of these were to influence subsequent generations of his family and provide the foundation for much of what they went on to achieve. Without the precedents set and the example shown by Joseph Rowntree as father, grandfather, mentor and employer, the stories of his descendants and of Rowntree's the company might be decidedly different.

So Henry would have much to thank his father for. Perhaps the most overt influence – which Henry witnessed at first hand and absorbed on a day-to-day basis in the grocer's shops in which they worked together in Scarborough and York – was the way his father systematically and meticulously conducted his business, the clockwork way he ran his shops, the high level of service he gave, his quality produce, and his insistence on being a fair, enlightened and generous employer. Joseph was a master grocer, a true professional in every respect and if anyone wanted to know how to sell groceries well, then they only had to turn to Joseph Rowntree of Pavement, York.

Joseph Rowntree died of cancer in November 1859, nursed to the end by Sarah, Hannah, their daughter, and Rachel, a half cousin. He is buried in the Friends' Burial Ground. Sarah never remarried in the thirty years she outlived her husband. She, along with Henry Isaac and Hannah, moved into Penn House (known as 'Top House'), which Joseph had built in the early 1850s on the corner of St Mary's and Bootham, with its distinctive Ionic columns on land that was bought from the London & Liverpool Railway. By now it had been converted into two houses with connecting doors; the young Joseph was to live in the other part with his bride, Julia.

Education and the Quakers

Education also played a major part in the elder Joseph's life. As mentioned above, with Samuel Tuke he helped establish two York Quaker schools: the Friends' School (later Bootham School for boys) in Lawrence Street and the girls' equivalent in Castlegate in 1831, later becoming the Mount School. Both survive and thrive today. The Mount School story begins with Esther Tuke, second wife of William Tuke (1732–1822), who in 1785 opened a boarding school in Trinity Lane, off Micklegate, known then as the Friends' Girl School. The aims of the York schools were heavily influenced by the Quaker school at Ackworth near Pontefract.

By 1796, Trinity Lane had become too small for the thirty or so girls and purpose-built premises were bought for £450 in Tower Street opposite Clifford's Tower and close to the Friends' Meeting House in Clifford Street. The next move, to Castlegate House, the 1763 mansion of the Recorder of York, took place in 1831. In 1855 the lease on Castlegate expired and Joseph Rowntree was charged with examining the school's future. He raised the question of its continuation at the Yorkshire Quarterly Meeting and was given an unequivocal yes, so as to safeguard 'the religious welfare of the children of our Society of every class ... maintaining and if possible extending the provision of the training of female teachers.' This led to a further move to the purpose-built buildings in Dalton Terrace off the Mount in what was then an acre of land in open countryside. By then 353 girls had been educated and fifty-four had completed teacher training at Castlegate. The Mount School opened its doors in 1857 under the supervision of Rachel Tregelles. Girls lived four or five to a bedroom rather than in dormitories and enjoyed the luxury of internal flushing toilets and hot water on tap.

It was William Tuke who, in 1818, floated the idea of establishing a boys' school in York for the sons of Quakers 'and any children of the opulent who will submit themselves to the general system of diet and discipline.' In 1822, premises on Lawrence Street, known as the Appendage, were leased from The Retreat, the revolutionary psychiatric hospital run by the Quaker Committee in York, and the school opened in early 1823 as the York Friends Boys' School. In 1829, it was known as Yorkshire Quarterly Meeting Boys' School – its official name until 1889 – even after it had moved to new premises at 20 (now 51) Bootham in 1846. The school's proximity to the River Foss had triggered the move to these more salubrious premises. One Lawrence Street master even carried a pistol to shoot rats with and cholera was also a problem. The mission statement then read: 'The cultivation of the individuality of the boy, leisure time pursuits, health-giving discipline, and education by contact with the outside world.'

Bootham was not the only Quaker boys' school in York. In 1827, the Hope Street British School off slum-ridden Walmgate was established and attended by many children of Friends; Joseph Rowntree was actively involved in its foundation and remained its secretary for the rest of his life. The school was slightly unusual because, in addition to the usual curriculum, it taught the working of the electric telegraph. The Electric Telegraph Company supplied the equipment and the school provided the company with a ready supply of clerks. So popular was it in its heyday and so good was its reputation that it was always over-subscribed and attracted applications from 'parents of higher rank' than that for which it was intended. In 1867 it peaked at 546 boys on the roll.

Significant as these schools were to York, and to the nation generally, Joseph Rowntree made a number of other important, far-reaching contributions to Quaker education. Apart from founding the Friends' Education Society, he set up with Benjamin Flounders the Flounders Institute at Ackworth in 1848 – a men's teacher training college for members of the Society of Friends. Flounders was a merchant and magistrate with estates at Culmington, near Ludlow, and Yarm; he was a director of the Stockton and Darlington Railway, and contributed more than half of the money needed to build Barnard Castle School, as well as helping to finance the Flounders Institute. Joseph worked closely with the British and Foreign School Society to find and fund provision for the education of the urban poor in York.

More specifically to York and Yorkshire, reports had been published in 1826 on educational provision for the poor in the city, backed up with statistics and exploding the popular, lazy and convenient myth that such provision was universal and adequate. Joseph's research was collected by painstaking door-knocking on a grand scale; his findings revealed that twenty-five per cent of children aged between 6 and 10 never went to school; seventeen per cent of children aged between 10 and 12 never attended school; while more than fifteen per cent of 12 to 14 year olds were illiterate. Fifty-six per cent of children not attending a day school went to Sunday school. He was also involved in establishing Rawdon Quaker school near Leeds in 1832 at Low Green, which was co-educational from 1835. The fees were means tested and ranged from £8 to £16 per annum. By 1851 there were fifty-three pupils here.

Joseph was also heavily involved in Ackworth School and helped modernise the curriculum there in 1843. Characteristically, he freighted his conclusions and recommendations with a raft of statistics on the destinations and careers of all Ackworth-leavers since 1799. The objective was to discover 'how many were living after a given interval, how many had gone to this or that trade, how many had failed in business, how many had emigrated, how many had married, how many were still Friends, for what causes those no longer Friends had left the Society.'

In 1829, Joseph became secretary to the York Schools Committee starting a 111-year period in which three generations of Rowntrees – Joseph, John Stephenson and Arnold – served as secretary or chairman, apart from one five-year gap. In 1837, with Samuel Tuke, he set up the Friends' Educational Society which explored the history of Quaker education and promoted its development.

Joseph's pre-occupation with the education of the under-privileged, and the concern he showed his apprentices, clearly indicate an abiding interest in the welfare of the youth of his day, especially the poor youth. Between 1842 and 1859, around fifty apprentices and shop assistants passed through the Pavement shop doors. The impact on his three sons was huge, as we will see.

Social welfare, social justice

Joseph was actively involved in an impressive number of other local good causes. His interests in religious education extended to include The Bible Society and The Religious Tract Society. His social work took in the York Soup Kitchen, City Mission, York Penitentiary Society – set up by the Gray family of lawyers – York County Hospital, York Dispensary and the Vagrant Office in 1822 in Little Shambles, for the 'suppression of mendicity' and to stem the flow into the city of those outside the law.

Many York prostitutes found scant reward in their non-industrial city and turned for support to the York Penitentiary Society, established in 1822 to rescue and rehabilitate fallen girls. The Refuge was set up in 1845 as a 'place of permanent refuge for such miserable young females as may seem in the spirit of true penitence'. The aim was to help them reform over a two-year period and allow them to escape from the brothels, many of which were clustered around York Minster, and Friargate, close to the Castlegate Meeting House, spreading south through the city. There are records of 1,400 prostitutes and brothel-keepers in the city between 1837 and 1887; sadly, of the 412 girls admitted to the Refuge between 1845 and

1887, only 142 were rehabilitated and found work in service, although many of these returned to their former ways.

Joseph set up the York Soup Kitchen in Black Horse Passage. By day it was a soup kitchen – a tavern in the evening – which provided many with their one and only meal of the day and was destined to run every winter from 1846. Joseph took a hands-on approach, establishing and controlling recipes, equipment, ticketing and distribution. By 1855 he must have been considered something of a national expert on coffee when Chancellor of the Exchequer William Gladstone consulted him on matters relating to the sale of coffee mixed with chicory.

To put Joseph's philanthropic and social work into context, it is useful to give some idea of the prodigious number of other, less familiar, philanthropic causes supported by Quakers in York between 1740 and 1860. They included the York Anti–Slavery Society; York Association for the Prosecution of Felons and Villains; York Society for the Prevention and Discouragement of Vice and Profaneness; Society to Assist the Labouring and Poor Classes of York; Mission to the Indians; Dr Choke's Society for Promoting Schools in Africa; Society for Promoting Permanent and Universal Peace; Society for Promoting the Education of Native Females in India; Society for the Prevention of Youthful Depravity; Female Temperance Association; York Society for the Encouragement of Faithful Female Servants and York Meeting Sewing Circle.

Joseph Rowntree's work at The Retreat, in education, temperance, with prostitution, the local soup kitchen, the hospital and The Dispensary was exemplary and indicative of a compelling and inexhaustible commitment to social welfare.

Chapter 4

Henry Isaac Rowntree (1838–1883): Early Days

H enry Isaac Rowntree was born at 28 Pavement, on 11 February 1838, the younger brother of John Stephenson and Joseph II. His parents were, as noted above, the elder Joseph Rowntree and Sarah Stephenson (1807–1888). Sarah was born in Stockton-on-Tees, the youngest child of Quakers Isaac and Hannah Stephenson. Isaac was a Quaker minister who moved the family to Manchester but died suddenly in 1828. In 1831, Sarah met Joseph Rowntree whom she married in 1832 at the new Meeting House in Manchester. After honeymooning in the Lake District, the couple set up home above the shop in Pavement. Sarah's hands were more than full, looking after and feeding the family and staff, working in the shop helping with the accounts and advising her husband. As a Quaker, she had her religious worship and good works: visiting the poor, serving on the managing committees of local schools and the York Penitentiary.

Henry was one of five children: three sons and two daughters, one of whom died in infancy. The eldest child, John Stephenson, was born in 1834, followed in 1836 by Joseph, and Henry Isaac in 1838, Hannah Elizabeth in 1840, and finally Sarah Jane (Sally), in 1843. Tragically, Sally died of whooping cough, aged 4 on 19 December 1847.

The children were home educated by a governess until 1845, when John, then aged 11, started at the Friends' School in Lawrence Street (later Bootham) as a day boarder. The morning and afternoon lessons were occasionally punctuated with rambles out in Langwith Wood, nature outings which were to leave a great impression on Henry and young Joseph. The Pavement business thrived but as a family home it left much to be desired and in 1845 the family were relieved to move to a doubled-fronted family house with large garden at 11 Blossom Street; three years later they were installed in elegant Bootham at number 39 in an even more capacious residence, before moving to palatial Top House in the early 1850s. Joseph's *Memoranda of Business and Household Arrangements* of 1852 meticulously covered the running of the Rowntree household, as well as the shop. On 22 January 2011, *The York Press* described Top House as follows:

> Go through the elegant porticoed front door and you find yourself in a stunning entrance hall. An oddly beautiful, geometric staircase winds up through three floors to a glass ceiling far above. Large, elegant rooms open off it from every floor, some looking out over the garden. The effect of the design is strangely Spartan, almost ascetic, yet beautiful.

Home life in Blossom Street and Bootham was, by all accounts, still somewhat wild despite the liberating garden, with their parents continuing to advocate and practise a decidedly liberal and relaxed upbringing for the children.

Bootham School

In the middle of the nineteenth century, Bootham School might be described as something of a paradox: refreshingly enlightened in some ways, frighteningly oppressive in others. Even the progressive second superintendent of the school, John Ford, still believed very much in the benefits of 'putting a hedge' between the Quaker boys and the big bad world outside. To that end there were no newspapers permitted and all incoming mail was opened and read by staff – mail, that is, that was only permitted to and from close family. Ford's regime allowed no corporal punishment but miscreants were dealt with by solitary standing instead – often thought to be much worse than a good thrashing. And then there were the 'columns', a system of punishment that comprised a copying out exercise masquerading as a spelling test, which opened with the words 'abrogate, absolute, adamant, admiral'. All this, though, was compensated by a liberal, boundless and holistic educational programme which nurtured the spirit, the mind and the body in equal measure. Ford was an enlightened man: over his thirty-seven years in post, he inculcated religion to an appropriate degree, melding it with a progressive programme of the classics, science and nature studies.

In the late nineteenth century, many of the Rowntree family boys were educated at Bootham; both Henry and Joseph went there, two of forty-five Rowntree boys to attend. Another of them, Arthur Rowntree (or Chocolate Jumbo to give him his nickname), was headmaster from 1899 to 1927. Arthur was at pains to promote the school's egalitarian principles: 'We are proud to be in the tradition of promoting friendship between all classes.' A number of staff and scholars went on to be opinion leaders, influential in the political and social reforms of their times, not least Seebohm Rowntree (Bootham 1882–1887), who used pioneering statistical methods to expose the fact that in York almost one third of the population lived at or below 'sustenance level'. Joseph Rowntree senior had been instrumental in the school's foundation and governance.

In 1862, John Ford visited Matthew Arnold at Rugby School and saw an unusual sight: a game of rugby football being played. He took the strange game back to Bootham, but had not taken into account the shape of the ball, obliging him to introduce rugby played with a round rather than an oval ball. Nor did he ever master the rules, and by 1867 the Bootham game was still 'an ill-regulated scramble for the leather by as many as could be got to take part!' Bootham's most famous athlete was Philip Noel-Baker, a silver-medallist runner in the 1920 Antwerp Olympic Games who was also awarded the Nobel Peace Prize in 1959 for his work on disarmament and international peace. Apart from the many boys from the Rowntree family and other Quakers from the Cadbury and Clark families, alumni include A. J. P. Taylor and J. B. Morrell. In 1850, Bootham became one of the first schools to have its own observatory, with the two telescopes and other 'astronomical apparatus' made for the school by local firm, Cooke, Troughton & Simms, instrument manufacturers of international repute.

The famous Natural History Society, the first of its kind in the UK, was started in 1834 by John Ford and would surely have attracted the attention of both Joseph and Henry. Its full name was the Natural History, Literary and Polytechnic Society and as such it was the umbrella organisation for many other clubs. Bootham's was the first School Natural History Society in the country and it gained an outstanding reputation, sharing its scientific findings with other schools and academic bodies. It also published its own journals, which covered the areas of astronomy, botany, geology, ornithology and the like. The society won for itself a strong tradition in photography and film, producing a range of fascinating early footage and photographic records that document the development of the school well into the twentieth century. The boys made their own collections of butterflies, moths and ferns and took specimens to the nearby Yorkshire Museum for identification. Many pupils went on to become eminent scientists in their field and fellows of the Royal Society.

In 1899, Bootham School was almost totally destroyed by fire. A keen pupil was boiling snail shells in the natural history room one evening when he was summoned by the bell for reading, and the snails were left boiling all night. On being informed by the fire brigade that his school was a smouldering shell, the headmaster promptly resigned. For a while, the school also owned No 54 Bootham, the birthplace of W. H. Auden, whose father was Medical Officer for York.

The school was evacuated to Roman Catholic Ampleforth during the Second World War. Donald Gray, the head at the time, is reputed to have addressed the combined school as 'Friends, Romans, Countrymen'.

Despite the absence of newspapers and magazines, students were encouraged to take an active interest in the political questions of the day. Anti-slavery; social justice; equality; humane treatment of prisoners and the mentally ill; temperance and giving a voice to women (women ministering was part of the Quaker tradition) were all up for discussion.

Henry followed his brothers John Stephenson and Joseph to Bootham School just over the road from the house. Henry was there for six years from the age of 10, from March 1848 until June 1854. He was never what you might call a star pupil or a studious one. He was much more attracted by the mechanical and practical – subjects not very high on Bootham's curriculum. Nevertheless, his father did what he could to nurture this non-academic interest as shown by two letters he sent to Henry; the first during a trip to Bangor in July 1850 in which he expatiated on the 'tubular bridge which like a vast gallery spans the Menai Straits ... I thought of my dear Harry ... I have got a little book which I intend sending thee.' Then from Bangor in July 1856, he sent Henry a description of the workings of a huge slate quarry he had visited. It was the norm in the Rowntree family, whenever they were away from home, to send back regular missives detailing what they had been up to; Henry though was a reluctant letter writer.

Bootham School results were disappointing to say the least – more a race to the bottom than anything like top of the class. In the 1853 summer examinations, Henry came bottom or next to bottom in a class of sixteen in Latin, Geography, Spelling, Dictation, Arithmetic, Mathematics, Science, Writing and Ancient History; but in History he was a creditable fifth. Things improved in his final year when he came tenth out of fourteen, even achieving top place in History. Extra tuition 'improving' reading bore little fruit and so his father, in desperation, forked out fees of £1006 to enrol him in Grove House School, Tottenham, where 'the sons of the Society of Friends' were educated in small classes. Henry was there from August 1854 until June 1855 but showed little sign of improvement, leading his father to conclude that he lacked irredeemably the skills required for a career in commerce.

No amount of encouragement had any impact. Even this letter sent by his father soon after Henry's arrival at Tottenham seems to have fallen on deaf ears:

> My dear Harry... . What art thou pursuing particularly? Do not be afraid of sending us details, anything which interests thee will ... be of interest to us. I hope thou finds that thou art making some progress in acquiring knowledge, and the power of completely executing what thou undertakes. Do not give up: be determined to spell correctly, to write legibly, and to place thy matter fairly on the paper ... I would fain hope that it is thy daily endeavour to act in such a manner as, while it benefits thyself, will give inexpressible comfort to Thy tenderly attached Father.

Leaving the Tottenham school after eleven months must have been a relief for Henry. He returned home to York and began his five-year apprenticeship in the shop on Pavement. But the distractions started to crowd in: he obviously went to Meeting as well as teaching boys' classes on Sundays. When Joseph was away working in London in 1857, Henry overcame his letter-writing block and wrote to him frequently, giving him the news from York. One of these letters describes just how busy he was outside work as he described 'the stress of business':

> On First Day I was at Osbaldwick [visiting Thomas Allis] on second I was engaged about the school till 9pm, on third John's lecture on money, on fourth a teachers' meeting, on fifth paying the bride's visit at C. Robinson's, and on sixth an election meeting ... John's lecture on money was short, interesting & inculcating sound anti-badger [*sic*] views.

Interestingly, he gives an opinion on one of the new apprentices:

> We had George Cadbury to dinner and tea ... our new hand, he has not been at all accustomed to the retail trade, and will never, I think, make much out of it, he seems kind and chearful [*sic*].

That winter was particularly harsh, causing the Ouse and Foss to freeze over. Despite the fun to be had skating, playing football and eating roast chestnuts on ice, the reality of the situation was that the York Soup Kitchen was forced to open. Henry's father had founded this in 1846 in Black Horse Passage close to his shop. Henry opened the kitchen before reporting for work and in February to March 1857, reported demand for soup was high, with over 6,400 pints sold every opening session.

Henry attempted to make his Sunday classes at Hope Street more enjoyable by introducing singing and general science. And he was no mean critic, as shown after a lecture on Palestine by A. Watson which he described in a letter to Joseph as 'well written but he sadly wants greater assurance of delivery, and the views only showed second rate, chiefly from want of light. If thou could get to know the source of Lenzes [*sic*] for a first rate magic lantern from Smith & Beck I should be much obliged.'

Chapter 5

York in the Mid-nineteenth Century

W hat was the commercial and industrial landscape in York into which Henry aimed to fit, along with the three other fledgling confectionery companies, Terry's in 1826, Craven in 1862 and York Confectionery Company in 1867? What sort of city was York in the mid-nineteenth century when John Stephenson and the younger Joseph Rowntree were building up the Pavement grocery business and Henry was learning his trade?

In the second half of the fourteenth century, York, on account of its cloth trade and the ancillary industries associated with it, had been described as 'the foremost industrial town in the North of England'. This did not last, and the trade in cloth declined to such a degree that a visitor to the city in the seventeenth century, Thomas Fuller, remarked, 'the foreign trade is like their river, low and flat'. According to Daniel Defoe, in *A Tour Through the Whole Island of Great Britain* (1724–1727): 'Here is no trade except such as depends upon the confluence of the gentry.' This was due to some extent to the high price of coal in York, which had to be shipped from the coalfields of the West Riding, and to the restrictive, exclusive attitude of the local Merchant Adventurers who insisted that the freedom regulations, whereby all traders had to be freemen of the city, be rigorously observed. Francis Drake in *Eboracum: or the History and Antiquities of the City of York* (1736) agreed: York in the eighteenth century had precious little industry, and the only real commercial activity was butter exports, corn and wine trading. Moreover, up until 1827 when a judgement went against them, it seems that only members of the Company of Merchant Adventurers could carry out trade in imported goods. But the high price of coal would only really affect any heavy industry, and the strictures of the Merchant Adventurers would not have impeded development and progress amongst established manufacturers and traders. Some of the reason for the industrial paralysis can probably be laid at the door of the corporation whose medieval constitution, financial straits and general lack of enterprise did little to attract, promote or sustain industry or commerce to any significant level.

If the 1775 register of freemen is to be believed, only 600 enfranchised members were actually engaged in manufacturing, while more were of the mercantile and hospitality classes: merchants, grocers or innkeepers. York, it seems, was now destined just to work as a parochial market town supplying its own, and the surrounding areas' basic needs, goods and services, and those of the Church and the gentry who frequented the city. Communications, though, were good by road and river and this facilitated the importation of coal – 98,000 tons annually in the 1830s – and the export of agricultural produce, for example, to Leeds, which, in the same period amounted to 110,000 sheep, 53,000 cattle and 30,000 tons of grain. But by the end of the century the butter trade had declined, and York, though still a major ecclesiastical centre, was no longer the magnet for the northern gentry it had once been and the traditional trade catering for these people suffered as a result.

The only real developments were small industries such as leather making (there were tanneries in Tanner's Moat, Walmgate on the Foss and at Marygate on the Ouse, as well as Strensall) and comb and horn breaking, which was active mainly around Hornpot Lane off Petergate (the comb makers worked in ivory and tortoiseshell as well as in horn). One of the more successful comb companies was Forbes and Fothergill near Toft Green. Joseph Rougier, descended from a Huguenot family of wigmakers and hairdressers, was also successful in Tanner Row. Other comb makers included B. Lund in St Andrewgate. Glass was made by Prince and Prest's Fishergate Glass Works which was established in 1797, and flour milling was in North Street and Skeldergate. The year 1780 saw the establishment of manufacturing and wholesale chemists Bleasdale Ltd behind Colliergate, while other pharmaceutical and chemical businesses included Wright and Prest in Pavement, Edward Wallis and Son in Bedern and Thomas Bishop at North Street Postern. Breweries were being run by the Wormald family and Thomas Hartley. A modest amount of shipbuilding came and quickly went after the construction of six brigantines outside Skeldergate Postern for butter exports around 1770, followed by a further three brigantines in 1776 and three more in 1781, 1783 and 1797. Heavy industries such as iron making were limited to Stodhart in Coney Street who produced lamps and kitchen tools, John Spence in Bootham Bar, Masterman and Gibson in Manor Yard and Prince and Holmes on the River Foss.

The 1841 census gives us the following figures for the industries of significance – glass making: fifty-four persons employed in three firms with an average workforce of eighteen persons; flax and linen manufacture: 118 employees in eight firms with an average of fifteen; iron making: twenty-five employees, six firms, average four; chemists and druggists: seventy-six workers in thirty-eight firms averaging two people per firm; 107 comb manufacturers in nine firms averaging twelve people per firm.

With regard to hospitality, coffee houses abounded in York from 1669. There are at least thirty recorded, amongst which were Parker's in Minster Yard – next to a bowling alley as shown on Horsley's 1896 map – the Garrick in Low Petergate, Wombwell and Wink's, Harrison's in Petergate (later Nessgate), Iveson's, also in Petergate, Duke's near to the Ouse Bridge, Brigg's on the corner of Stonegate and Coffee Yard – as well as William Tuke's roasting house. As one of thirty-one York tea dealers in 1823 and importers of tea, coffee and chocolate, the Tukes were the sole holders in the north of England of a licence which permitted the processing of coffee beans and the sale of roasted coffee, tea and chocolate in the north of England. Once drinking chocolate and cocoa became popular then, as elsewhere, they would have been added to the list of beverages available in York's coffee shops.

At the beginning of the nineteenth century the population of York (municipal borough) was 16,846; by the end of the century this had increased by over 200 per cent to 54,742, with the biggest annual increase (twenty-six per cent) coming in the 1840s, soon after the arrival of the railways. Towns and cities such as Leeds, Huddersfield and Bradford, which were directly affected by the Industrial Revolution, nevertheless showed much bigger increases. As we know, the Industrial Revolution was an event which largely passed York by. Indeed, in 1851 we can appreciate the different commercial complexions of these cities when we see that York had twice as many domestic servants in employment as the other three, and an above-national average number of small artisan trades and shopkeepers: one shop for every fifty-five people. At the time, 2,800 people or seventeen per cent of the city's workforce were in service (for women the figure was twenty-five per cent) and a further ninety-one (five and a half per cent) in hospitality – hotels and inns. By comparison, manufacturing accounted for 3,170 persons, or just over nineteen per cent of the economically active. Furthermore, at the dawn of the nineteenth century, York was England's sixteenth largest city and the fourth largest in Yorkshire after Leeds, Sheffield and Hull. By the end of the century it had plummeted to forty-first in the country and in Yorkshire, York had been surpassed by Bradford, Middlesbrough, Halifax and Huddersfield.

Before the railways, many goods were transported in and out of the city on the River Ouse. *White's 1840 Directory* had high hopes for the future:

> The formation of railways to open a better communication with the West of Yorkshire and the North and South of England, are in progress and with these improved modes of transit for goods, it is to be hoped that the trade of York will improve.

In the event, the railways may not have led to a seismic expansion of the industrial base in York, even though six main line companies were soon calling regularly at York. But they did bring their own opportunities for employment and the obvious benefit in communication with the rest of the country, and indeed, with the world, as access to Hull and other east coast ports was improved. When the railways came to the city in 1839, with the first services to London a year later, they brought with them not only a vastly quicker and more comfortable journey for Joseph when he attended meetings in the capital but also a massive influx of visitors – and more trade. The Railway King, scurrilous George Hudson, was prominent in York's development as a major railway city; his advice to George Stephenson was to make it a hub: 'Mak all t'railways cum t'York,' he thundered. Stephenson took that advice and with the lines came a significant industry. The number of people employed in York in railway-related work increased from forty-one in 1841 to 513 in 1851, of whom 390 came for the work from other towns. Many of these were involved in engine repair and building at the railway works where there was a 1,200-strong workforce by 1855. Carriage and wagon building followed; this all moved from Queen Street to a 45-acre site at Holgate and became York's first large-scale industry and its biggest employer. By the end of the century there were 5,500 railway workers in the city, nearly 2,000 of whom were skilled with disposable income-a-plenty.

Other industries in 1851 were still small fry by comparison. The glassworks in Fishergate was ailing and was taken over by Joseph Spence, a Quaker analytical chemist, James Meek and Thomas Spence, to become the successful York Flint Glass Company. It employed 223 men turning out chemists' jars, railway lamps, beetle and wasp traps, cake shades, cruets and Daffy's Elixir bottles. The metal industry was shared between John Walker with fifty-two men, Edwin Thompson, (forty-eight men) and William Knapton, (eighteen men). George Steward's comb manufacturing had thirty men while E. Steward had eighteen in the same industry; William Hebden, linen maker, had a workforce of thirty-five men, seven boys and one woman. In 1823 there were nine toy and household trinket manufacturers including John Barber of Coney Street, John Bell in Stonegate and John Jameson of College Street. Chemicals, flour milling and printing were the only other industries of any size, with 150 chemical workers at the end of the century, ninety-eight millers (mainly at Leetham's in Wormald's Cut in 1891 rising to 600 in 1911) and, also in 1891, almost 500 employed in the printing and publishing trade.

Printing had been established in York since the fifteenth century and by 1750 there were four printing houses in the city. The largest of these was run by the Quaker William Alexander from 1811 in Lower Ousegate and was taken over in 1865 by another Quaker, William Sessions, who moved the firm to Coney Street in 1894. Alexander was following in the tradition of Thomas Gent, author and printer, who operated out of Coffee Yard from 1724 and published the first local newspaper and scores of chapbooks. Ben Johnson and Co Ltd was established as a lithographic printer by Johnson and John Lancaster and specialised in railway timetables and other jobs associated with the railways. Newspapers obviously also provided employment in the shape of the *Whig York Courant*, set up by Caesar Ward in the 1750s. Ward was also the publisher of the first edition of Laurence Sterne's *The Life and Opinions of Tristram Shandy*, the *York Daily Herald* (which changed from a weekly in 1874 and absorbed the *Courant* in 1848), and the 1882 *York Evening Press*, now *The York Press*.

Apart from Bleasdale Ltd in the chemical and drug-making industry, there was Raimes and Company from 1818 in Micklegate, and Henry Richardson and Company, fertiliser makers founded in 1824 at Skeldergate Postern in Clementhorpe. John Walker's iron foundry was very successful and received Queen Victoria's royal warrant in 1847. In 1850, it won the contract to supply the extensive railings and gates for the British Museum and for the Sandringham Estate. In addition, much of its work was in gates and railings for the many country houses around York and at British embassies and foreign government buildings abroad, an example being the Botanical Gardens in Mauritius. The Adams Patent Sewage Lift Company Ltd was established in Peaseholme Green in 1887 to make sanitary equipment. It merged in 1919 with the 1885 iron foundry, G. W. Kirk, its biggest supplier.

A specialist and high-tech company for the time was optical engineers, Thomas Cooke who went on to make sundials, microscopes and world-renowned telescopes from 1837, and became one of York's first, if not the first, global companies. The firm moved from Stonegate to the

Buckingham Works on Bishophill in 1856 and was run by Cooke's two sons after his death in 1868. By the end of the century it had diversified into clock making and employed 500 workers. Cooke also invented a steam car which carried fifteen passengers at a speed of fifteen mph, but which was outlawed by the Road Act prohibiting vehicles which travelled above four mph. His sons invented the pneumatic despatch system.

The development of flour milling in York was particularly important. Henry Leetham set up his milling industry in Hungate on the banks of the River Foss in 1850, replacing his old steam mills with state-of-the-art Hungarian steel rollers for milling the corn. In 1888, he flexed his industrial muscle by threatening to relocate to Hull if the City Corporation refused to enlarge the lock at the entry to the Foss at Castle Mills. This they duly did, and grain replaced coal as the largest river cargo. At the same time, very favourable terms were negotiated for the transport of Leetham's goods. Leetham went on to build his landmark five-storey warehouse in 1896 on Wormald's Cut with its nine-storey castellated water tower linked to the Hungate Mill by bridges. At the time, it was one of the largest mills in Europe. By then, the firm had operations in Hull, Newcastle and Cardiff, as well as in York and was showing handsome profits of around £50,000 per year with a wholesale customer base of around 9,000.

This then was the environment in which Mary, and then Henry Tuke, set up their chocolate, cocoa and tea business in their Castlegate shop, and in which Bayldon and Berry opened their confectionery business in St Helen's Square, and in which Mary Craven established her operation in Coppergate, not far from Mr Henderson of York Confectionery Company in Fossgate. This was the environment in which the businesses which were to become Rowntree's, Terry's and Craven's began their respective commercial lives.

Joseph Rowntree's grocery shop was one of forty-nine grocer's-cum-tea dealers in the city in 1851 and as such faced intense local competition. Success would only come with top quality in both goods and service. Indeed, the choice of Pavement as a location cannot have been a coincidence or accident – more likely a shrewd business decision. Pavement was, as we have seen, the commercial hub of the town, particularly on Saturdays when it hosted the heaving Saturday market and the associated crowds and the visitor business it brought. Add in the hiring fairs and the processions which regularly assembled here and Pavement was often seething with activity all the way down to Parliament Street where a new market had opened in 1836. As we have seen, during the 1850s Joseph's elder sons, John, now 23 and Joseph, 21, became partners in the business, joined by a Christopher Robinson as manager and William Hughes who looked after the live-in apprentices which included Henry, his elder brothers and a Cadbury.

Chapter 6

The Confectionery Industry in Mid-nineteenth Century England

Chocolate – the science

A 100-gram serving of milk chocolate delivers 540 calories. It is fifty-nine per cent carbohydrates (fifty-two per cent as sugar and three per cent as dietary fibre), thirty per cent fat and eight per cent protein. About sixty-five per cent of the fat in milk chocolate is saturated, mainly palmitic acid and stearic acid, while the main unsaturated fat is oleic acid.

One hundred grams of milk chocolate is an excellent source – more than nineteen per cent of the recommended daily amount – of riboflavin, vitamin B12 and the dietary minerals, manganese, phosphorus and zinc. Chocolate is a good source of calcium, magnesium and iron.

Chocolate contains alkaloids such as theobromine and phenethylamine, which have physiological effects in humans, but the presence of theobromine makes it toxic to some animals, such as dogs and cats.

Research has also shown that consuming dark chocolate does not substantially affect blood pressure. Research is ongoing to determine if consumption affects the risk of certain cardiovascular diseases or cognitive abilities.

Chocolate is a mild stimulant and is slightly addictive – hence the fashionable coining of the term 'chocoholic', worn as a badge by some. A tablespoon (5 gram) serving of dry unsweetened cocoa powder has 12.1 mg of caffeine and a 25 gram single serving of dark chocolate has 22.4 mg of caffeine. Although a single 7 oz serving of coffee may contain 80-175 mg, studies have shown psychoactive effects in caffeine doses as low as 9 mg, and a dose as low as 12.5 mg was shown to have effects on cognitive performance.

Chocolate – the commodity

Chocolate grows on trees; so, then, does money, as Montezuma II (reigned 1502–1520) and the Aztecs first proved. Later, western companies such as Rowntree's, Hershey, Cadbury's, Mars and Nestlé were to enjoy the same warming experience when the money started rolling in. Chocolate grows on trees in the form of cocoa powder from the seeds or beans of the cacao tree, *Theobroma cacao,* literally, 'cocoa, food of the gods'. 'Cacao' means 'bitter juice' in Mayan. The main growing areas are central and eastern South America and West Africa, all within 20 degrees of the Equator, below 1,000 feet in the shade and at a minimum temperature of 16°C. Global warming will no doubt have an impact, one way or another. Between thirty and forty white pulp-covered seeds are in the average, football-sized pod; it fruits all year round. In the very early days the beans were sun dried and the kernels or nibs (up to half their weight is made up of fat, or cacao butter) were roasted, shelled and crushed into a paste called cacao liquor – liquor in the liquid essence sense – and then made into cakes. These were then crumbled and immersed in water to form liquid chocolate. The drink was taken both hot and cold, thickened to make a soup or redried to make cakes. Four hundred or so beans make 1 lb of chocolate.

Chocolate comes to England

England's early encounters with chocolate were far from auspicious. Thomas Gage noted in 1579:

> When we have taken a good prize, a ship laden with cocoa, in anger and wrath we have hurled overboard this good commodity not regarding the worth and goodness of it, but calling it in bad Spanish *cagaruta de carnero,* or sheep shit in good English.

José deAcosta in his 1590 *Natural and Moral History* tells us that an English corsair burnt 100,000 loads of cacao in the port of Guatulco in New Spain, the equivalent of 2.4 billion beans. It was a Parisian shopkeeper who opened the first chocolate shop in London, in June 1657. The 23 June 1659 edition of Needham's *Mercurius Politicus* ran the following advertisement:

> An excellent West India drink called chocolate, in Bishopsgate Street, in Queen's Head Alley, at a Frenchman's house being the first man who did sell it in England ... ready at any time, and also unmade at reasonable rates ... it cures and preserves the body of many diseases.

Chocolate makes an appearance in 1658 as a 'compounded Indian drink, whose chief ingredient is a fruit called Cacao' in Edward Phillips' *The New World of English Words, or, A General Dictionary Containing the Interpretation of such Hard Words as are Derived from other Languages*. M. Sury's Oxford chocolate house pamphlet in 1660 describes chocolate as a panacea; 'chocolate goggles' in another time:

> By this pleasing drink health is preserved, sickness diverted. It cures consumptions and Coughs of the Lungs; it expels poison, cleanseth the teeth, and sweetneth the Breath; provoketh Urine; cureth the stone and strangury, maketh Fatt and Corpulent, faire and aimeable.

And when it comes to its benefits to infertile women he is quite poetic: 'Nor need the Women longer grieve, Who spend their oyle yet not Conceive, For 'tis a Help Immediate, If such but Lick of Chocolate.'

James Wadsworth wittily declared in his *Curious History of the Nature and Quality of Chocolate*: 'Twill make Old Women Young and Fresh, Create New Motion of the Flesh, And cause them Long for you know what, If they but taste of Chocolate.'

Pepys' diary entries show how it was very much part of his seventeenth-century society, thus confirming chocolate as one of the drinks of choice among men of influence and affluence. On the morning of 24 April 1661, he used it as a hangover cure after Charles II's coronation, waking up 'with my head in a sad taking through last night's drink which I am sorry for. So rose and went out with Mr Creede to drink our morning draft, which he did give me chocolate to settle my stomach.'

Sex and chocolate, then, had formed an association which endures to this day. However, what was happening in England was nothing compared to the chocolate goings-on over in France.

Louis XVI's mistresses, Mesdames du Barry and de Pompadour, played their parts in sexing up chocolate, however unwittingly: du Barry was scurrilously accused of exciting her lovers with chocolate to satisfy her own lust. Pompadour, on the other hand, was reputedly frigid and, according to Stanley Loomis, used hot chocolate along with 'aphrodisiacs, truffle and celery soup to stir a sensuality that was at best sluggish.' Voltaire's *Candide* learns that the spread of syphilis throughout Europe by Columbus' explorers was a fair price to pay for the simultaneous introduction of chocolate and cochineal.

The works of the notorious Marquis de Sade have frequent references to chocolate, consumed before and after sex, and it features regularly as a prop in his orgies. His petulant letters from prison to Madame de Sade (Renée de Montreuil) betray a genuine personal craving – our first sadomasochist chocoholic; this from 16 May 1779:

> The sponge cake is not at all what I asked for. 1st, I wanted it iced all over ... 2nd I wanted it to have chocolate inside as black as the devil's arse is black from smoke, and there isn't even the least trace of chocolate. I beg you to have it sent to me at the first opportunity ... the cakes must smell of it, as if you're biting into a bar of chocolate.

However, de Sade's greatest chocolate moment is told by Louis Petit de Bachaumont in his *Mémoires secrets pour servir à l'histoire de la République des lettres*: at a ball given by de Sade, the host laced the chocolate pastilles with Spanish fly, a well-known aphrodisiac:

> It proved to be so potent that those who ate the pastilles began to burn with unchaste ardour and to carry on as if in the grip of the most amorous frenzy ... even the most respectable of women were unable to resist the uterine rage that stirred within them. And so it was that M de Sade enjoyed the favours of his sister-in-law ... several persons died of their frightful priapic excesses, and others are still quite sick.

In the beginning in the west, chocolate manufacture was the preserve of small, local workshops and apothecaries; only in the mid 1850s did sizeable chocolate companies emerge to exploit economies of scale in the roasting and grinding processes. They churned out finished chocolate, and cocoa butter and cocoa powder, which were often sold on to other manufacturers. Unsweetened plain chocolate was bought up by numerous confectioners, grocery shops and bakers, many of which were small family concerns. Cartels amongst the large producers were rare, and largely restricted to England: Fry's, Cadbury's, Rowntree's and Caley's.

Chocolate manufacture in Europe

Rowntree's were obviously affected and influenced by the productivity of their main rivals Fry's, Packard's, Dunn's, Caley's and Cadbury's, but competition came too from those foreign companies who were setting up offices, agencies and factories in England. Moreover, the existence of chocolate manufacturing on the continent, even by those companies without a UK presence, would have had an impact, albeit an indirect one, notably on exports. In the 1760s, Lombart was established, claiming to be the oldest chocolate manufactory in France; Pelletier followed in 1770 – both seem to have experimented, unsuccessfully, with pressing out cocoa butter. By 1778 water power was applied to grinding and mixing liquor. In 1819, François Pelletier caused a stir when he fitted a four-horse power-steam mixer in his Paris factory; this allowed him to turn out 75 kilos of cocoa mass in half a day. Louit was established in Bordeaux in 1825 with satellite factories, all steam powered by 1850. Bayonne's chocolate-making firms grew from twenty-one in 1822 to thirty-three in 1856. Jean-Baptiste Létang was making moulds for eating chocolate in Paris in 1832, making use of new developments in metal working and chocolate making.

In 1798, Austria and Germany could boast factories in eight cities. Germany, and more specifically Dresden, were famous for their cocoa bean-processing machinery, spearheaded by the firm of Lehmann. Stollwerck followed them into that market in 1866. Lehmann's booth at the 1893 Chicago International Exposition inspired Milton Hershey to go into chocolate. In 1870, Anton Reiche set up in Dresden and became the world's largest producer of chocolate machinery in 1910, with 500 workers on the payroll, while pioneering the use of nickel plating. British chocolate makers bought some of their chocolate machinery from Joseph Baker & Sons but relied mainly on imported machines.

The Dutch chocolate industry was centred on Zeeland, probably using wind power. There were twelve manufacturers in 1888 exporting 750 tons of chocolate powder per year to Britain and Germany, and 1,000 tons into other markets. Van Houten were a smallish company, even in the nineteenth century when, in 1850, they installed their first steam engine, employing only seventy-eight workers in 1871. It is also argued that the novelty and impact of the Van Houten press has been exaggerated, from its patenting in 1828 to the end of the century. The first cocoa butter press is attested in 1687 with repeated attempts to improve it. Demand for cocoa butter was very low so there was little to be gained by anyone pressing it out – hence the long gap between the invention of the Van Houten press and its adoption by manufacturers in Britain, France, Germany and Switzerland.

The real break came in 1879 when the eating of chocolate went through the roof, largely due to Roderich Lindt's invention of 'melting chocolate', enriched by added cocoa butter with an enhanced texture created by extra mechanical conching (smoothing) of the cocoa mass. Chocolate became a popular and common ingredient in all manner of baking and confectionery products. Small amounts of cocoa butter were also used in the manufacture of suppositories, pessaries, ointments, perfumes and toothpaste. Shells were drunk in Ireland and Italy as a cheap beverage and went into livestock fodder; they were also burned to produce potassium-enriched fertilisers.

The advent of the modern chocolate factory from 1890, with its state-of-the-art machinery and enhanced energy supplies, allowed the factory worker to produce 500 kilos per day of chocolate paste; his pre-industrial workshop counterpart could only manage 10 kilos per day. Of the 144 German chocolate factories we know much about in 1895, 109 were powered by steam, eighteen by water, and seventeen by petroleum, gas or electricity.

The temperance movement and taxes

The temperance movement took to chocolate with gusto, establishing British Workman houses to compete with alcohol-serving public houses. It even published a guide instructing how to set up and run these establishments. The Quakers had strong links with the movement and so began the association of Quakers with chocolate. When Messrs Fry, Cadbury and Rowntree (and non-Quaker Terry) made 'conversation lozenges' and dragées which carried such romantic messages as 'Do you love me?' and 'No, I won't ask Mama', the Quakers poured sobering cold water (or flat beer) on it all by distributing their sweets with such killjoy and cautionary messages as 'Misery, sickness and poverty are the effect of drunkenness'. Right message, wrong medium.

Cocoa had to compete with other non-alcoholic drinks, most notably coffee and tea, since all three required mixing with boiled liquids, which obviated the need for drinking cold drinks and their often-diseased cold water. Coffee, however, was the main beneficiary of the temperance movement's activities discouraging all alcohol – not just spirits – and it thus became popular with the working classes, with consumption per head rising to nearly that of tea by 1840. Chicory from Belgium or that grown in England was still being mixed with it. Generally, cocoa remained the Cinderella drink: around 1880, estimates put 500 million people drinking tea, 200 million coffee, and only fifty million imbibing cocoa. But things soon changed for the better, helped by public revulsion at the routine adulteration of all beverages, the advertising onslaught promoting the health-giving qualities of all three and the efforts of the temperance movement. Between 1870 and 1897, world imports of cocoa beans grew ninefold whereas tea could only manage a doubling and coffee a half. Between 1870 and 1910, cocoa consumption per head in Britain increased by a factor of six; tea failed to double while coffee fell by a half.

Alkaloids extracted from coca leaves and kola nuts were added to industrially produced soft drinks from the 1870s, notably Coca-Cola which was launched in Atlanta in 1886 as a temperance drink and a 'brain, tonic'. It lost its cocaine in 1906.

Customs duties on cocoa beans and sales taxes on the end product obviously dictated the ebb and flow of demand when it translated into prices in the shops. A sign of how things were getting serious amongst chocolate and cocoa industrialists came with the launch of the German-language trade magazine *Der Gordian*, founded in 1895. Slavery provided the engine of cultivation, with slaves working at it on estates from at least 1765, although coerced labour was finally dying out by 1914.

This had an enormous impact on the commodity chain which saw the 'one hat fits all' merchant, who controlled everything from the purchase of beans to final sale, be replaced by huge mechanised factories benefitting from those elastic economies of scale and employing enormous numbers of workers. What was originally a heavily taxed luxury product for the wealthy few became affordable and a 'nice to have' food, a discretionary purchase for industrial workers. The geographical profile of cocoa production changed too: from Spanish-driven Mesoamerica to the northern fringes of South America with increasing incursions by Brazilian Bahia, Trinidad and the Dominican Republic and, more significantly, the Portuguese colony of São Tomé and Príncipe and what was the Gold Coast from 1911.

As might be expected, the USA, Britain, France and Germany were the major recipients of cocoa imports, but the party was gatecrashed by the Dutch and the Swiss who dominated the markets for drinking chocolate and eating and milk chocolate respectively.

Coffee houses and chocolate houses

Drinking chocolate did not just happen. It was part of that triumvirate of hot liquors, along with tea and coffee, which became fashionable in Europe in various places and at various times. Often the three were consumed in the same establishments, usually coffee houses or tea houses. Sometimes they were served in the same cup.

For example, Turin's oldest surviving coffee house opened in 1763: Caffè Al Bicerin (literally 'The Little Cup' in the local Piemontese dialect), is situated on Piazza della Consolata, and is home to the traditional drink of Turin, the *bicerin*, the exact recipe for which remains a secret. It is made of espresso, drinking chocolate and whole milk served layered in a small rounded glass. The beverage has been known since the eighteenth century and was much beloved of Alexandre Dumas around 1852. It is believed to be based on the seventeenth-century drink *bavareisa*: the key difference being that in a *bicerin*, the three components are carefully layered in the glass rather than being mixed together. Once frequented by aristocracy, including Puccini, Cavour and Dumas, the tiny and ancient coffee house has only eight marble-topped tables.

In Trentino, ask for a *cappuccino Viennese* and you are served with a frothy coffee with chocolate and cinnamon. In the Marche region, stop for a *caffè anisette* for an aniseed-flavoured espresso. In Naples, enjoy coffee flavoured with hazelnut cream and, while in Sicily, indulge in a *caffè d'u parrinu* – an Arabic-inspired coffee flavoured with cloves, cinnamon and cocoa powder.

In English coffee houses, for one penny customers bought a cup of coffee and admission, with access to newspapers and the opinions, advice and attitude of fellow patrons. The early coffee houses also served tea and chocolate but not alcohol. It is this that did much to foster an atmosphere in which it was possible to engage in more serious and nuanced conversation than was usually possible in the rowdy drink-fuelled alehouse. The low admission price made them comparatively inclusive, in Oxford (and presumably Cambridge) and an exciting alternative to the exclusive and much more formal university lecture and tutorial.

London's second coffee house opened in 1656 as the Rainbow, near Temple Bar in Fleet Street. It also served tea and chocolate and was run by a man named Farr. He was arraigned on charges of causing a nuisance by his neighbours who complained of the strange smell of roasting coffee:

> we present James Farr, barber, for making and selling of a drink called coffee, whereby in making the same he annoyeth his neighbours by evil smells; and for keeping of fire for the most part night and day, whereby his chimney and chamber hath been set on fire, to the great danger and affrightment of his neighbours.

The Great Turk Coffee House (also known as *Morat Ye Great*) in Exchange Alley in 1662 was famous for its bust of Sultan Amurath IV himself, 'the most detestable tyrant that ever ruled the Ottoman Empire'. Customers could buy coffee, tea and tobacco here, as well as chocolate and a range of sherbets, which, in the words of the *Mercurius Publicus* (12–19 March 1662), was 'made in Turkie; made of lemons, roses, and violets perfumed'.

Exclusively chocolate houses included the famous White's, the Cocoa Tree, Arthur's and St James but, no doubt, a cup of coffee could also be had in each. They offered the same ambience and character as coffee houses and gave off the same literary, social and commercial atmosphere, attracting the same clientele. In April 1773, a fire destroyed White's Chocolate House which reopened as White's Club, the first of many London houses to become an exclusive gentleman's club. The Cocoa Tree was the haunt of Tories, Arthur's that of Whigs.

Jonathan Swift was not impressed: he described White's Chocolate House as a place to be 'fleeced and corrupted by fashionable gamblers and profligates'. White's was opened in 1693 by the Italian Francis White and by 1709 had achieved such a fashionable reputation that Richard Steele wrote his pieces for *The Tatler* there: 'All accounts of Gallantry, Pleasure and Entertainment shall be under the article of White's Chocolate House, Poetry under that of … .' In Alexander Pope's *Dunciad* it was where you went to 'teach oaths to youngsters and to nobles wit'. The Cocoa Tree also enjoyed Steele's patronage, this time along with Joseph Addison, who wrote articles for *The Spectator* from there when it was launched in 1711. Addison ranked chocolate alongside 'romances' and 'novels' as one of life's great 'inflamers'.

Soon, chocolate house owners were realising the business opportunities their establishments offered and rewrote their business plans to convert them into havens for the rich, the privileged and the male and, in doing so, forged the origins of the English gentlemen's club. Disorder of one sort or another – be it prostitution at the notorious Moll King's coffee house, brawling or highwaymen conspiring to waylay well-heeled guests – led coffee houses and chocolate houses such as St James and The Cocoa Tree, to follow White's into a private membership business model. This paved the way for the demise of the coffee shop and its culture.

The memorial plaque at 32 Cornhill is all that is left of Garraway's. It reads: 'Garraway's Coffee House, a place of great commercial transaction and frequented by people of quality'. According to the barber Thomas Rugg, writing in his *Diurnal*, 'Coffee, chocolate and a kind of drink called *tee* [were] sold in almost every street in 1659'.

So coffee, tea and chocolate frequently rubbed shoulders: Thomas Twining purchased Tom's Coffee House at 216 the Strand in 1706 and set up his tea empire with cocoa on his supply list. In 1824, John Cadbury opened his tea, coffee and cocoa shop in Bull Street, Birmingham after apprenticeships first at John Cudworth's grocers in Leeds, and then in London at the East India Company's bonded warehouse and at the Sanderson, Fox and Company teahouse. In York, as we have seen, Joseph Rowntree senior laid down the law for apprentices in their shop in Pavement:

> be explicit in stating the particular kind of article wanted: e.g. if Coffee is ordered, state on order, whether whole, ground, mixed or genuine is wanted. – if Tea, – Black, Mixed, Assam, or whole-leaf: if Sugar, Lump, Raw or Moist.

In 1754 Robert Bartholomew advertised his White Conduit House tavern-cum-pleasure garden with the following copy:

> I have completed a long walk, with a handsome circular fish-pond, a number of shady pleasant arbours, enclosed with a fence seven feet high to prevent being the least incommoded from people in the fields; hot loaves and butter every day, milk directly from the cows, coffee, tea, and all manner of liquors in the greatest perfection.

In Charing Cross there was the Cannon; the coffee house run by Alexander Man, and known, unsurprisingly, as Man's. Man was appointed coffee, tea, and chocolate maker to William III, which allowed his establishment to be described as the royal coffee house. It had a third name, Old Man's Coffee House, to distinguish it from Young Man's on the other side of the street.

Tea, however, was resurgent in and around 1790 and was enjoying a period of mass consumption amongst an ever-fickle public. The knock-on effect was a ruinous decline in sales of coffee, cocoa and chocolate which in turn did for many a coffee and chocolate house. The Royal Navy did what it could by sending slabs of chocolate to its sailors in the Caribbean in the 1780s – a move which helped the appreciation of the beverage amongst the lower classes, especially when the sailors got back home to their families. In 1824, the Navy went a step further by replacing breakfast gruel with an ounce of chocolate. While this may have seemed a reasonable trade off, the halving of the rum ration in 1825 and issuing more chocolate will not have gone down so well. By 1830 the Navy was getting through 179 tons per year, quite astonishing when we remember that most of England's cocoa at the time was made in pharmacies.

On the scientific front, Faustus Nairon Banesius published the first printed treatise devoted to coffee in Rome, in 1671. The same year Dufour brought out the first treatise in French, followed in 1684 by *The manner of making coffee, tea, and chocolate*. John Ray praised coffee in his *Universal Botany of Plants* (London 1686). Leonardus Ferdinandus Meisner published a Latin treatise on coffee, tea, and chocolate in 1721. Dr James Douglas released *A description and history of the coffee tree* in London in 1727.

Marie de Rabutin-Chantal, the Marquise de Sévigné, the socialite and letter-writing gossip, declared chocolate to have a defining role in embryology. One of her missives in 1671 tells us that the Marquise de Coetlogon took so much chocolate during her pregnancy the previous year that she produced 'a small boy as black as the devil'. He died. Black magic?

Indeed, cocoa was frequently tarred with the same brush as coffee, a veritable stimulant of simmering sedition. In 1672, Charles II issued his 'Proclamation to restrain the spreading of false news, and licentious talking of matters of State and Government'. Coffee houses were seen by the state as 'nurseries of sedition' and the public was urged to report any such anti-government scandal-mongering. They were looked upon with suspicion, especially by royalists and Tories who were fearful of a return to civil war. They were 'places of promiscuous resort' according to the socially conservative lawyer and biographer Roger North where 'gentlemen, citizens and underlings mingled' – a potentially explosive combination.   Charles II saw them as centres of the 'most seditious, indecent and scandalous discourses'. He banned coffee houses from receiving any newspapers apart from the official *London Gazette*. Coffee houses seemed to have escaped the strictures of Cromwell's Puritanism but were, ironically, assaulted during the comparative liberalism in Charles' restoration reign.

Unsurprisingly, nothing much changed, so in 1674 a similar proclamation was published, and another, more punitive still, at the end of 1675: 'A proclamation for the suppression of coffee-houses'. How far this was really done for commercial reasons, or for genuine concern over simmering revolution we can only speculate. It is worth remembering, though, that the Popish Plot and the hysteria it was to cause from 1678 to 1681 was not far away. No doubt Charles' spies were good customers of the coffee houses, eavesdropping, stoking paranoia and inciting suspected enemies of the state in the verbal rough and tumble and indiscretions so commonly found there. Who exactly was spreading the alleged sedition? Impossible to police and in the face of public disapproval, the proclamation was rescinded within eleven short days. Coffee and coffee houses, unlike the Stuarts, had come to stay. In 1676 the poet Andrew Marvell scorned Charles in his *Dialogue between Two Horses*:

> Though tyrants make laws, which they strictly proclaim,
> To conceal their own faults and to cover their shame...
> Let the city drink coffee and quietly groan, –
> They who conquered the father won't be slaves to the son.
> For wine and strong drink make tumults increase,
> Chocolate, tea, and coffee, are liquors of peace;
> No quarrels, or oaths are among those who drink'em
> 'Tis Bacchus and the brewer swear, damn'em! And sink'em!
> Then Charles thy edict against coffee recall,
> There's ten times more treason in brandy and ale.

Charles Edward Taylor, a Quaker, and son of a York master grocer, set up his business with kiosk tea and coffee shops in fashionable Harrogate – at 11 Parliament Street – and Ilkley after an apprenticeship at James Ashby, the London tea dealers. The kiosks were followed by Cafe Imperials in both towns: Ilkley opened in 1896; the Harrogate branch in 1907, in the mock baronial castle now occupied by Bettys. The Ilkley Bettys is the old Taylor's kiosk cafe and Bettys in Stonegate York occupies the former Taylor's kiosk cafe.

Chocolate in York

When Henry Rowntree made that momentous decision to buy the Tuke business and graduate to the manufacture of cocoa, he was aware that there was plenty of aggressive and talented competition on his very doorstep. Was this a prescient Henry subscribing to an early form of cluster economics in order to increase the productivity of his company as part of the cluster, to drive innovation in the field, and stimulate new businesses in the sector? Or was this a determined Henry believing that if Terry and Craven could make a success of it then so could he? Or was this Henry blithely unaware of the impact any such competition might have on his potential market share? Probably the first, but he is unlikely to have realised it, with elements of the second and third.

Joseph Terry

When Henry signed on the dotted line, the confectionery industry in York was beginning to emerge as a major force, helped in part by the freighting opportunities the railways offered. By 1851, Joseph Terry employed 127 workers in his smart St Helen's Square premises and Thomas Craven was working with sixty-three men and sixty boys; both manufacturing sugar confectionery and chocolate (of sorts) for the nation.

Joseph Terry was making cocoa and chocolate from 1886 and by the end of the 1920s, the firm had become the market leader in chocolate assortments and was building a sound reputation for producing the best in dark and bitter chocolate. The origins of the company go right back to 1767 when:

> there was founded near Bootham Bar, York, a confectionery business which was destined to develop, at first into a centre where the elite of the County enjoyed their sweetmeats, and, at last after phases of success with various specialties and operation at different centres in the City, into a Chocolate Factory the name of which is recognised throughout the World as synonymous with excellence of quality.

This confectionery business was run by Messrs William Bayldon and Robert Berry.

Joseph Terry came to York from nearby Pocklington to serve an apprenticeship in an apothecary in Stonegate. An advertisement in the *York Courant* in 1813 tells us that he is established 'opposite the Castle, selling spices, pickling vinegar, essence of spruce, patent medicines and perfumery' – the usual stock in trade for an apothecary. In those days, there was a very thin grey line separating the chemist and druggist from the confectioner. The very word 'confectionery' is derived from the medical term 'confection', which originally meant a sweetened pill.

In 1823 Joseph married Harriet Atkinson, a sister-in-law of Robert Berry's. He then threw in his lot as a chemist and joined Berry, who had moved from Bootham to St Helen's Square in 1824 – the site of the first old factory. George Berry succeeded his father to form the pleasantly rhyming Terry & Berry, but George departed in 1828 leaving Joseph to develop what then was essentially an expanding confectionery business.

Terry's wasted no time in going national; by 1840 their products were reaching seventy-five towns all over England. They included candied eringo, coltsfoot rock, gum balls and lozenges made from squill, camphor and horehound. Apart from boiled sweets, production included marmalade, marzipan, mushroom ketchup and calves' jelly. Conversation Lozenges, precursors of Love Hearts, with risqué slogans such as 'Can you polka?', 'I want a wife', 'Do you love me?' and 'How do you flirt?' were particularly popular. Chocolate production began in earnest around 1867 with thirteen chocolate products (including chocolate creams and batons), although the company would remain essentially a confectionery company for some thirty more years. The chocolate complemented the other 380 or so confectionery lines.

When he died in 1850, Joseph left the business to his son, Joseph junior, then aged 22. In 1864, Joseph leased a riverside factory at Clementhorpe on the River Ouse. St Helen's Square was retained and converted into a fashionable shop, ballroom and restaurant; you can still see the Terry name on the building's façade. Joseph junior died in 1898 and was succeeded by his sons Thomas Walker Leaper Terry and Frank Terry. The famous Neapolitans brand was launched in 1899.

In 1926 the company moved again to the purpose-built Chocolate Works in Bishopthorpe Road.

M. A. Craven & Son

Craven's opened their doors in 1803 when 29-year-old Joseph Hick set up as Kilner and Hick, confectioners. Kilner left town leaving Hick to run the business, which he relocated to 47 Coney Street (see *White's 1858 City of York Directory*), next door to what was then the Leopard Inn, opposite St Martin le Grand. Joseph's daughter Mary Ann Hick was born in 1826. At around the same time George Berry, a former partner of confectioner Joseph Terry, was setting up in business with his brother-in-law, Thomas Hide, at 20 High Ousegate. Thomas' wife Frances (née Craven) was from an East Yorkshire farming family and in 1833 her brother, Thomas Craven, then aged 16, moved to York to become apprentice to Berry and Hide. After seven years of apprenticeship, Thomas was able to buy the right to trade in York when he became a freeman in 1840.

Thomas Hide died in 1843 and Thomas Craven then set up his own business next door at 19 High Ousegate as a 'purveyor of confectionery, teas, coffees etc'. He worked from there for a short while but, on 1 May 1845, moved to 21 Pavement, which he rented at £70 a year from William Dove, with an additional property in Foss Islands Road. Thomas Craven married Mary Ann Hick on 29 April 1851. They bought the Pavement building outright for £1,300 from Dove, and a further site at

10 Coppergate. William Dove was an ironmonger with close connections to the Craven family. He was their next-door neighbour when they moved to Heworth in the 1870s and Mary's daughter, Susan, married William's son, also William.

In 1860, Joseph Hick died and his estate was divided up between his three children. In 1862 Mary Ann's husband, Thomas Craven, died at the age of 43, leaving her with three young children – Joseph William aged 7, Annie 5 and Susan 3 – and, at the same time, she was faced with the challenging prospect of bringing up the children with two businesses to run. On the verge of starvation she took up the challenge, amalgamated and reanimated the businesses, changed the name of the company to M. A. Craven, and ran it until her death in 1900. In 1881 her son, Joseph William, had joined the firm which became M.A. Craven & Son.

We have noted above how, as elsewhere, York traders were required to register as freemen and freewomen before they were allowed to conduct business. The three usual routes were through 'patrimony' as children of existing freemen; completing an apprenticeship with a York freeman or woman and paying £1; or by 'Order of the City Corporation' and the payment of a substantial fee. In the eighteenth century that fee was between £20 and £35, usually £25.

Widowhood allowed women to take up or change their occupation. In York they were allowed to carry on their husband's trade or occupation without needing to take up their own freedom, and were allowed to take on apprenticeships, as long as their husbands had been free. It is therefore likely that at least some of these widows, such as Mary Ann Craven, were already familiar with their husbands' businesses. Magdalena Clubley, confectioner, grocer and tea dealer, widowed 1791, is another example.

In 1861, just before Mary Ann's husband died, there were fifty men and forty boys on the books. Ten years later she had 110 employees; by 1908 this had increased to 800 – a sizeable business by York standards. In addition to production, packaging, despatch and marketing, there were four Craven's retail shops in the city. One of these, 'Mary Ann's Sweet Shop', was in the Shambles and featured a sweet museum on the first floor where visitors could see 150 years of the 'Art, Trade, Mystery and Business of the Confectioner'.

On her death, her son Joseph William took a business trip to Paris – at that time the centre of the world's sugar confectionery trade – and bought the recipe for Original French Almonds. He brought this back to York in 1904 and kept it and the manufacturing process a closely guarded secret from Craven's competitors. So important were French Almonds to their business sales that, in 1920, the Coppergate factory was renamed the French Almond Works. In 1925, Rowntree's made a takeover bid for Craven's which was rejected.

In the summer of 2011, a surprise find of priceless material from Craven's heyday was discovered in an old Craven warehouse. The horde included the famous painting of Mary Craven which hung in the company's boardroom for many years; various sweet and chocolate tins and other bits and pieces. Tony Wade of Tangerine Confectionery, which owns the Craven brand and who made the discovery, remembers the painting from his early apprenticeship days at the firm as well as anecdotes about Mary Craven as reported in *The York Press*. 'She wasn't very tall,' he said. 'Apparently, she used to have a high chair she would sit on so she could oversee the packing.' He points out that the company is making many of the same products now as they made in the early days: 'We still use the same techniques. The stripes on the humbugs are still painted by hand.'

The York Confectionery Company

The York Confectionery Company was founded in 1867 in Fossgate, moving to Fenwick Street off Bishopthorpe Road. It specialised in candied peel and did a good line in red and white mint rock which was all the rage for the burgeoning seaside market, aided and abetted by the railway and the railway excursion. The company is listed in the *1879 Post Office Directory* where the address is given as Fenwick Street and the manager as George Irving. It booked a small advertisement in the directory in which the company is described as 'Wholesale and Export Confectioners ... Peel manufacturers & C ... Nunthorpe, York'.

York Confectionery Company was run by a man called Henderson who suffered from dyspnoea – laboured breathing – and thereby won for his firm the nickname 'Puffy's'. Its factory was Nunthorpe Peel Works but the firm finally ran out of breath in 1909 and Henderson was declared bankrupt. When chocolate became readily available, candied peel lost its popularity.

The York Herald of 10 June 1876 reported a fire at the Nunthorpe Peel Works. This gives us an illuminating description of the premises:

The works ... consist of three large blocks of buildings running parallel with each other, and contain lemon peel, bags of sugar, sweets, and confectionery of almost every description. It was in the centre block of buildings, known as the lemon peel and lozenge departments, at one end of which are a couple of inhabited cottages belonging to Mr Keswick builder, and at the other the offices of the [York Confectionery] Company. [Once the fire was extinguished] nothing but the bare and blackened walls of the building [were] remaining. Several tons of lemon peel, lozenges, sugar, etc., were destroyed.

Other confectionery manufacturers listed in 1879 are Craven, Terry, William Borman Seaman (12 Railway Street) and William Henry Stott (11 Feasegate). Rowntree is not listed. *White's 1867 City of York Directory* lists a Chas Craven at 56a Micklegate, specialising in butterscotch with M. A. Craven at 31 Pavement, 47 Coney Street and 56a Micklegate (as Chas above).

H. Backhouse & Co

Cook's York Directory of 1900 lists some of York's main cocoa and chocolate manufacturers. Not only are the usual suspects there but we also discover H. Backhouse & Co of Clementhorpe.

Herbert Backhouse and his colleague, who delighted in the wonderful name of Xavier Marb, ran the Criterion Cocoa Works on Walmgate with a subsidiary business in Ogleforth. They ran these operations until around 1900, trading as Backhouse & Marb, when they went into liquidation. Parts of the business continued as separate entities including 'Backhouses' of River Street, Clementhorpe, which survived until 1935, when it too was liquidated.

Backhouse & Marb was mentioned in the local press down the years, all of which shines a light on the workings of a confectionery company at the time:

Yorkshire Post 14 November 1900 wanted 'An experienced moulder, H. Backhouse & Co., Clementhorpe.'

Yorkshire Evening Post 27 October 1899 wanted 'Experienced starch hand well up in fondants, creams and chocolate centres. H. Backhouse and Co., Clementhorpe.'

Leeds Mercury 27 September 1898 described a meeting of creditors of Backhouse & Marb, listing all the known liabilities and assets.

The *Manchester Evening News* of 22 January 1901 ran an advertisement for staff placed by H. Backhouse and Co. The company was looking for skilled chocolate moulders.

The 1914 edition of *Who's Who in Business* included the following entry:

Backhouse, H. & Company Limited. Chocolate Manufacturers, Clementhorpe, York. Hours of Business: 8 a.m. to 6 p.m.; Saturdays 8 a.m. to 12.30 p.m. Established in 1899 by H. Backhouse, the present Managing Director. Incorporated as a Private Limited Company in 1911. Speciality: Fine Chocolate.

The Yorkshire Post and Leeds Intelligencer of 24 November 1930 had an advertisement for sales representatives at Backhouse & Co's chocolate and toffee house. Applicants needed to demonstrate good connections, and preferably to own a car. Payment would be by commission only.

The Yorkshire Post and Leeds Intelligencer of 18 June 1934 featured an advertisement for Backhouse's chocolate and fruit dessert, 'only the purest ingredients'.

The *Leeds Mercury* of 18 June 1934 had an advertisement which read:

Backhouses Chocolate Fruit Dessert 4d Per Qr. The MOST DELICIOUS SWEETMEAT YOU CAN BUY. Delicious fruit jellies with real fruit flavours covered with that rich, smooth chocolate for which BACKHOUSES have been famous since 1898. Only the best and purest ingredients are used for all BACKHOUSE lines ... Backhouses Ltd., Makers of Good Chocolate since 1839.

On 23 February 1935, the *Yorkshire Post and Leeds Intelligencer* reported the liquidation and sale of Backhouses Ltd of River Street.

The same edition contained a notice announcing the sale by public auction of the Backhouse premises in River Street, Clementhorpe. The sale included all manner of chocolate-making machinery and equipment.

The owner, Herbert E. P. Backhouse, was born in Ilfracombe, North Devon, in 1865. He lived at 110 Bishopthorpe Road in 1911, but by 1939 he was retired and living at Pine Crest, 100 Acomb Road with his wife Florence. He was then described as a retired cocoa and chocolate manufacturer. He died in 1950. The house still stands, opposite the Mormon church.

England

Henry Mayhew's 1851 *London Labour and the London Poor* gives us some idea of the relative size of the UK confectionery market at the time. Confectionery was worth £10,000 per annum compared with £31,200 for tea and coffee, £19,448 for hot eels, £14,000 for baked potatoes, £11,400 for fried fish, £6,000 for muffins and crumpets and £3,000 for pies. There were 230 sweet sellers in the capital. In Manchester, there were two confectioners' shops in 1772, rising to 308 in 1872 (by comparison there were 804 butchers and 374 bakers). Confectionery schools were established, the most famous being the Ladies' Confiserie Company and the piping and ornamentation school on Tottenham Court Road.

Henry Rowntree was wise enough to realise that confectionery was a national industry and that not only was the proximity of Terry's and Craven's incidental to some degree, but also that companies nationwide had a bearing on his market and an impact on prospective sales. And it was not only British companies which provided the competition: serious rivalry was flooding into the ports of England and onto the railways for nationwide sweet shop distribution from France, the Netherlands and Switzerland, some of whom even established UK offices and local distribution networks. The railways had revolutionised the industry with its profound effects on imports and exports, domestic transportation of raw materials and finished goods and workforce mobility. Competition was legion.

The English were at the forefront of attempts to make chocolate more palatable. Once the beans are ground the resulting essence produces about fifty-five per cent cocoa butter. Various trials to counteract the viscosity and greasiness of the liquid had been made. The English tried arrowroot, potato starch, sago flour and powdered seashells; and to darken the colour they added iron rust or brick dust until such practice was made illegal under the Food and Drugs Act 1860 and the Adulteration of Food Act 1872 (these are dealt with in the chapter on adulteration).

But it was a Dutch chemist and confectioner, Casparus Van Houten, who made the real breakthrough. In 1828, notwithstanding a mention in Diderot's *Encyclopedia* – where tablets of chocolate were recommended as a good snack for the busy man who had no time for a real breakfast – he invented a hydraulic press which squeezed out most of the cocoa butter from the liquor, thus reducing the cocoa butter content from fifty-five per cent to twenty-seven per cent, and leaving chocolate powder or, as we know it, cocoa. Then, in the 1880s, by adding alkalis such as potassium or sodium carbonate in to the liquor (known as Dutching), Van Houten was able to render it darker, mellower, more mixable and softer and, with added sugar, sweeter. Much to the dismay of his English competitors at the time, Van Houten's new soluble, unadulterated cocoa was winning the approval of eminent scientists at such august institutions as the Pharmaceutical Society of Great Britain and the Society of Public Analysts.

This revolution led the way to mass production of cheaper chocolate in powder and solid form. In the eighteenth and earlier part of the nineteenth centuries, the Spanish still had a virtual monopoly on cocoa bean cultivation, with Venezuela alone supplying half the world's cocoa in 1810 and the Spanish drinking about a third of the global crop on their own. Casanova, writing at the end of the eighteenth century, tells us that, 'The Spaniards offer visitors chocolate so frequently at all hours, that if one accepted, one would be choked.' Between 1730 and 1784, 43,000 tons of cacao were exported to Spain by one company alone, the Compañia Gipuzcoana.

This was all to change with the political upheaval caused by the Venezuelan revolution in 1811, and the resulting loss of cheap labour to the warring factions. To maintain supply to meet the ongoing demand, the French developed cocoa plantations in Martinique and Madagascar, the Dutch in Java and Sumatra, the Germans in the Cameroons, the Portuguese on São Tomé and Príncipe islands off the west coast of Africa, the Spanish on Fernando Po (Bioko) and the British in their colonies in Gold Coast (Ghana), Ceylon (Sri Lanka) and the West Indies, notably Trinidad and Jamaica. In 1825, gastronome Brillat-Savarin tells us that in France chocolate 'had become quite ordinary' and that 'Spanish Ladies of the New World love chocolate to the point of madness'. In fact, so popular had it become that Proust considered it too vulgar to take at tea time.

Along with the squalid deployment of tens of thousands of slaves, mechanisation soon began to help increase production and foster commercialisation. It was Joseph Fry & Sons of Bristol who led the way when, in 1761, they bought a watermill and warehouse and established a sales agency network in fifty-three English towns. Companies in France, Germany and Austria followed suit with watermill power while the Dutch used the windmill and the Spanish mules. The advent of steam power in the nineteenth century led to more significant change. In 1776, Doret patented a hydraulic chocolate grinding machine which reduced it to a paste and in 1795, Joseph Fry industrialised chocolate production in England when he started using a James Watt steam engine to grind his beans. In 1834, J. M. Lehmann of Dresden set up a plant specialising in making cocoa-processing machinery. Reductions by Gladstone in the punitive duty on chocolate in 1852 from 2 shillings to 1 penny per pound also had a profound effect on consumer affordability and demand. This was met not just by grocers and confectioners but also by chemists; the medicinal properties attributed to chocolate led to a demand for chocolate-coated pills and lozenges, or confectionery.

Fry's, Bristol

In 1795 Joseph Storrs Fry took control of what was then Anna Fry & Company and patented a technique of grinding cocoa beans using a Watt steam engine, thus ushering factory techniques into the cocoa business. In 1835, Fry's were consuming forty per cent of the cocoa imported into Britain with sales of £12,000 per annum. But the cocoa and chocolate makers had a problem: what to do with all the cocoa butter, that discarded by-product, which represented up to thirty per cent wastage? The answer was to make it into *eating* chocolate suitable for large-scale production. Joseph Fry & Sons were again the pioneers; they had been making drinking chocolate since the 1820s and in 1847 they developed eating chocolate in the shape of chocolate bars, by adding some of the cocoa butter back in to the mix and producing a thinner paste that was easier to mould. That year, 1847, was pivotal as it was the year Joseph Fry II produced the first chocolate bar which could be eaten. French chocolate enjoyed the highest reputation in Britain up to the mid-nineteenth century: anything British simply could not compete. But then Fry's came up with their Cream Stick – the first chocolate confectionery to be produced on an industrial scale. Hitherto, chocolate had exclusively been a drink and a luxury beyond the budgets of most people but this was a 'value for money bar' and marked the start of chocolate as a confectionery for the masses.

The Fry's chocolate bar launch took place at an 1849 Birmingham trade show and two years later the new moulded chocolate was on the market branded as *'chocolate délicieux à manger'*. This was to exploit the cachet associated with French-sounding food and to counter the popularity of French imports into the UK. The next generation Fry's Chocolate Cream bar started to roll off the production lines in 1866 with over 220 products launched in the succeeding decades, including production of the first chocolate Easter egg in the UK in 1873.

H. J. Packer, a former Fry's employee and a Quaker, began trading in 1881, making chocolate from his house in Armoury Square, Bristol under the name of Packer & Co.

Cadbury, Bournville

In 1824, John Cadbury, son of a prosperous Quaker, set up shop selling tea, coffee and sixteen varieties of drinking chocolate at 93 Bull Street, Birmingham, after completing an apprenticeship in London at the Sanderson, Fox & Company teahouse. The shop was certainly remarkable: it featured an eye-catching window filled with Chinese vases and figures and, appropriately for a tea merchant's, a Chinese shop assistant dressed in full Chinese regalia.

By 1861, John had retired and his sons, George and Richard, had taken over the business. A year later the Cadbury catalogue was filled with such exotic brands as Chocolat du Mexique, Crystal Palace Chocolate, Dietetic Cocoa, Trinidad Rock Cocoa and Churchman's Cocoa. Cadbury's produced Britain's first chocolate box in 1868. Around the same time the firm produced the first Valentine's Day chocolate assortment. But on the shop floor, things were not going well; that is, until George's 1866 visit to Casparus van Houten's son, Coenraad, Dutch chocolate manufacturer of some repute, to acquire one of his family's revolutionary presses. Business at Bournville was perilously close to collapsing: 'All the brothers' industry and virtue made no difference. At the end of four years they were facing disaster.'

'All my brother's money had disappeared,' George admitted. 'I had but £1,500 left … I was preparing to go to the Himalayas as a tea planter … Richard was intending to be a surveyor.' In 1860, sales had been around £27,800 but much of this was from the tea side of the business and capital injections of £8,000 had made little appreciable difference.

This visit to the Netherlands was pivotal and eventually led a company teetering on the brink of failure to the success it was soon to become. This revolutionary machine enabled the firm to start producing their Cocoa Essence from 1866. Sales of chocolate in 1852 were 9 tons rising to 12,000 tons in 1904. How did it revolutionise chocolate production? It quite simply squeezed all the fat out of the cocoa bean, thus obviating the need for absorbents such as potato starch or sago to soak it up and eliminate the mildly offensive fatty taste. No potato, no bad taste, leaving a drink that was much more pleasant and drinkable.

In short, the Van Houten process enabled drinking chocolate to be made as conveniently and easily as a cup of tea. Introduced in 1828, this revolutionary new patented method allowed the fats to be extracted from the cocoa, instead of adding sugar and farina to soak up the fats, thus leaving a pure, unadulterated cocoa. A fortunate by-product was the extracted fats or cocoa butter, which could be used to make eating chocolate. Cadbury's Cocoa Essence demanded a high retail price to cover costs and make a margin but this was never a problem: George Cadbury presciently recognised that the only way forward was to boost sales by advertising and marketing: 'desperation drove the Cadbury brothers to a different view' to the prevailing Quaker opinion that advertising was insincere and no replacement for the intrinsic quality of the product.

Eschewing those dusty Quaker reservations about advertising, the Cadburys set about gaining medical testimonials and establishing the health-giving credentials of their products – no doubt with an eye on manufacturers in other industries whose eye-catching posters featured glamorous women and children exuding healthiness. Both *The British Medical Journal* and *The Lancet* endorsed Cocoa Essence when it was launched in late 1866, with the former calling it 'one of the most nutritious, digestible and restorative drinks'. *The Grocer* chimed in, emphasising the absence of adulteration. The advertising campaign devised to maximise these endorsements asserted the cocoa to be 'Absolutely Pure, Therefore Best. No Chemicals Used'. The early 1870s saw the launch of the plush, decidedly un-Quakerly French-influenced Fancy Box, complete with silk lining and mirror. *Chemist & Druggist* called it 'Divine. The most exquisite chocolate ever to come under our notice'.

Van Houten, Weesp, the Netherlands

In 1815, Casparus van Houten (1770–1858) opened a chocolate factory in Amsterdam powered with a mill; then cocoa beans were ground into a fine mass, which could be mixed with milk to create a chocolate drink or, with addition of sugar, cinnamon, and vanilla, made into cakes.

In 1828, Casparus patented an inexpensive method for pressing the fat from roasted cocoa beans. The centre of the bean, the 'nib', contains an average of fifty-five per cent cocoa butter, which is a natural fat. Van Houten's machine – a hydraulic press – reduced the cocoa butter content by nearly half. This created a 'cake' that could be pulverised into cocoa powder, which would soon become the foundation of all chocolate products.

The introduction of cocoa powder not only made creating chocolate drinks much easier, but also made it possible to combine the powder with sugar and then remix it with cocoa butter to create a solid, similar to today's eating chocolate. In 1866, John Cadbury went to Weesp to buy a Van Houten press and started using it in production in 1875.

Fierce competition to English chocolate manufacturers flooded in from the French (Chocolat Menier, for example), the Dutch (Van Houten) and Swiss (Suchard, Cailler, Kohler, Tobler and Nestlé), as well as companies such as Taylor's in Spitalfields, manufacturers of more than fifty brands of cocoa and mustard. Also, Dunn & Hewett of Pentonville who sold chocolate sticks and patent Lentilised Chocolate (made from lentils, tapioca, sago or dried peas) and the disarmingly descriptive 'Plain Chocolate Sold in Drab Paper'.

Chocolat Menier, Noisiel

Menier were a chocolate manufacturing business founded in 1816 by Jean-Antoine Brutus Menier (1795–1853), initially as a pharmaceutical manufacturer in Paris, at a time when chocolate was aggressively vaunted as a medicinal product. Chocolate was just one part of the overall business; their main use of cocoa under Jean Menier was as a medicinal powder and for coating bitter-tasting pills; the market was Paris pharmacies, particularly in the Marais Quarter.

Under the founder's son, Émile-Justin Menier, the company concentrated solely on chocolate products, moving the pharmaceuticals to Saint Denis and then selling the business in 1879. In the beginning they used horses to power an old mill but later graduated to a watermill in Noisiel on the river Marne. The magnificent factory built there earned the name 'the cathedral'. In 1864, Menier began a period of expansion that made the Menier chocolate company the largest chocolate manufacturer in France, winning many medals at international exhibitions from 1832. At the 1878 World's Fair in Paris, for example, the company was awarded seven gold medals plus the Grand Prize for the excellence of its products, as well as praise for its modern production methods and the importance the company placed on the welfare and value of its employees.

Menier also pioneered packaging in France, wrapping his cylindrical bars in yellow chrome paper in 1849, depicting the firm's medals and his signature. By 1853, annual chocolate production reached 688 tons and by 1855 it reached 2,502, which was twenty-five per cent of total French output. By 1872 this had reached 4,000 tons, mostly for export. Hitherto unheard of vertical integration followed when Menier purchased cocoa-growing estates in Nicaragua, a fleet of cargo ships along with sugar beet fields and a sugar refinery at Roye on the Somme. By 1893, Menier were the world's largest manufacturers of chocolate; they opened their London office in 1863 in Southwark Street which in 1873 was producing 500 tons per annum of chocolate.

To a large extent Menier anticipated the paternalism of the English Quaker chocolate companies, Fry's, Cadbury's and Rowntree's, when they built a village for their workers and rolled out a whole suite of benefits. By the mid-1880s, production capacity at the Noisiel plant reached 125,000 tons annually and the company employed 2,000 people. Labour was an immediate problem because of the company's rapid growth and the shortage of workers available from the small village of Noisiel. Attempts to attract workers from other towns and cities failed due to a lack of local housing so, in 1874, Menier built 312 residences on 30 hectares of land near the factory. They also built a school for their employees' children and thirty years later, a senior citizens' home for their retired workers. In the 1870s, the Meniers also constructed the Noisiel town hall where a family member would serve as mayor without interruption from 11 May 1871 to 8 November 1959.

Menier's main competitors were Marquis and the Compagnie Coloniale in Paris, and Compagnie Française des Chocolats et des Thès established by Pelletier in 1853, who were unusual as they had planters from Venezuela and Brazil amongst their shareholders. La Maison Chocolat Guérin-Boutron was a luxury brand with two shops and a factory in Paris, operating from 1775 to 1942. By 1910 they were employing 280 workers in the factory at 23 and 25 de la Rue du Maroc. The upmarket shops were at 29 Boulevard Poissonnière and 28 Rue Saint-Sulpice. Debauve & Gallais were founded by Sulpice Debauve in 1800. They were suppliers to Napoléon, Louis XVIII, Charles X and Louis-Philippe. Sulpice Debauve (1757–1836) had been pharmacist to Louis XVI.

Menier pioneered developments in industrial refrigeration and factory design. Their famous chocolate graffiti posters, designed by Firmin Bouisset, showed a girl scrawling 'Chocolate Menier' on a wall or window. The old Menier Chocolate Factory building in South London is today a thriving arts complex comprising an art gallery, restaurant and theatre.

Mazawattee Tea Company

The Mazawattee Tea Company was at the forefront of the huge expansion of the British tea trade which followed the start of cultivation of tea in India and Ceylon. Set up by John Boon Densham who had been an apothecary in Plymouth and was a strict Baptist; his teetotalism would have influenced his decision to promote and sell tea in 1865 London.

His youngest son, John Lane Densham, joined in 1881 and drove the company's growth, adopting the revolutionary retail innovation introduced in 1826 by John Horniman of packaging tea so that customers could buy a known brand rather than rely on the grocer's (such as Rowntree's) personal selection of loose tea. The Denshams offered their first packets of Ceylon tea in 1884. John Lane was clearly a keen advocate of branding and advertising as he set about selecting a new name and an image which would sell his tea, coming up with the exotic 'Mazawattee' in 1887. It is a fusion of the Hindi word *mazza*, meaning pleasure, and the

Sinhalese word *wattee*, or garden. The image of an elderly, bespectacled and edentulous grandmother with her granddaughter and cup of tea was chosen to star in adverts and posters, and became very popular, redolent of the warmth and security of home and family. The picture was called *Old Folks at Home* and the striking advertisements were to appear on every station platform in the British Isles.

In 1901 the firm diversified into chocolate with a new factory in New Cross in which 2,000 people worked. This was an ill-advised move, as indeed was the expansion into retail tea shops. Despite a number of stunts – one of which involved using four zebras to haul the delivery vans in Tunbridge Wells while another was to design vans with a large Mazawattee teapot on the roof with the exhaust smoke coming out of the teapot's spout – the company was on the slide by 1936. Severe damage to the company's buildings in the Blitz did not help and the company, and the name, were sold off in the 1950s.

J. Caley & Sons Ltd, Norwich

Caley's were originally manufacturers of mineral waters founded in 1863; their entry into the confectionery market was a strategic move to balance out the seasonal water market. In 1857, Albert Jarman Caley opened a chemist's business in London Street, Norwich and in 1883 he started manufacturing drinking chocolate as a winter drink as part of his product balancing act. This was followed by eating chocolate in 1886, all made at the Fleur-de-Lys factory. In 1898 Christmas cracker manufacture began, and kept the girls who wrapped and decorated the chocolate boxes busy all year round.

Nestlé, Vevey, Switzerland

Henri Nestlé was born in Frankfurt in 1814. In 1875, thirty-two years after moving to Vevey on Lake Geneva in 1843, the chemist started making *farine lactée*, a baby food (initially called *Kindermehl*) made from Alpine milk in powder form and ground cereal. It was essentially infant formula for babies who had difficulty breastfeeding. Henri Nestlé, with his chocolate-manufacturing neighbours Daniel Peter with Jean-Jacques Kohler, then went on to develop the first real milk chocolate when the businessmen combined their products to produce Chocolat au Lait Gala Peter – 'The Original Milk Chocolate' – in 1874.

Henri opened a sales office in London in 1883 for the Farine Lactée Henri Nestlé Company and in 1901, the first UK factory began production. Nestlé merged with the 1866-established Anglo–Swiss Condensed Milk Company in 1905 to form the Nestlé and Anglo-Swiss Milk Company.

Toblerone, Berne, Switzerland

In 1868 Jean Tobler was running a confectionery shop called Confiserie Spéciale in Bern, Switzerland, producing chocolate sweets from products supplied by other manufacturers. By 1899 Tobler's chocolates were so successful that he set up his own factory with his sons: the Fabrique de Chocolat Berne, Tobler & Cie. In 1900, his son Theodor Tobler took over the business and exports to countries including Britain began that year. In 1908, with his cousin Emil Baumann, he invented the unique and distinctive milk chocolate bar that is Toblerone.

The name Toblerone is derived from the chocolatier's family name Tobler and *torrone*, the Italian for nougat. It is commonly believed that Theodor Tobler fashioned the shape of his unique and iconic chocolate – a series of joined-up triangular prisms – on the beautiful Alpine scenery of Switzerland, and on the Matterhorn in particular. But the truth is much more exotic, erotic even: according to Theodor's sons, the bar was inspired by the red-and-cream-frilled line of dancers at the Folies Bergères in Paris, which formed a shapely pyramid at the finale of each show.

Prudently, Theodor Tobler and his then company, Tobler AG, applied for a patent in 1909 in Bern to cover the manufacture and shape of the bar, and Toblerone thus became the first patented milk chocolate bar. The official who gave the authorising signature was one Albert Einstein who was working in the Swiss Federal Institute of Intellectual Property in Bern at the time. A picture of a bear – the civic symbol of Bern – lurks in the (disputed) Matterhorn mountain image on the packaging. In 2000, after cigarettes, the biggest selling line in airport duty free shops was Toblerone.

Switzerland then took centre stage. Philippe Suchard first came across chocolate when his mother sent him to collect a supply from an apothecary in Neuchâtel (at a cost of six francs, equivalent to three days' pay for a workman) and he set up his confectionery business in 1826. Charles-Amédée Kohler introduced hazelnuts into chocolate in 1831 in his Lausanne factory. The high point though was the development of milk chocolate in 1876 by Swiss manufacturer Daniel Peter. Peter was the son-in-law of Francois-Louis Cailler, the owner of Switzerland's first chocolate factory established in Corsier near Vevey in 1819, having worked at Caffarel's chocolate factory in Milan before that. He combined powdered milk – which had recently been developed by Henri Nestlé as an infant food – with chocolate and cocoa butter to produce a solid that was easy to mould and shape. Soon after, in 1876, Rodolphe Lindt introduced conching – a process which resulted in a smoother, more pleasant flavour we now know as fondant chocolate. The same year, Lindt merged with Johann Rudolf Sprüngli-Schifferli of Zurich to form Chocoladefabriken Lindt und Sprüngli.

Thanks largely to Fry, the milk chocolate bar and the chocolate-coated sweet were thus born. With the mechanisation that came along, the chocolate industry was totally transformed in England and the rest of Europe. Chocolate was now being eaten as well as drunk, although it would not be until the early years of the twentieth century before sales of eating chocolate outstripped drinking chocolate.

Chapter 7

Chocolate and Quakers

W hat was it that so inextricably linked the manufacture of chocolate with Quakers? Both the Fry and Cadbury families were Quakers and, like the Quaker Rowntrees in York, they were concerned with providing their workers with clean, safe and relatively pleasant working conditions that were environmentally and ergonomically friendly. In addition, outside the factory, sanitary and comfortable housing, educational, social and recreational facilities were provided. Fry's employed a nurse and a doctor; ran 'continuation classes' (further education) for the girls, provided a gym with instructors, facilities and pitches for football, tennis, cricket and bowls and set up the Operatic Society, the Camera Club and the Debating and Dramatic societies. Girls leaving to get married received a copy of *Mrs Beeton's Book of Household Management*. Joseph Storrs II was particularly philanthropic: he habitually visited sick workers in their homes.

George Cadbury financed the Sweating Exhibition in 1904 to expose the parlous state of British industry where sweat shops were rampant, and he financed the Anti-Sweating League. As an illustration of what he was combating, sweating of an altogether different kind was a major problem at R. S. Murray's confectionery factory in Clerkenwell, London. Women workers went on strike complaining of the sweltering conditions they endured there, and eventually won their case.

Fry's characterises well the close connection of chocolate with Quakerism. Until the 1870s, Friends were excluded by the 1673 Test Act from studying at Oxford or Cambridge, because of their non-conformism and the universities' close ties with Anglicanism. The Act also debarred them from public office and from Parliament, and to some extent the guilds, and medicine was only accessible via an apprenticeship to an apothecary. Friends were restricted in what they could and could not do as lawyers because they refused to take oaths in the belief that this implied the existence of two types of oath – one with your hand on the Bible and one not. The arts were considered by many as frivolous; Quakers were disqualified by their peace testimony from the armed services because they were, largely, pacifists and they rarely farmed because they would not pay tithes as this was tantamount to supporting a church of which they disapproved.

What then was a young Quaker to do in life? One of the few options left to privileged and well-to-do young Quakers was to follow a life in industry or business, and this is what Henry, Joseph, Seebohm Rowntree and many others did. They often brought with them a tradition of high, fastidious management and ethical trading practices, rigorous scientific research supported by statistics and innovative technical development, as well as an almost obsessive preoccupation with quality and a forensic attention to robust business administration. Much of this was clearly evident in both Joseph Rowntrees.

Years of work in trade by generation after Quaker generation had built up a tradition, and expectation, of success. In short, Quaker families in general were usually very good in commerce; they knew how to form and develop a successful industry. Moreover, one of the legacies of the frequent Meetings routinely held by the Society of Friends, and the travelling required to get to these Meetings, was the building up of a strong network of dependable friends and contacts. This in turn, along with frequent intermarriage amongst Quaker families, led to a tradition of mutual assistance in business and industry, and to those strong business networks and industrial partnerships, all underpinned by unfaltering service to the community at large.

When they were not trading, the Quaker typically might bury him or herself in a book or newspaper, avidly seeking the knowledge they were denied by the barred gates of Oxbridge colleges. As a result of their prodigious curiosity, Quakers excelled in such disciplines as natural history, politics and social justice and welfare in the community. Their non-conformism, of course, did not help them because it was not just religion which set them apart from society at large. The Society of Friends was socially aloof; not only did its people cling together and depend on other Friends when help or advice was needed but trade and commerce – be it banking, shoes, mining, iron, biscuits or chocolates – bound them together, at arm's length from the outside world. Indeed, Seebohm Rowntree tells us in 1909 that 'many [Friends] did not have personal friends outside the society'.

Cocoa and chocolate were attractive to Fry, Cadbury and Rowntree because of all the attendant social and workplace productivity benefits of an alcohol-free beverage.

Early concerns over the intrinsic insincerity of advertising in business and accusations of price fixing and a Quaker chocolate cartel were overcome to a greater (Fry's and Cadbury's) or lesser (Rowntree's) degree, allowing the companies to get on with building a largely contented workforce, introducing enlightened industrial relations, fair dealing and relatively pleasant factories, with an air of homeliness provided by potted plants and pictures on the walls. Managers used workers' Christian names and the extra-curricular provision of housing, entertainment, sport and education was welcomed by staff; it was all years ahead of its time.

In terms of industrial relations generally, Fry and the other chocolate Quakers were at the forefront, providing terms of employment and working conditions introduced in other industries and companies only after legislation made them mandatory. Rules and guidelines were laid down as to how Quakers should conduct themselves in business: the 1738 *Advices* promoted fair dealing and absolute honesty; the 1783 *Book of Extracts* unequivocally banned paper credit; the 1833 *Rules of Discipline* reminded adherents that the root of all evil was money and the 1861 *Doctrine, Practice and Discipline* summarised the whole code covering debt, seeking advice from other Friends, inappropriate speculation and much more. An early Fry's company booklet, *Into the Open Country*, typifies the orthodoxy when it gives the firm's mission statement and a flavour of the corporate ethos:

> Fry's have kept before them two guiding principles; one, giving the public the best possible value in cocoa and chocolate manufactured under the best possible conditions; the other, of giving the workpeople the best facilities for recreation and happiness.

Paternalism and philanthropy were not, of course, confined to Quakers, or indeed to England. In the global chocolate industry, Philippe Suchard in Switzerland, Menier in France and the Mennonite Milton Hershey in the US also offered enlightened industrial welfare – but England was exceptional with its Quaker triumvirate.

All the industrial welfare in the world, though, could not eradicate industrial injury or occupational diseases – daily hazards shared by all industries at the time. An example is the boy soldering tins at Clarnico's toffee tin department who presented to his doctor with a headache and a blue rash on his upper torso. The doctor's diagnosis was lead poisoning; verdict (unfortunately, as encouraged by the firm): death by natural causes. In April 1914, 'the very dangerous practice of wearing unprotected hat-pins' was highlighted in Rowntree's staff magazine, *Cocoa Works Magazine*: 'in January during the first few days one girl has had her eye pierced, another her eye badly scratched ... since then 14 accidents have happened in the clock room and corridors through unguarded pins.' Hat-pin protectors were made available for sale at 1d each. Still in York, Alex Smith, a worker in the Aero plant fell into an 8-foot deep mixer and narrowly escaped being immersed in a boiling hot torrent of liquid peppermint.

In addition to his purpose-built, worker-friendly factory, a further 120 acres had been bought by George Cadbury in 1893 and a groundbreaking, life-changing model village was built to 'alleviate the evils of more modern cramped living conditions' – inner city slums in other words. This visionary achievement was inspired by what Cadbury witnessed all around him: 'It is not easy to describe or imagine the dreary desolation which acre after acre of the very heart of the town presents ... hundreds of leaky, damp, wretched houses, wholly unfit for human habitation.' Within seven years the new village comprised 313 sound, clean and sanitary houses complete with front and back gardens on 330 acres of land. Only initially were the houses intended exclusively for Cadbury's employees: the later objective was to provide a village of mixed housing for a wide range of inhabitants and thereby establish a mixed community.

Residents were provided with a booklet laying down rules for keeping houses and gardens in good order, abstaining from alcohol on the Sabbath and the advantages of single beds for married couples. The area was alcohol-free until 1940 with no pubs and no alcohol sold in local shops until a licensed members' bar opened in the Rowheath Pavilion. This abstinence was a reflection of John Cadbury's strict temperance beliefs and a manifestation of his work in social reform, which also included campaigns for workhouse reform and against industrial pollution, child labour, particularly child chimney sweeps, and animal cruelty. He founded the Animals Friend Society which led to the RSPCA. Cadbury's own research showed that one in every thirty houses in Birmingham was given over to the sale of alcohol and that ten per cent of the city's 6,593 alcoholics died of alcohol-related diseases each year. The many gin shops and gin palaces nevertheless provided a ready supply of replacements for these casualties of a gin-soaked retail trade but John and Candia, his wife, successfully persisted with their Total Abstinence Plan, counting even the moderate Moderation Society amongst their conquests.

Bournville was truly pioneering in all sorts of ways: socially, environmentally and architecturally in particular, but it also had great influence throughout Europe in areas as diverse as housing, urban planning, community health and local education. Visitors who came to look at this template included architects from Krupp's in Germany, Dame Henrietta Barnett who went on to inspire the development of Hampstead Garden Suburb, William Hesketh Lever who founded the garden village of Port Sunlight in 1888 and the Rowntrees who established New Earswick garden village just north of their factory in York.

Cadbury's were one of the first companies in the UK to introduce half-day holidays, at Bridge Street. Philanthropy and paternalism continued in the workplace with groundbreaking pension schemes, a sick club, medical services, outings, in-service education, staff committees (the Works Councils) and decent wages. George and Richard Cadbury had been fervent believers in the value of education – they both taught at the Birmingham adult schools – and this was maintained at Bournville where continuation classes were set up in 1913 to provide free further education, during working hours, for younger employees from when they left school and joined Cadbury's aged 14 until they were 16 – later extended to 18. A wide range of apprenticeships was established for the boys and a sewing club for the girls. Employees were, as a matter of course, treated with respect. The Works Councils, segregated until 1964, worked in concert with the trade unions, which had also always been encouraged. The councils were made up of management and shop floor representatives and were primarily responsible for the company's welfare schemes.

In common with other factories of the time, male and female workers were segregated with separate entrances, working, rest and dining areas and, as noted, Works Councils. Technicians going in to women's areas of the factory had to wear armbands showing that they had obtained permission to be there. Married women were not employed and betrothed girls had to leave on marriage – but not before they were presented with a Bible and a carnation and a talk from one of the directors. It wasn't until the shortage of male workers caused by the Second World War that married women began to be kept on or recruited.

Social and recreational facilities were a vital part of the Cadbury's community. Land was bought at Rowheath for football and hockey pitches and a running track; the pavilion opened in 1924, not just as a clubhouse and changing facility for the sportsmen and women, but also as a social venue for dinners and dances. In addition, there were bowling greens, a fishing lake and an outdoor lido. An indoor swimming pool was built in Bournville Lane, and a boating lake and the cricket pitch made famous on the Milk Tray boxes followed. All the sports facilities were free of charge. The Bournville Village Trust set up in 1900 looked after, amongst other things, the primary and junior school, the School of Art and the Day Continuation School. Why was it called Milk Tray? Because it was trays with which chocolates were delivered to shops – on a tray containing five ½ lb boxes from which the shopkeeper selected his order.

Up in York, meanwhile, on the social welfare side, Joseph Rowntree emulated the Cadburys by establishing the Joseph Rowntree Trust and beginning the building of New Earswick, a new and attractive garden village, at the turn of the century. The objective was to provide the worker of even the most modest means with a new type of house that was clean, sanitary and efficient. Rowntree's deep concern for the welfare of his workers, his research findings and those of his son, Seebohm, into the plight of the urban poor, his Quaker beliefs, Cadbury's achievements at Bournville and the pioneering work on garden cities by Ebenezer Howard all combined to drive the establishment of New Earswick just minutes away from the Haxby Road factory.

Chapter 8

H. I. Rowntree & Co: 'The Cocoa, Chocolate & Chicory Works'

Henry's new firm, on the corner of Coppergate and Castlegate, was, to say the least, a modest enterprise with twelve men on the payroll and an output of around 610 kg of cocoa per week. The Tukes' sales of cocoa and chocolate in 1859 had amounted to £2,645.18s.4d and in Henry's first year of ownership it did not go up by very much. By comparison, Cadbury's sales were nearer £27,000, and Fry's £55,000. Henry had a lot of catching up to do.

One of the first things he did was take the firm upmarket by moving to new premises. By 1864 he had bought and was installed in a four-storey block in Tanner's Moat facing the south-west end of Lendal Bridge, bounded by Tanner's Moat, Wellington Row and Queen Street (not the one we know today which goes from the station to Micklegate Bar). This imposing block comprised a pub, The Old Ebor, Calvert's foundry, cottages and houses. Its close proximity to the railway station with good road and river transport links made it the perfect spot for an import-export company. Henry paid £1,000 for his factory space. We see from his cash book that by 1865 he had received his £1,000 legacy (in May 1860) and could also point to a gift of £95 from his mother in 1864 and £2,000 from his father's estate in 1865.

The business that Henry Isaac bought was small and financially precarious: two thirds of his output was Tuke's Superior Rock Cocoa – a blend of pure cocoa and sugar compressed into a cake on sale at 9d per lb wholesale. Other lines in 1873 included Homoeopathic Cocoa with its alleged health-giving qualities, Iceland Moss Cocoa, Hexagon Cocoa, Pearl Cocoa, Farinaceous Cocoa, Flake Cocoa, Shilling Chocolate, Sweet Shield Chocolate, Chicory and 1d and ½d balls. Brands such as Tuke's Rich Cocoa, Tuke's Plain Chocolate, British Cocoa Coffee and Tuke's Milk Chocolate were also brought to market. As just stated, sales were under £3,000 or put another way, ten per cent of Cadbury's and five per cent of Fry's.

Henry was saddled with a number of inherent problems. Crucially, two thirds of his output of about 12 hundredweight (cwt) was Rock Cocoa made with old school technology. Nevertheless it was of comparably higher quality than most – fine ground, mixed with sugar and sold in cakes – less coarse and more soluble than other cocoas, which were often cut with flour, sago and other farinaceous substances.

At this point only Van Houten enjoyed the luxury of their famous press which extracted most of the surplus fat or cocoa butter from the bean, resulting in a purer cocoa essence or powder with which to make a more appetising hot drink, and leaving the by-product butter to be used for eating chocolate. Cadbury's, as we have seen, acquired their machine in 1865 – a substantial but shrewd capital investment – but Henry simply did not have the money or the burning desire to buy and was left to work with old technology and traditional products. Most of the firm's production was, as we have seen, Tuke's Superior Rock Cocoa – later to be rebranded Rowntree's Prize Medal Rock Cocoa when his leading product fortuitously won one of the 113 medals awarded at the Yorkshire Fine Art and Industrial Exhibition, held in York from July to October 1866. This, at 9d per lb, was a blend of pure cocoa and sugar made, using pre-Van Houten technology, into fine ground cakes. Consequently, despite the relative quality, the cakes suffered from the oiliness characteristic of this old manufacturing process. The absence of a Van Houten press also meant an absence of the cocoa butter, essential in the production of eating chocolate, a product line which Henry later abandoned. It should be noted, however, that at the time in England, eating chocolate was a rare commodity compared with the established drinking cocoa brands such as Rock. The 1862 Ledger Account shows that he had 250 or so regular customers.

The service and quality promised by the Tukes and his own notices of sale did not, unfortunately, quite materialise. There is no reason to doubt Henry's knowledge of the business – his experience from the Scarborough and Pavement shops and his management position with Tukes should have guaranteed that. However, his business focus and administrative abilities obviously left much to be desired.

After the huge success of the 1851 Great Exhibition at Crystal Palace, it was natural that provincial towns would want a slice of the action. Henry and his friend William Pumphrey were no different and, after they had visited Wakefield's Industrial and Fine Art Exhibition in 1865, they were convinced that York could do just as well, and were 'determined to agitate the question'. Henry was on the executive committee, which included the great and good of York, including the lord mayor, the Dean of York, George Leeman MP and local newspaper magnates the Hargroves.

And so it was that a large, ornate temporary pavilion was erected in the grounds of Bootham Park Hospital and the Prince and Princess of Wales arrived by train on 10 August 1866.

Henry was responsible for procuring facsimiles of *Magna Carta* and the death warrant of Charles I, beehives stocked with buzzing bees, a working model of a steam engine, a boiler with pressure and water gauges, whistles (no bells) and so on, all heated by gas.

To paraphrase the Yorkshire Fine Art & Industrial Exhibition 1866 Catalogue and Awards, Henry won his medal for the purity and excellence of his Rock Cocoa and other preparations from the cocoa nut, and for the interesting way in which raw materials and stages of production were exhibited. A second exhibition was held from May to November 1879 at the newly built art gallery building. H. I. Rowntree & Co were decorated again for their excellent Rock and other cocoa and chocolate. The manufacture of their latest products, Queen chocolate cakes and Exhibition Creams, was demonstrated on their stand, with their 'shaker' machine' taking pride of place. This pleased Henry no end because, according to T. H. Appleton in *The Evolution of a Modern Business*, 'whenever the moulding of Queen chocolate was being shown a crowd was soon attracted, much to Henry's satisfaction, but not to that of the other exhibitors.' George Barker, who from 1877 was in charge of grinding sugar and mixing cocoa powders, remembers doing 'six months hard [labour]' working the machinery at the exhibition.

Henry, nevertheless, remained optimistic about the business and often quoted *Deuteronomy 23* in defence of his strategy: 'their Rock is not as our Rock, even our enemies themselves being judges'. Witty as this might have been, it was not the answer to what was a serious issue for the fledgling business. As one would expect from a Quaker, and as demonstrated already by Cadbury, the highest standards were essential, and Henry's dilemma was that he was never going to make false claims about his products. It seems, though, that he could not see the fundamental deficiencies of what was now a rather second-rate product in the European cocoa market, thanks to Van Houten and, later, Cadbury's implementation of the Van Houten process.

What was the working experience at Tanner's Moat? Manufacturing processes were primitive and out of date. There were machines for roasting and grinding cocoa beans, sifting the powder and 'caking' the final product, but crucially no Van Houten press. Power was by steam boiler and engine. Protective clothing was unheard of. Henry was often seen up to his elbows in oily cocoa, sleeves rolled up. Hours, as in the shop, were long: 6 am to 6 pm, weekdays, and until 2 pm on Saturday. No work on the Sabbath, of course.

A donkey and cart took goods and brought raw materials through the streets. Heavy sacks full of those raw materials and ingredients were manhandled from room to room, floor to floor, to each manufacturing stage. Back injuries and incapacitation were common, as noted in this letter young Joseph wrote to Julia on 5 August 1863: Joseph reported that Henry was helping his man to lift a bag of cocoa yesterday and 'quite strained himself, so that this morning he found he could not get up'.

As we have noted, Henry Hipsley was the manager when Henry started with the Tukes. Soon after he took over, however, in November 1862 he was given leave by York Quaker Meeting to 'travel in the ministry' to India and did not return until July 1864 at which point he retired. Henry was fortunate, though, to have inherited four other key employees from the Tuke business: William Wise, Isaac Dickinson, William Fearby and William Wood (who soon retired due to ill health). Fearby was works foreman in charge of machinery, in particular the grinding and sifting processes for Rock Cocoa, and stayed until 1872. Isaac Dickinson looked after the steam engine and boiler. William Wise stayed until the 1880s in the packing room as foreman, handling all goods despatched on the cart. The move to Tanner's Moat saw Dickinson and Wise living rent-free on the premises, Dickinson at the top of the building and Wise at the bottom. Everyone gained: the two men had no rent to pay and the firm, in return for the accommodation, procured round-the-clock security. On the all-important sales side, Richard Wilson was already in post as the only traveller, until John Alexander Bevington was taken on in 1865 as London representative. He had served his grocery apprenticeship at the Rowntree shop and remained in the job for an impressive forty-six years, retiring in 1911.

The meagre, shoestring staff had to learn versatility; they shared the tasks of grinding and roasting the cocoa on the two available machines, and of heaving the sugar around. S. C. Hanks ran the chocolate cream department assisted by one girl. He was also wages clerk. His wages would have been about 16 shillings per week. This musical chairs method of staffing persisted into the 1880s and 1890s. An employee originally hired as a timekeeper moved on to general manager and then took charge of the *mélangeur* and cake room departments. Another man hired as a junior clerk transferred to the cream rooms as manager to twenty staff. On retirement, he was responsible for nearly 1,000 workers.

Henry was obviously at pains to avoid any suggestion that his company was provincial in any way. His printed memo paper reads: 'Henry I Rowntree & Co, Cocoa and Chocolate Manufacturers, York – Prize medals 1866, 1867, 1875, 1879; London address: Cowper's Court, Cornhill, EC.' By February 1888 this had changed to the Jerusalem Subscription Room EC.

Chapter 9

Henry the Quaker:
Life Outside Tanner's Moat

We have already seen how great an influence, how good a mentor and how dependable a role model Henry's father was to him, and to his siblings. Apart from instilling in his son the desire – despite his perceived intellectual shortcomings – to go into the grocery trade, Joseph, an ardent Quaker, imbued him with a similar passion to embrace the Quaker faith. Henry was shrewd enough to see the real benefits offered by the Ebor Permanent Benefit Society, established in May 1868 by George Leeman 'for Liberals and railwaymen'. Involvement would gain him and his business access to York's commercial and civic inner sanctum and Henry eagerly accepted the invitation to be its first chairman. *The Yorkshire Express*, which he owned, told readers that shares were within reach of all who could save about 1 shilling per week, and investing was recommended 'as a safe and easy medium by which to get rid of those very disagreeable things – rent days'.

His father's political achievements also had an impact – thirteen years as a Liberal councillor and in 1853, York's first Quaker alderman. Henry saw the advantages of emulating him and served one three-year term as a Liberal councillor until November 1870. He also did time as chairman, and later vice-president, of the Micklegate Liberal Association and chairman of the North Riding Liberal Association.

Henry followed Joseph onto the local board of health, a sub-committee of fourteen councillors chaired by the lord mayor, which met weekly, working on the mundane but necessary work of city management. It dealt with everyday matters but matters that were essential to the common man and woman. Paving, drains, maintenance of urinals, removal of night soil, scavenging, slaughter houses, lighting, all sorts of 'nuisances' such as smoke and steam belching from industrial premises, or butchers leaving offal lying around from slaughtered sheep and cattle. Lodgers in households had to be licensed, the numbers of gallons of petroleum allowed to be stored had to be controlled, operators of Hackney carriages must be listed and foot and mouth outbreaks had to be dealt with. Henry regularly attended the monthly council meetings at which all the reports were heard. Here he voted against the outrageous proposal to demolish the Assembly Rooms portico in March 1868. He opposed a reduction in the rates from 1s 5d to 1s 4d in the pound that August in 1868. He joined a sub-committee to report on the price which should be paid for land near Layerthorpe Bridge in September 1868. He voted in favour of paying £1,300 to purchase a Church Lane property for the purpose of improvements in July 1869. He met with the North Eastern Railway and voted in favour of building a bridge to connect the Mount with Holgate Lane, replacing a level crossing there in February 1870. He was heavily involved in, and had a view on, the proposal to build a covered market in York and its site. This dragged on and on and was finally scotched, after many an inconclusive meeting, on the grounds of cost. York still has no covered market.

The York adult schools

In 1832, Henry's father was part of a movement of Friends involved in setting up the non-denominational British School in Hope Street in the midst of the Walmgate slums. This first adult school (which emerged from 'first-day' schools, referring to the first day of the week, Sunday) was set up by Joseph Rowntree senior and other prominent Quakers for boys aged between 8 and 15. It opened in 1848, under the aegis of Quakers Joseph Theobald and Richard Cadbury Barrow, in the premises of the British School in Hope Street; this was where Henry cut his teeth teaching his boys' class. Over time, many members of the Rowntree family, and especially John Stephenson Rowntree, were involved at Hope Street, united in the aim of teaching adolescents 'to apply the teaching of the Bible to everyday life and the problems of society.'

An inspector's report of 1850 tells us that the schoolmaster, William Osborn, had increased the roll from twenty to 200, and in 1854 it received its first annual grant. The school enjoyed a good reputation and by 1867 the number on its roll reached 546. Discipline was strict: 'No scholar shall be allowed to talk or leave his desk or class without permission' and expulsion followed four successive weeks' absence. By 1856, 860 boys and twenty-five men had received an education. The boys' classes were augmented by a class for 16 to 25 year olds, which developed into the adult schools, aimed at educating illiterate adults through Bible teachings. The scripture readings were not compulsory as the teachers were aware that they could be a disincentive to attend. Prizes were awarded for good work, usually booklets published by the Religious Tract Society.

Yet it wasn't all work and no play. A judicious blend of the religious and educational, the adult school was also about leisure and the well-being of the whole person; in other words. it was an holistic experience breaking new educational ground by teaching useful life skills. The aim was to create 'a band of thoughtful men' and give encouragement to people to find fellowship in their everyday lives. There was a social club, an allotments society with 150 plots of land, a savings bank, a library, 'to refine the taste and improve the morals', and temperance coffee carts. There were choral competitions, cricket and fishing matches, and unusual activities such as linnet singing and aircraft building – all indicative of the dearth of leisure provision in York generally. There were also communal breakfasts and lending libraries, as well as annual excursions – to Sheriff Hutton in 1860, for example. Between 1902 and 1906, the membership of the four schools open in York rose from 729 to 2,373.

Adult schools were a major force in combating adult illiteracy, giving working people a chance to catch up on the basic schooling they had been denied as children. The work and achievements of the Rowntrees here have to be seen in the context that, at the time, one man in five and one woman in three could neither read nor write in York, as elsewhere. In 1857, they moved first into a room in Thomas Herbert's house on the corner of Pavement and then into Cumberland House on King's Staith to join the girls' Sunday school. Numbers peaked at 263 in 1867. The Methodist Chapel in Lady Peckett's Yard was pressed into use until it was pulled down and in 1875, a new building was constructed in the yard behind the Pavement shop. The foundation stone was laid by Sarah Rowntree and 600 people attended the celebratory tea. Women's classes started here in 1876.

The schools were non-denominational and included Methodists, Anglicans, Wesleyans, a Brethren and a Roman Catholic at one time or another. They were also different from other similar philanthropic institutions in that they provided education for poorer citizens with no access to other forms of education, mainly semi-skilled tradesmen such as tinners, cabinet makers and cobblers. Although it was never a recruiting ground for Quakers or an opportunity 'to proselytise Quakerism', Joseph reported that the hope was that 'the example of teachers might lead their scholars to it'.

Lady Peckett's Yard was divided into two groups, brothers John taking 'A' and Joseph 'B'. In 1871 there was a further subdivision when the two were divided into five: 'A' to 'D' plus Elementary. The new teachers were Henry, George Baker, William Pumphrey and James Backwell – the latter three being apprentices at the Rowntree shop. The school day was from 8.15 am to 10 am every Sunday, with at least one hour of Bible-based reading and a half hour of writing.

Nationally, the first adult school was set up in Nottingham in 1798 to educate young women in the lace and hosiery factories. It was non-denominational and run by a Methodist, William Singleton, and Samuel Fox, a Quaker. Their focus was on Bible reading (notably from the New Testament), and then writing out passages from dictation. From the early days, there was a social welfare side to many of the schools, which often included savings funds to encourage thrift (with very attractive rates of interest) and, as in York, coffee carts to promote temperance, book clubs and sick clubs. The Quakers set up the Friends' First Day School Association around 1845 with Birmingham the first member, soon followed by sixteen others. Advertisements for such schools would typically be aimed at 'Working Men who desire instruction in Reading and Writing'. Two Quaker businessmen – Joseph Sturge and William White – were the driving forces behind Birmingham with Sturge's Severn Street School extending its curriculum to include evening classes in arithmetic, geography and grammar. By 1900 there were about 350 adult schools nationwide, supported by one non-conformist denomination or another and catering for approximately 45,000 students, 29,000 of which were directly attributable to schools run by the Society of Friends. The National Council of Adult Schools was set up in 1899 to coordinate adult school associations and to promote their work.

These educational initiatives had wider implications, exposing as they did the teachers and organisers to local and national social and political issues and challenges. For example, in 1848, Joseph took his sons John and Joseph, 16 and 14 at the time, on a three-week visit to Ireland (ostensibly as a botanical field trip) where they would see at first hand 'the horrors of the dead and dying in a famine-stricken countryside [which] left on them a lasting impression that poverty was an evil which needed to be tackled by more than palliative measures.' Starvation, prostitution, homelessness, housing conditions, slavery, alcoholism, prison reform and psychiatric care were other social and humanitarian problems which came under the Quaker spotlight, as indeed with nonconformists generally. We can clearly see an example of the influence slavery had on Joseph Rowntree when, in 1827, he published *An Address on Colonial Slavery* and spoke on the subject in public in May 1828; from 1824 Joseph was a member of The Retreat hospital committee.

Henry could not fail to have been influenced by the experiences of his father and brothers who, no doubt, would have shared their observations with him. Although Henry was not on the Irish trip he must have learnt much about the causes and consequences of the potato famine and its effect on so many Irish families. Moreover, the fact that the adult school was in Hope Street was no random coincidence. Research published by Philip Batman in 2019 shows how Irish émigré families settled in the already impoverished slums of Walmgate in the second half of the nineteenth century:

The 1840s were a turning point in the demographic history of York. This decade heralded two mass migrations into the City, one driven by the Industrial Revolution and the other by an ecological disaster. The arrival of the railway brought with it an expanding workforce to service this new burgeoning [confectionery] industry. The other influx was not a workforce, but a desperate, impoverished people fleeing the potato famine in Ireland.

As we know, the potato crop completely failed during the Irish winter of 1846 to 1847, when starvation was at its most critical. The population subsisted entirely from the land it lived on, rendering the poor fatally vulnerable to harvest failure. For his part, the Irish landlord's response to his newly unproductive, unprofitable tenants – 'useless mouths' to use a phrase adopted by the Nazis just under 100 years later in a different land – was to forcibly evict them. Result: mass migration of tens of thousands of poor people out of Ireland to America or Britain.

The 1841 census tells us that 57,000 migrants crossed to England each year and that the first wave of famine-driven immigrants – most of them came from western Ireland – began to arrive in York in late 1846, soon after the outbreak of the first ruinous attack of potato blight. By spring 1847 they flooded in at about forty-five people a day, settling in parishes in the south east of the city, up against the city walls and the stagnant, stinking River Foss.

The opportunities for unskilled casual labour within York, and agricultural employment in the surrounding villages, acted as a magnet to the Irish immigrants. The emergence of York's industrial chicory cultivation coincided with the arrival of the first immigrants, many of whom would have come to the area before the 1840s as seasonal and seasoned chicory harvesters, moving on to another commodity elsewhere before returning to Ireland. What they were doing in the 1840s was simply

making permanent what they had hitherto been doing on a seasonal basis.
Batman reveals that:

> about 70% of Irish male workers were concentrated in the six
> occupations of farm worker and field labourer, labourer, army,
> ordnance survey, glassblower and bricklayer's labourer. Farmworkers
> and labourers accounted for most of the working men, and many
> of the soldiers at York barracks or attached to the ordnance survey
> were also Irish. A good number of labourers worked in surrounding
> villages, some several miles from the City. The immigrants were
> often hired in families or groups, often on a piecework basis, as the
> seasons dictated.

Indeed, we know that towards the end of the nineteenth century,
grandchildren of the early immigrants obtained work on the production
lines of Rowntree's factory as chocolate, confectionery and gum packers.
Three groups of sisters at least were employed here.

The York 'ghetto' acted as a barrier to mobility, its inhabitants
remaining in the Irish neighbourhood regardless of how many times they
might change address. They monopolised particular streets, courts and
alleys, such as Long Close Lane and Hope Street. It was only when these
slums were demolished in the 1920s that the Irish communities were
dispersed.

Typically, the houses had two floors with a single room on each, and
had access at the rear to communal yards with privies. Narrow passages
between houses connected the streets to some of these yards, for example
Pawson's and Skelton's Yards, Wood's Yard, Square & Compass Yard and
Lewis Yard behind Long Close Lane, and Place's Yard and Hotham's Yard
between the two streets. There were two pubs, the Brown Cow which
was an integral part of the terracing in Hope Street and the Square &
Compass at the end of Long Close Lane.

Grinding and life-shortening poverty characterised Hope Street and
it was here and in similar places that Joseph Rowntree senior and others
saw the greatest need for inculcating education as a potential passport
to better things and better places. Henry Rowntree was one of those
other people. His father's example of actually doing something about
the situation, and what Henry knew about the plight of the Irish poor
from what his brothers and father would have told him, all combined
to make him eager to work in, and contribute to, the Hope Street Adult
School.

And it was by no means just the teaching that was consuming Henry's time. Henry threw himself into the organisation and management of the many social events which accompanied the adult school. One of these was the annual tea meeting. A good meal was followed by the annual report and then speeches. Entertainment came next, in which Henry usually played a starring role. Family letters reveal that, 'When the gases were turned down Henry's magic lantern with its hydrogen light threw out upon a large screen some exquisite photographs.' His repertoire included such diverse subjects as English scenery, Paris, the Mont Cenis Tunnel, the Suez Canal, and cocoa manufacturing. Sometimes he and William Pumphrey performed exciting 'experiments' with oxygen and hydrogen gas, as well as something called the 'fairy fountain'. On other occasions William Osborn, the Hope Street school headmaster, 'exhibited and explained a model of Vesuvius in volcanic action'.

Summer outings were also organised. In September 1866 after cricket on the Knavesmire, croquet in John's garden, tea, hymns, and a lecture by Henry on the contents of the Fine Art Exhibition, members and wives were shuttled in ten carriages to the Bootham pavilion to visit the exhibition there. In August 1867, a party of 140 no less took a trip along the Ouse in a steamer. Perhaps the most ambitious event was in September 1867 when Henry took a party of ninety working men to Paris for a week, setting off from York at 4 am. As if that wasn't enough, Henry was also chairman of the Micklegate Liberal Association.

Temperance and the coffee carts

The presence of at least two public houses in the poverty-stricken area of Hope Street and the antisocial, violent behaviour this frequently gave rise to, not least recurrent domestic violence, is not without its significance. Henry's father, as we have seen, was implacably opposed to the evils he saw associated with drink and Henry was greatly influenced by this. He believed that the appalling conditions endured by the residents in the Walmgate area were exacerbated by liquor. He and his father often saw pupils at the adult schools somewhat the worse for wear or depressed by hard drinking and constantly tempted by easily obtainable and affordable alcohol.

The temperance movement and the Quakers became inextricably linked; in May 1850 a meeting of the Friends interested in temperance was held at the London Yearly Meeting. Members of the provisional committee included James Backhouse and Joseph Spence of York and in August that year a further meeting was held in York to confirm this as a national organisation. York Temperance Society was formed in 1830 (*Yorkshire Gazette*, August 1830) with forty subscribers; Joseph Rowntree was an early, and active member. *The Yorkshire Herald* of 17 November 1832 reported on the copious statistics he provided to outline the extent of the alcohol abuse problem in York: 50,000 gallons of spirits were consumed annually while some streets, for example Water Lane, were awash with beer and spirit shops – four within the space of just under 100 yards (*York Courant*, 19 November 1840). Noting that there were 302 public houses and dram shops in the city in 1851 – or one for every 142 citizens and one for every twenty-six families – Joseph petitioned the magistrates to grant no further licences. *White's Trade Directory* of 1830 lists twenty pubs in Walmgate alone. By contrast, leafy Bootham had only two taverns – private cellars did the work of the pub for the gentry.

The meeting house in Castlegate hosted the temperance meetings and no doubt many of the largely affluent members donated generously. By 1830 the society could boast almost 1,000 members, which is a significant number in a city of 30,000 people. Nationwide, the temperance societies got the credit for a zero rise in alcohol consumption since 1928. But the temperance society was, by its nature, vulnerable. It only advocated temperance from spirits – beer was tolerated partly because it was considered nutritious by the medical profession and because it was seen as a healthy alternative to readily available water polluted by poor sanitation and other filth. This inevitably gave rise to the teetotaller who advocated abstention from all alcohol except where dispensed for medicinal reasons, and questioned the validity of the view that beer was a wholesome part of the working man's and woman's diet. In 1837, the new York Teetotal Society, also called New Temperance, Total Abstinence or Teetotal, held its inaugural meeting in the Protestant Methodist Chapel.

So now there were two temperance societies in York. The difference between total abstinence and moderation was at times tantamount to a chasm, and rivalry between the two ensued, with the teetotallers insisting that the moderates 'neutralised' (or more aptly, watered down) their message and their work. They believed, and told their audiences, that social success or failure depended on one's resistance to alcohol.

The prohibition-focused United Kingdom Alliance was founded in 1853, 'to procure the Total and Immediate Legislative Suppression of the Traffic in all Intoxicating Liquors'.

In 1851, Joseph Rowntree senior had warned:

beware the necessity of cheap beer, or 'liquid food' for the support and comfort of the working man and the desirableness of affording him every facility of obtaining it ... the Beer Act has done more to demoralize our youthful population and neutralize the labours of the Sabbath School Teacher.

But the society remained optimistic despite this doom and gloom: 'light finds its way through the smallest crevice ... we already perceive a vast change in the public mind.' The York Temperance Society actively campaigned against such issues as the extension of licensing hours to 11 pm, and for Sunday closing and prohibiting the sale of alcohol to children. It was also instrumental in stopping license renewals at The Golden Slipper Inn in Goodramgate and The Corporation Arms in Friargate.

In 1841, a temperance coffee house opened in Colliergate, which transformed into The Commercial Temperance Hotel when it changed hands and moved to Low Ousegate in 1843. York's Temperance Hall opened in Goodramgate in 1845 at a cost of £2,500.

A branch of the Leeds-based Band of Hope was set up and educated 1,200 children in temperance principles; a trip to Moreby Hall, south of York, took 800 children; 3,000 copies of their magazine, *The Visitor*, were regularly distributed each edition.

On his father's death, Henry took over the temperance mantle and on 4 December 1869, published in *The Yorkshire Express* the astonishing statistic that £30 million was spent per year in the UK on 'ardent spirits' and £43,749,556 annually on beer alone. The temperance message of resisting temptation became an integral element of the adult school curriculum and a temperance society was set up at the school in 1861. For the first ten years it went about its work quietly until, in the words of Gilman: 'largely as a result of a "concern" on the part of Henry Isaac Rowntree ... it entered on a vigorous forward movement based around Saturday evening temperance meetings held in the large schoolroom.'

Henry was in his element, delivering powerful presentations. Not only was this excellent education but the meetings themselves provided a welcoming alternative to the public house. They were always crowded and drew in a wider audience than meetings where just adult scholars came for their lessons. According to the York Adult School annual report December 1871:

Under the superintendence of Henry Isaac ... the large schoolroom
is filled every Saturday night ... . Meetings consist of temperance
addresses, recitations, reading and melodies ... . The total number
of names in the [temperance] pledge book is 227, about 100 being
scholars.

The next year the figures went up to 531, 139 of which were scholars,
and the number 'signing the pledge' continued to rise too. A harmonium
was procured, played by William Osborn's younger daughter Fanny.
Henry's 'realistic slides of the human stomach with and without alcohol
are remembered to this day'. With continued growth in attendance, the
temperance meetings continued steadily, attracting 'numerous pledges'
(according to the 1880 annual report) until 1887, when 'the Temperance
Society has been practically confined to fortnightly Saturday evening
entertainments'. A sad indication that after Henry's sudden death the
society lost its impulse. An Association of Abstainers started in 1874.

Coffee carts were another of Henry's inspired ideas in the fight against
'the drink misery' among working people. George Pattinson, an adult
scholar and carpenter at the cocoa works, built the carts in his spare time
under Henry's supervision and they were hauled into position by the
company donkey. Strategically sited, where people passed by in large
numbers on their way to and from work, they would divert workers from
the 'swift-half' alehouses with a cheap hot drink – coffee cost a halfpenny
with buns the same. Initially one stood outside the Queen Street railway
workshops with another at the market on Saturdays. The 1873 annual
report declared that five morning coffee carts were up and running, were
self-supporting and would eventually clear off the heavy set-up costs. To
bring in more money, and reduce the debt, an exhibition and bazaar was
organised. Such was its success that the idea was adopted in other cities
and towns so that Mr Pattison was required to supply carts further afield
than York.

Family life

Besides everything else Henry was leading a rather hectic family life.

His eldest brother, John Stephenson Rowntree, married Elizabeth
Hotham in summer 1858 and at first, they lived over the Pavement shop,
managing the apprentices as well as running the shop. They then moved
to Mount Villa on Tadcaster Road.

Henry Rowntree about the time he bought the Tuke business. (*Public domain*)

Mary Tuke's shop in Walmgate. (*Public domain*)

The Rowntrees in Bootham School in 1845: Joseph on the extreme left; Henry Isaac on the extreme right. (*Courtesy of Bootham School Archives*)

A busy Pavement with the Rowntree shop the second building on the left, now in the ownership of T. Coning. (*Public domain*)

Apprentices at the 28 Pavement shop: Joseph Rowntree (middle front), George Cadbury (left front). (*Public domain*)

This wonderful card is advertising the sumptuous fare available from all first-class grocers; no doubt many grocers, including Rowntree, aspired to this standard. (*Public domain*)

Rowntrees' Tanner's Moat building for sale or rent around the time of the move to Haxby Road. (*Courtesy of Yorkshire Architectural and York Archaeological Society*)

Part of Wellington Row and the old Rowntree's factory, which was off North Street, in about 1933. The castellations on the right of the picture belong to the building marking the end of Lendal Bridge. (*York Explore*)

Billingham's Yard, Sherwood's Yard and Midgeley Place in about 1933. This area was between Tanner Row and North Street. The tall industrial building dominating the rear of the photograph is Rowntree's factory. The foreground is filled with terraced housing and some washing can be seen in some of the back yards. (*York Explore*)

Four views of the Tanner's Moat cocoa factory. (*York Explore*)

Arthur Hemmen's grocer's shop on North Street, 1920s looking towards Tanner Row. (*York Explore*)

A typical view of the slum conditions, here exacerbated by perennial flooding, endured by the residents around Walmgate. (*Yorkshire Architectural and York Archaeological Society*)

Slum area of York, 1920. (*Images reproduced courtesy of the Joseph Rowntree Foundation Archive, Borthwick Institute for Archives, University of York*)

In 1907, the York adult schools celebrated their jubilee and residents of Hungate decorated their street. Many will have been members of the school. (*York Explore*)

Elegant brickwork for Elect on the cocoa building at Haxby Road. (*Courtesy of York Press*)

Children attending the St Lawrence's Temperance Treat in July 1893. (*York Explore*)

Henry Isaac Rowntree was a strong supporter of the adult school movement, as were the rest of his family. Henry launched the society's coffee cart scheme in 1871. He suggested selling coffee as an alternative to alcohol for the young men working at the markets. The first cart was built by George Pattinson. (*Public domain*)

An 1880 temperance magazine advert by F. Allen, cocoa, chocolate and confectionery manufacturer of London. It graphically shows the stark difference between the lives of a temperance family – everything is happy – while the home of the drinking man is squalid. (*Public domain*)

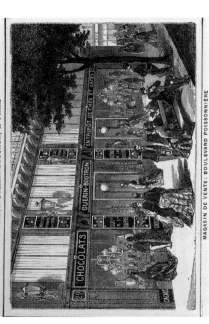

Four engravings from the catalogue of Chocolat Guérin–Boutron, luxury chocolate makers and retailers in Paris. The images depict the shop at 29, Boulevard Poissonnière and inside the factory at 23 and 25 de la Rue du Maroc showing the steam-powered machinery, grinding and packing departments. (*Images courtesy of Borthwick Institute for Archives, University of York*)

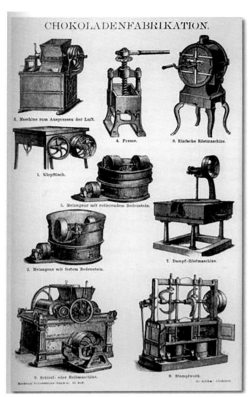

CHOKOLADENFABRIKATION.

German chocolate-making machinery.
(*Public domain*)

Late-nineteenth-century chocolate-making machinery as depicted in Brockhaus's *Konversations Lexikon*; the Germans were leaders in this field. The machines are: (1) shell hammering table; (2) mixer with fixed stones; (3) grinder; (4) cocoa butter extractor press; (5) mixer with rotating stones; (6) air bubble extractor; (7) steam roaster; (8) moulder; (9) roaster.

Joseph Rowntree aged 84.
(*Public domain*)

WANTED
MEN who thoroughly understand the Manufacture of SOLUBLE COCOAS.

Apply, by letter, to H. H., 19, Lordship Road, Stoke Newington, N.

One of the leaflets distributed by Joseph Rowntree in his industrial espionage campaign.
(*Public domain*)

A Van Houten press, which was the shape of the future. Rowntree hesitated to buy one although competitors such as Cadbury wasted no time at all and soon reaped the benefit.
(*Public domain*)

Advertisements showing the focus on the health-giving benefits of eating chocolate. Rowntree's launched their homoeopathic chocolate to capture this relatively more health-conscious market. Thorne's (the Quaker company in Leeds), Bovril, and F. Allen all exhibited at the International Health Exhibition in 1884. Bovril claimed their chocolate 'contained 300% more nourishment than any other chocolate extant'. It was especially recommended for children, invalids, cyclists, sportsmen and travellers. Oxo and Horlicks followed suit in pursuit of the same markets. (*Public domain*)

Fry's and Cadbury's (later to merge) were Rowntree's main competition. Adverts like these gave the two rivals the edge over Rowntree's who remained suspicious of, and averse to, advertising until the 1930s. It enabled both to promote the purity and health and strength-giving aspects of their chocolate, while Rowntree's largely deprived themselves of this opportunity. (*Public domain*)

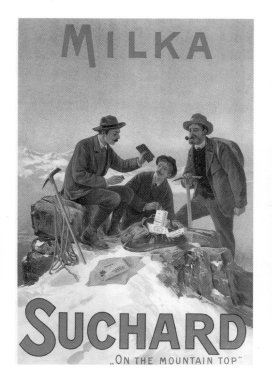

Foreign competition for Rowntree's – again making the most of advertising while Rowntree's languished on the sidelines. (*Public domain*)

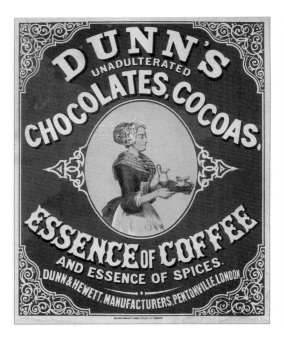
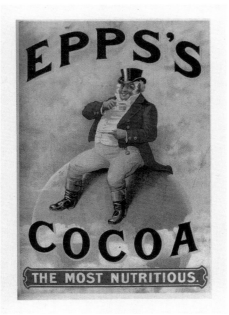

Competition nearer home with some outstanding advertising. The Terry's advert is from the 1880s when everything French was à la mode; the Dunn's showcard was from the same time. The mildly erotic Caley's poster is from the late 1920s. (*Public domain*)

Next, his brother Joseph married Julia Seebohm in August 1862. She was a Quaker of German extraction, and well known to the Rowntrees, as she had been at school in York. Julia was the daughter and youngest child of Esther and Benjamin Seebohm, who were both Quakers. She was from Hitchin and he was a German from Friedensthal (Dale of Peace) near Bad Pyrmont, Hameln, and the epicentre of the Religious Society of Friends in Germany. Friedensthal had been founded in 1792 by Benjamin's father, Johann Georg Ludwig Seebohm (1757–1835), and other disaffected Lutherans. They were given land and building materials by Friederich of Waldeck, Prince of Pyrmont, on condition that they promoted and developed local business. Benjamin was reputedly descended from a Swedish Army officer who served under Gustavus Adolphus in the Thirty Years War (1618–1648). His family's Quakerism was inspired by the visit of one of William Tuke's daughters, Sarah Grubb, in 1800. Benjamin was persuaded to move to Undercliffe near Bradford by a Sarah Hustler in 1814 who took him to Meetings and introduced him to the local Quaker community. He then began travelling ceaselessly on Quaker business; his 'real job' – exporting wool with Sarah's nephew to his three brothers, Wilhelm in Hamburg, August in Dusseldorf and John in Friedensthal – suffered accordingly. Benjamin married Esther in 1833. On retirement he edited the *Annual Monitor* and wrote several of the Quaker *Lives of Weighty Friends*. Her brother Frederic (1833–1912) went into banking and wrote influential books on economic history, notably *English Village Community* published in 1883; in 1856 he became a barrister in the Middle Temple. Other books were published on the Black Death and on education. Her other brother, Henry (1832–1895) went into the iron and steel industry and became a noted ornithologist and zoologist. His collections were bequeathed to the British Museum; he left over £100,000 – a staggering fortune.

In the months before the wedding, Henry's widowed mother, Sarah Rowntree, set about extensively reworking the marital home, Top House, to accommodate the couple. The kitchen was moved up from the basement into what was the dining room and the drawing room was split in half and became the dining room and a living room for Joseph and Julia. One of the bedrooms was turned into the drawing room. Joseph's and Julia's bedroom was in the basement next to the scullery and coal cellar.

Henry described conditions as thus: 'the whole house is delivered up to men, women, and dress makers. They begin at six and end, well there is no end, their name is legion, for they are many.'

A year after their marriage, on 30 May 1863, their daughter, Julia Seebohm Rowntree, or Lilley, was born but the birth so weakened her mother that by September, after a period of recuperation in Scarborough, she fell critically ill, finally succumbing to 'congestion of the brain' (probably a form of meningitis) on 21 September. Her father, who was in Germany at the time and reluctant to come home, arrived too late. Lilley, then three months old, was looked after by her aunt Hannah; Lilley herself was to die of scarlet fever in 1869. Hannah Rowntree remained at home to help care for Lilley until Joseph remarried in November 1867. Brother John, in the meantime, had initiated an expensive refit of the shop.

Henry was never averse to dropping the odd bombshell. His determination to purchase the Tuke business and his reinvention as a newspaper editor and proprietor (as we shall see) can only be described as decisions which must have astonished his family and friends. On 28 February 1868, York Meeting woke up to learn that Henry Isaac Rowntree had married Harriet Selina Osborn by licence at Scarborough Registry Office. No problem there but further enquiries revealed that Harriet Selina Osborn was neither a member nor an attender of any Quaker Meeting.

Before 1860, Quakers who 'married out' (which was what Henry had done) were ostracised by their Meetings and only the best efforts of Henry's father and brother John won the relaxation of this rule. The elder Joseph saw that the diktat was responsible for an irreversible decline in Quaker numbers and he lobbied unsuccessfully at Yearly Meeting for a change, urging his son John, aged 24, to produce statistical evidence on Quaker births, marriages and deaths to prove that reforms were urgently needed. The argument was finally accepted and the change agreed a month before Joseph's death in 1859.

When the widower Joseph married Emma Antoinette Seebohm (Tonie), his first wife's cousin, he did things by the book, mindful that she was not a Quaker by birth. Two months before the wedding day, he gave notice to York Meeting of his intended marriage to 'a person professing with us and an attender of our meetings for worship for whom the necessary certificate has been received.' Members of each Meeting (York and Hitchin, where the couple met) made 'the needful enquiries' as to the couple's 'clearness to marry' and attended the ceremony to see that it was conducted correctly.

Henry, however, did none of this. Two York Meeting overseers were appointed to look into the case and interviewed Henry in April 1868.

Selina (as she was known) was living at the couple's Melrose Villa, Avenue Road house in Scarborough and so avoided being interviewed herself. This is where, on 31 October 1868, 18-year-old Selina gave birth to their son, Francis Henry.

John Stephenson Rowntree and Selina's father William Osborn, headmaster of the Hope Street school, witnessed the marriage.

Henry and Selina's second child, Alice Mary, was born at their York address, 13 Blossom Street – which the family rented through the Ebor Building Society for £5 per month – on 19 January 1870. Another daughter, Ethel, was born in Scarborough on 5 April 1873. After Alice's birth, Selina applied to be admitted to York Meeting on behalf of herself and her two infant children. She was admitted in May 1870. In 1872 the family moved to 22 The Mount, a fine town house which boasted stables at the bottom of a long garden.

Henry's politics

Politics coursed through the veins of many of the Rowntree men. Henry's father would no doubt have influenced him greatly with his Liberal views and preoccupation with social welfare. His brothers, John and Joseph, who were similarly impacted, would only have reinforced Henry's own political stance.

We have seen how Henry followed his father as a Liberal councillor and did much good work on the Board of Health. One of the other ways in which Henry's liberalism is perhaps best exemplified is through another of the many diverting and distracting activities he was embroiled in: this was the York Institute of Mechanics. The aim of Mechanics' Institutes was to provide a technical education for the working man and for professionals: to 'address societal needs by incorporating fundamental scientific thinking and research into engineering solutions'. They transformed science and technology education for the man in the street. The world's first opened in Edinburgh in 1821 as the School of Arts of Edinburgh and later became Heriot-Watt University. This was followed in 1823 by the institute in Glasgow, which was founded on the institution set up in 1800 by George Birkbeck and the Andersonian University, offering free lectures on arts, science and technical subjects. It moved to London in 1804 and became The London Mechanics' Institute from 1823 and later, Birkbeck College. Liverpool opened in July 1823 and Manchester (later to become University of Manchester Institute of Science and Technology) in 1824. By 1850, there were over 700 institutes in the UK and abroad, many of which developed into libraries, colleges and universities.

According to Jefferson in 1969, they were a product of the Industrial Revolution in which as:

> a consequence of the introduction of machinery a class of workmen emerged to build, maintain and repair the machines on which the blessing of progress depended, at a time when population shifts and the dissolving influences of industrialization in the new urban areas, where these were concentrated, destroyed the inadequate old apprentice system and threw into relief the connection between material advancement and the necessity of education to take part in its advantages.

Apart from providing a free lending library, Mechanics' Institutes also offered lectures, laboratories, and occasionally a museum.

The York institute had its stimulus from a Whig newspaper article about the London Society for the Diffusion of Useful Knowledge. The Tories, on the other hand, were suspicious of the 'efforts to awaken the dormant powers of the mind in the middling, but more especially in the lower classes of society.' Nevertheless, it opened in 1827 in Bedern with a membership of 272 while appeals for books for the library produced over 500 by the end of the year. The institute struggled, though, and did not hold the attraction for the working classes the founders hoped it would. Indeed, the 1834 annual report was naively indignant about the lack of support for an institute that was 'designed and adapted to check the progress of Frivolity, Dissipation and Vice' – in line with Quaker support for the York Society for the Prevention and Discouragement of Profaneness and Vice (lewdness, brothel-keeping, intoxication, swearing and Sabbath-breaking) which, in turn, was lampooned as a society for the suppression of the 'vice of persons whose income does not exceed £500 per annum'. By and large the institute was not a success for the simple reason that its agenda was at odds with the needs of its students: 'values and ideals which were totally out of touch with the reality of the lives of its students. Much of its curriculum was beyond the comprehension and ability of most of its pupils.'

In 1838 the institute was rebadged to reflect a new focus and became the York Institute of Popular Science and Literature. Lectures became more populist; they included phrenology and one on the American Phineas Taylor Barnum in 1855. Musical entertainment was introduced in 1846. The evening classes were an enduring success: Society of Arts examinations were taken from 1851, leading to the opening of the Institute School of Art in 1881 in King Street. City and Guilds technological examinations and commercial examinations of the Yorkshire Union of Mechanics' Institutes were also introduced. These paved the way for the institute to transform itself into a technical college, which is what it became when it moved into a new building in the newly constructed Clifford Street in 1883, the year that Henry Isaac died.

Henry was a devotee of the Quaker Liberal reformer John Bright (1811–1889), whom the family knew well. While in his early twenties, Joseph had stayed with Bright in Rochdale and in turn Bright visited the family when in York. Bright was a British Radical and one of the greatest orators of his generation; a champion of free trade policies. Charismatic and dynamic, Bright was born in Rochdale and after schooling at both Ackworth and Bootham, went to work in his father's cotton mill where he became a partner. Member of Parliament at one time or another for Durham (from 1843), Manchester (from 1847) and Birmingham (from 1858), he worked tirelessly with Richard Cobden against the Corn Laws in the Anti-Corn Law League until its repeal. Other causes included campaigns against capital punishment, church rates, flogging in the Army, and the disestablishment of the Irish Church. His opposition to the Crimean War inspired, on 23 February 1855, his moving 'The angel of death has been abroad throughout the land. You may almost hear the beating of his wings' speech in the House.

His fight for parliamentary reform resulted in the Reform Act of 1867, the parliamentary apathy surrounding which he described as 'like flogging a dead horse to make it pull a load', the first use of the phrase. He also coined (on 18 January 1865) 'England is the mother of parliaments'. It is usually wrongly applied to the Parliament of the United Kingdom. Such was the man who probably had the greatest political influence on Henry.

While Joseph was in London, aged 19, and still under the age of being eligible to vote, Henry was also transfixed by his descriptions of the debates in the Commons, which he attended regularly during his few months spent working in the capital. 'It must be very satisfactory to hear all the great men one after another in so short a space of time, so as to be able to compare one with the other,' he said. The 1857 election was the first in which he took a keen interest: 'the account of Lord John [Russell] at the head of the pole [*sic*] was very pleasant' but the loss of 'good men' such as Bright, Gibson and Cobden was not.

The election took place under the system established by the 1832 Reform Act. The electorate consisted of all male heads of households with property valued at £10 a year, and in York the great majority of these were freemen of the city. In order to vote, their names had to be published in the electors' list (poll book), they cast their votes publicly, and afterwards poll books were published showing how everyone had voted. In two-member constituencies, such as York, electors had two votes. 'Plumpers' were people who voted for one candidate only, 'straights' supported one party interest with both votes, and those who chose one Liberal and one Conservative, were 'splitters'. Bribery, 'treating' and intimidation were rife, with voters fearful of offending patrons, landlords or employers. Polling (hustings) went on for several days and was frequently accompanied by rowdyism and mass inebriation.

Henry sent Joseph his animated impressions of election-gripped York: 'We are in a very curious state [about the election], no one seems able to guess, although many persons knowing very little talk very large.' In the event Joshua Brown Westhead (moderate Whig Liberal) and J. G. Smyth (Conservative) each polled about '1500 a piece' and took the seats, while 'our own man Malcolm Lewin' polled 1,006 votes, 'most of them plumpers'. He continues:

> This was considered a great triumph ... Lewin is very popular and Smyth just the reverse. His hotel 'Harkers' has to be guarded by the police.... Whenever he attempted [to speak] either on the hustings or from his own committee room window they first hooted him, and then sang 'Rule Britannia' and drowned his voice. On 5th and 6th Day they smashed the windows and pelted the police with stones. We expect a row tomorrow but as we have imported 40 police from Wakefield and have 4 to 600 specials, and the military ordered to be ready at any moment, I hope we shall get over pretty well.

In the event, the crowd's ardour was cooled by heavy rain and by 'being kept [waiting] from 10 till 20 minutes to 1 before anything was done owing to a mistake in one of the pole [*sic*] books.'

Lewin, 'our own man', was seconded by Quaker grocer Thomas Coning. T. Coning and Sons later bought the Pavement shop, and continued as a grocer's shop where the new owners made and sold their own cocoa. The Rowntree name remained prominent on the façade for many years after the sale to Coning; a sure indication that the Rowntree name was synonymous with quality and was well worth cashing in on.

The 1867 Representation of the People Act enfranchised male urban householders and male lodgers paying £10 a year rent and created an electorate of two-and-a-half million voters, or one in three adult males. The York electorate more than doubled to 9,088.

In the next election of autumn 1868, the first under the new Act, the York Liberal MP George Leeman was unable to stand for health reasons. The Rowntree brothers, by now more confident in and au fait with the machinery of politics, decided to take direct action in the matter of selecting a radical candidate. Their choice was Dr John Hall Gladstone, a scientist, Fellow of the Royal Society and an educationalist, with excellent credentials in philanthropic and religious work. His election notice in the York newspapers outlined his platform – the recent Reform Act required further revision regarding rate-paying clauses and redistribution of seats, voting by ballot should be adopted for parliamentary elections 'to put an end to intimidation', Oxford and Cambridge should admit nonconformists, there should be a national system of primary education and proper legal protection in the workplace for both masters and employees. In other words his views accorded completely with those of his Rowntree sponsors, or as the Tory *Yorkshire Gazette* called them, the 'fussy section', led by the 'Quaker Junta who seek to rule the Liberal Party in York'.

The Yorkshire Express

Henry, it seems, also aspired to be a newspaper proprietor, and to that end he established *The Yorkshire Express*. In Henry's day, the newspaper *was* the media; a newspaper informed and dictated the choices of those who could vote, and stimulated an enthusiasm for reform in those who remained debarred. John Bright had 'demonstrated the right way to use the cheap press' when he and Richard Cobden founded the radical pro-peace London daily the *Morning Star*, which ran from 1856 to 1865. In the provinces, the Liberal press already dominated and gave rise to a surge in fledgling local newspapers with a decidedly reforming agenda. In Leeds, for example, the prevailing moderate Liberal daily was the *Leeds Mercury*, but in 1857 the more radical *Leeds Express* was founded by W. E. Forster and the former Chartist Robert Meek Carter. In Newcastle in 1858, Joseph Cowen bought the *Newcastle Daily Chronicle* and the *Newcastle Weekly Chronicle* which both became vehicles for reform. In Manchester in 1861, John Taylor revived the early radicalism of the long-established *Manchester Guardian*. In York meanwhile, on the eve of the

1868 election, there was still no newspaper espousing a radical point of view. Henry was not going to allow this lamentable situation to continue so he decided that the best way he could help Dr Gladstone and further the radical cause was to establish a newspaper himself. A few weeks before the hustings, on 5 September 1868, he published the inaugural edition of a new weekly, *The Yorkshire Express*: four sheets, eight pages printed at the Tanner's Moat factory and sold for one penny on a Saturday by cocoa works errand boys.

In theory this was not a bad time to launch a newspaper. In 1853 advertisement duty had been removed; in 1855 newspaper stamp duty was abolished, and duty on paper was rescinded in 1861. A. J. Lee tells us that it was commonly perceived that owning a newspaper had 'for some minds a singular fascination, just as there are men who *must* have race horses'. With a fairly modest capital investment, a small newspaper could be run on a shoestring by the inexperienced amateur. Nevertheless, Henry enjoyed none of the benefits of new technology in the printing process; instead he used a ramshackle printing machine left behind in the Calvert's foundry building; printing was done overnight on a Friday by Isaac Dickinson, ready to hit the streets of York next morning from 7 am. It is unlikely too that he could benefit from progress in cutting-edge news gathering and news-distribution services. Reuters Telegram Company was now supplying foreign news and stock market information from around the world and the National Press Agency and Central News offered provincial newspapers 'social and political leaders ... in manuscript, proof or stereotype'. They would even supply partially printed sheets in which provincial editors could insert their local material and advertisements. The Press Association, founded in 1868, could furnish parliamentary, Stock Exchange, commercial, sporting, markets, and general news, summarised from daily London papers – 'by telegraph once a week for £7.5s. per annum'.

What was Henry up against in York? Established competition comprised two Saturday papers offering twelve pages for 3d; the *York Herald* had been run by the Hargrove family since 1820 and had swallowed up *The Yorkshireman* in 1858; the *York Gazette* was founded in 1819. According to the *Newspaper Press Directory*, the *Herald* claimed a circulation of 8,000, with a readership estimated at 140,000 in Yorkshire, Lancashire, the North East and Lincolnshire. It was 'the organ of the agriculturalists ... and the principal provincial sporting paper in England'. The *Gazette*'s entry stated: 'as an advertising medium it cannot be surpassed, being read by the leading gentry, clergy and agricultural and commercial classes in the district.' By contrast Henry's *Yorkshire Express* claimed it had the largest circulation in the city of York. An office was opened in Market Street, Scarborough, in November 1868, but the *Express* circulation was never anywhere near that of its rivals.

By the sixth issue (7 October) there were six columns of adverts. Leak & Thorp was usually prominent. House ads for Rowntree products were obviously always a feature: 'Ask for Rowntree's Rock Cocoa and see that you get it: see also that you get the best quality'... 'Rowntree's Homoeopathic Cocoa is specially recommended to invalids and to all who find the best Rock Cocoa too rich.' By May 1869, adverts filled three of the eight pages, but still with a noticeably local, urban York bias.

Henry never held back in exposing the corruption of the Tories. When hustings had been marred by violence, intimidation and treating, it was usual for defeated candidates to present a petition to Parliament disputing the result. Even if such petitions were then overturned, their evidence claiming bribery and corruption increased pressure for legislation to introduce the secret ballot. Whereas the *York Gazette* and *York Herald* merely reported on results, Henry's coverage made a point of emphasising the unedifying aspects of the hustings, and detailed unseemly conduct at York, Whitby, Scarborough, Ripon, Knaresborough and Thirsk.

Henry fulfilled his mission to use the paper to further the Liberal cause generally and, more personally, specific local issues on which he had a view – the siting of the covered market being a good example. On other matters, though, he certainly overstepped the mark and probably alienated more readers than he persuaded.

Under the headline 'Priest and vestments' he hysterically accused York Minster of being 'dedicated to the sensuous rites of ritualistic worship' when there was 'misery and squalor of the worst description' to be found in its shadow, and demanded 'Priests, what are they?' with their 'mystical incantations and mumbo jumbo ceremonies'. (*The Yorkshire Express*, 4 September 1869.) He denounced horse racing as 'a mere basis for gambling': 'if a tree is to be known by its fruit, most assuredly York Races are accursed', always characterised by thieving, inebriation and prostitution. He dismissed Yeomanry musters as 'when 500 men and horses come to York for 8 days ... playing at soldiers' and a 'costly relic of a bygone age' as they 'exercise on the Asylum field to the great edification of the Bootham nurse girls'. Balanced and appropriate this was not; judgemental and without foundation it certainly was. When the Prince of Wales visited Scarborough for a shoot, the *Herald* simply reported how much game had been bagged, while Henry condemned the 'flunkeyism' of the local dignitaries who 'built arches' and 'got up illuminations'. As for the House of Lords, it was 'an irresponsible debating club'.

Such views were, of course, born of Quakerly hostility to gambling, intemperance, militarism, a professional clergy, and class-based condescension, but they were unwanted by, and unpalatable to, the average impartial newspaper reader. Henry continued as editor-proprietor until 23 October 1869 when the business was sold to William Oxlade of 7 Nessgate, York. But he could still not let go completely: advertisers were still referred to Tanner's Moat, and leading articles would continue to be written by the same 'gentlemen'. This arrangement lasted until issue seventy-nine on 5 March 1870, when the paper folded without notice or explanation. One of the boys who sold the papers got it absolutely right when asked what he thought was the cause of its failure, saying, 'Mr Henry put too many of his own opinions into it.'

It is obvious that the time, money and energy that Henry devoted to the newspaper distracted him away from managing the cocoa works in any meaningful way, and was a drain financially on himself and the business. His 1870 accounts show expenditure on the 'Express newspaper' of £100.14s.3d in January and £68.6s.4d in July. It also diverted employees from their day jobs. For example, Stephen Henry Sidney, who was taken on in 1872 to work in the cream boiling section, had as his first job 'the paper business to clear up and destroy'.

Henry then was clearly something of a butterfly, unpredictably flitting from one attractive-looking flower to the next. His liberal outlook and his Quaker principles made it difficult for him not to be involved and immersed in anything that ignited his interest and compassion – anything really that benefited his fellow man, particularly those fellow men who were less well off than himself. And all the while Henry was supposed to be running that time-consuming cocoa business.

Chapter 10

Enter Joseph Rowntree Junior

S omething had to change. The damaging effects of Henry's well-intentioned but unworkable preoccupation with Quaker-related activities, his role as publisher and writer on *The Yorkshire Express*, the old cocoa technology and small scale, short-run manufacturing techniques with an antiquated factory plant and utterly disorganised organisation, and his apparent commercial ineptitude, all conspired to compromise any real progress. In short, the Rowntree business was ailing and ailing fast; it was not long before it was revealed to be teetering on the edge of a very un-Quakerly bankruptcy.

The dramatic change that was so urgently needed for Rowntree's took place on 5 July 1869 when Henry was joined at Tanner's Moat by his 33-year-old brother, Joseph Rowntree II, and the firm H. I. Rowntree & Co was established. The news was announced to their customer base – 'Respected friends' – in a somewhat enigmatic, somewhat delayed sales letter of 3 January 1870 stating that a 'partner has joined the concern'. John Stephenson continued to manage the Pavement shop for the time being.

Joseph injected much-needed capital into Tanner's Moat, using money he had invested in, and now withdrew from, Pavement. More importantly, he brought experience and sound, rational business acumen to the company, focusing on the accounts, financials and sales side while leaving manufacturing to Henry. Joseph began building up the sales force so that by 1897, not before time, 'Sales' had become an official department of the company. In effect he saved the 'hopelessly embarrassed' company from that decidedly un-Quakerly bankruptcy, bailing out a brother who 'knew next to nothing of the business'; 'left alone he must have succumbed to circumstances'. Joseph sheds more light on the desperate situation he walked into in an uncompromising and withering letter to Selina much later in 1890.

Joseph Rowntree had cut his teeth in statistics and accountancy with his earlier work at Pavement and with his involvement in various Quaker campaigns and activities. He was also a first-rate grocer with experience and aptitude in tea and coffee blending and tasting. In particular, his own extensive research into poverty in England had given him a facility with statistics and a meticulousness which was to manifest itself in his neat and precise ledgers and accounts and other instances of deft business administration.

How very different in that respect Henry was, not just to his brother, but also to his father who, as we have seen, was similarly wedded to statistical evidence, exactitude and empirical precision. The Pavement shop was sold to Thomas Coning & Sons on 1 August 1892.

Why did Joseph forsake his comfort zone and the security of Pavement when the business there continued to thrive? After all, he had not insignificant domestic concerns which would have benefitted from the stability Pavement offered. In May 1869, his daughter Julia (Lilley) died from scarlet fever, and there was anxiety for some weeks that his 8-month-old son John Wilhelm might succumb to the infection as well.

There are three good reasons why Joseph made that move. First, Henry was family and he patently needed help in bringing some order to the shambolic state of his financials before imminent forthcoming changes in the bankruptcy law. Quite by chance Joseph's intervention here revealed the real mess Henry was in. Second, Quakerly responsibility played a big part: the Society of Friends' Christian doctrine, practice and discipline taught Quakers 'the duty of watching over one another for good ... whether it be in the family, in the shop, in the market, the bank or the boardroom'. Looking after fellow Quakers was a cornerstone of the faith. Third, as alluded to above, Friends had a very dim view of bankruptcy. They were advised to 'be very careful not to contract extravagant debts', nor to burden themselves with 'too much trading and commerce, beyond their capacities to discharge with a good conscience ... and be very cautious of running themselves into debt.' For Quakers, business failure was regarded as a very serious matter. In the elder Joseph's day, Friends could be disowned by their Meetings for bankruptcy. The young Joseph was in the unique position of being able to discharge all three responsibilities in a bid to help and save his younger brother.

Moreover, the stigma incurred by an insolvency, especially in Quaker circles, had ramifications for the whole family, and for the family's reputation at Pavement and at Tanner's Moat. It affected them all. Not just that, John had to agree to Joseph's severance payment from the Pavement shop which thereby lost a not insignificant £7,500, and obliged John to enlist a new partner, his neighbour Thomas Hills.

Joseph's display of brotherly love, however, was neither absolute nor unconditional. When he sat down to organise and assess the accounts from the balance sheets in the first half of 1869, he found the firm to be under-capitalised with just the legacy from their father's will, a bank loan of £2,000. On the debit side there were sundry business debts. Henry owed the business £2,057, and the loss for the year was £381.2s.6d. Joseph must have been livid, and his anger must have simmered for a long time after because, years later, on 25 November 1890, he penned that rather harsh letter to Henry's widow in which he described the cocoa business that he joined as 'hopelessly embarrassed [with] the book keeping in a state of confusion', and that if he had not intervened 'Henry would have had to call his creditors together.' He made it abundantly clear that his intervention had cost him dear: 'At the age of 33 I found I must begin and learn a new business. The struggle was severe and at times it seemed doubtful what the result would be.' He went on to say that he had ploughed virtually his entire fortune into a business whose owner had not only demonstrated a 'singular inaptitude in business' but was also still concerned to publish a newspaper every Saturday. After his move to Tanner's Moat, Joseph was obviously stunned to find that Henry knew surprisingly little about basic elements of his own business, such as recipes, brands of raw cocoa, specialised machinery and the wholesale trade. Undoubtedly, these shortcomings resulted in part from the disproportionate amount of time and attention he had been devoting to the newspaper, as well as all the many other distractions in his life. Joseph may even have insisted that he divested himself of *The Yorkshire Express* as a condition of his intervention. *The Yorkshire Express* was sold just sixteen weeks after Joseph arrived at Tanner's Moat.

No accurate figures or accounts earlier than 1869 survive. Maybe what Joseph found in the chaos at Tanner's Moat was indecipherable and unaccountable and he binned the lot. He later confided to a widowed Selina that 'the power of rescuing a drunkard', which Henry possessed in spades, was a far higher power than 'the power of making money'. However, a Rowntree was expected to make money; he continued, 'to many who knew how brilliant H. was and his remarkable power of managing men, this statement of his singular inaptitude in business would excite surprise.'

The jumble of improvised buildings at Henry's Tanner's Moat, which would have greeted, and presumably appalled Joseph, was nothing if not full of character. Apart from the resident parrot there was a somewhat temperamental donkey, obedient to one man and one man only, and a serious danger to everyone else. On its dismissal, deliveries were relegated to a hand cart. Night-shift workers were sustained by cocoa and pork pies

on the firm, and most communications to and from Joseph Rowntree
were through a trapdoor in the floor of his Lendal Bridge-facing office.
S. C. Hanks, the foreman, paid the wages each Saturday from a hat full
of silver and coppers (£60 a week usually covered it). Each employee
would be asked 'how much time has thee got?' and be duly paid his or her
going rate from the contents of the hat. Mistakes were inevitable, which
prompted the disarmingly honest 'What did I give thee?' Girls aged
about 14 would have earned around 3 shillings per week, boys a shilling
more and men earned 18 shillings at most – fairly standard money for
the times.

The purchase of a horse and wagonette in 1874 proved injudicious –
an overhead the company could ill afford as food, farriers' and veterinary
bills, and tolls amounted to 12s 7d ¾ per week. The horse was duly sold
and the wagonette mothballed. Factory production was steam driven
but hampered by the use of different machines for each of the processes
involved (grinding, sifting, roasting and so on) with raw materials
laboriously manhandled between machines. Hours were long by later
standards: Monday to Saturday, 6 am to 6 pm or 2 pm on Saturdays.
Indeed, Tanner's Moat was inadequate in every way; Seebohm Rowntree
said of it: 'Tanner's Moat was Hell'. Coming from a man not usually
given over to such language, these were strong words indeed.

Other staff at the time included John Fenwick, Joseph's assistant and
works manager from 1883; George Barker, head of the Gum Department
from 1895; William Farrow who started in the offices in 1880, became
a traveller and then the Travel Department supervisor. B. Grantham
worked for G. Mansfield of Layerthorpe who had the contract for all
building work and joinery; he joined Rowntree as foreman joiner in 1890
and T. H. Appleton did the expenses, purchase ledger and company
accounts, as well as working as a traveller.

From 1869 it is difficult to tell which decisions were made by Henry
and which by Joseph. It seems reasonable, nevertheless, to assume that
on most key issues they were of one mind and that the resolution of
these issues was coloured by their shared faith in, and devotion to,
Quakerism. As we shall see, this faith was largely responsible for their
rejection of advertising, fervently but naively believing instead that their
products would sell themselves, not just because of a hard-earned, sound
reputation but also because they were Quakers with Quaker standards of
ethical business practice and financial fairness. They rejected branding
because they believed it to be ostentatious and shallow, maintaining that
their clientele much preferred a well-stocked shop to a flashy display.

Joseph was still very much the 'master grocer'. He and Henry would also have shared a belief in, and derived satisfaction from, the knowledge that the production of cocoa was a potent weapon in the battle for temperance and that the well-provisioned shop in Pavement, and the very act of manufacturing cocoa at Tanner's Moat, was an essential service to the community.

There were other, more commercial, reasons for not branding and not advertising: the main one being that many shopkeepers, including grocers, would have seen packaging as the beginning of the end for the specialist shopkeeper. Packaged goods, as opposed to loose goods, allowed the customer to be persuaded at the point of sale and to make an independent choice of what to buy, reliant much less on the experience and advice of the master grocer who, for example, might well be an expert in tea blending, ham curing, coffee roasting and the like and, therefore influential in what was bought and sold. The Rowntrees, because of their Pavement shop experience, and despite the cocoa manufactory, still had a vested interest in protecting the traditional grocery trade and its ways of trading. The Rowntree brothers looked both ways.

Team Henry and Joseph

Despite Joseph's simmering anger and the prevailing shambles, things soon started to improve for Henry and for the company with Joseph's intervention. Henry, it seems, was much more relaxed and efficiencies started to show.

When Joseph first installed himself in his office above the 'finance office', with its large window facing on to Lendal Bridge, H. I. Rowntree & Co was still a small concern with fewer than thirty employees. As noted, Joseph took control of sales, purchasing of raw materials and ingredients, and costing and pricing of each line. Henry, on the other hand, focused on the manufacturing, the machinery and the 'hands'. Joseph's forensic attention to order and details soon started to show, not least on costs: waste was reducing and efficiencies were increasing. Indeed, expansion was in the air when four cottages on Queen Street and a stable on Tanner's Moat were purchased in 1870, with another four cottages adding to the estate in 1880. These were all demolished and replaced by extensions to the factory.

But manufacturing and the processes involved remained antediluvian by industry standards, or non-existent. The creams for chocolate centres were handmade, with sugar boiled over a fire. Couverture (chocolate made with extra cocoa butter to give a high gloss) was mixed manually. Thermometers were non-existent and temperatures were established by the baby bathwater technique. There was still no refrigeration, which made extracting chocolate from moulds nigh on impossible with a lot of wastage, mitigated in part only by selling it on to the trade as 'waste tablets'. Making the chocolate cream castles introduced in 1876 proved particularly difficult with Henry using cooling air, and then having moulds filled overnight with plain chocolate. Both were unsuccessful.

More relaxed and happier Henry may have been with his new focus, but he still showed signs of an impetuousness and an inability to think things through before launching headlong into their, often disappointing, execution. Thomas Appleton, an early colleague who went on to rise to general manager at Rowntree & Co, remembered him, tactfully, as:

> a real pragmatist ... in the sense of over-leaping obstacles, meeting difficulties, fitting means to ends. Henry loved making alterations, always seeing some possible improvement in the layout or methods of work. Immediately an idea occurred to him he had ... to act upon it straightaway. He did not want plans and estimates.

Presumably this cavalier approach led to at least as many aborted plans as it did to successes, but the slapdash modus operandi led to Bentley Grantham from George Mansfield's building firm being almost resident at the factory, carrying out modifications under Henry's instructions. In 1880, Grantham was made foreman of the works joinery department. Another consequence of his constant experimentation and ill-advised projects was damage to the machinery because it was constantly pushed beyond its capacities and limits by Henry, who was intent on ignoring the advice of those who knew much better than he.

In 1882, Joseph sanctioned the purchase of a new boiler from Horsfields of Dewsbury. The man who came to install it, James Archer, so impressed Joseph and Henry that he was taken on permanently and soon transformed the old mechanics shop, where the tools were mainly hammers, chisels and files, into a proper, well-oiled engineering department by overhauling all the plant, most of which was virtually obsolete.

Henry's firm boasted an all-male workforce, the essential qualification being an ability to lug a 10-ton sack of flour up numerous steps. As we shall see, the future development of the company led to a dramatic change in the gender mix with many more girls and women by the end of the century.

Antiquated machinery obviously had its effect on productivity, product line expansion, pricing, order lead times and efficiency. But there were even graver consequences. A fire in August 1876 caused £591.11s.4d worth of damage. Joseph had a hard time with the Yorkshire Insurance Company getting payment for a devastating loss which 'was so much more than the amount for which we are insured'. And then there were the industrial injuries: the steam boiler killed Isaac Dickinson in May 1872 when 'by some unaccountable carelessness' he opened the manhole before letting off the steam with the inevitable consequence that the steam and boiling hot water cascaded tsunami-like out of the boiler and fatally scalded him. In December 1874, the factory foreman Thomas Butterfield also died in an accident.

The Auguste Claude Gaget effect 1879

It seems a great shame that the man who started it all is forgotten. Perhaps we should raise a monument to Auguste Claude Gaget. Or maybe remember the Frenchman with an annual Pastille Day.

York Evening Press

In the 1870s, turnover increased from around £7,400 per annum to nearly £31,000 at the end of the decade. Unfortunately, profits were wretched with an average net profit of £372 and losses were recorded in 1873 and 1876.

However, a combination of Joseph's fastidiousness, increased product lines and a rise in national demand, raised the company's fortunes. Cocoa consumption in the UK was going through a boom: in 1820 it had been 267,000 lb with a consumption per head of 0.01 lb; by 1860 this had risen to 4,583,000 lb (0.16) with the following inexorable rises: 1870: 6,944,000 (0.22); 1880: 10,527,000 (0.30); 1890: 20,224,000 (0.53) and 1900: 43,680 (1.06). Population growth – in 1820 it was 21.3 million growing to 41.1 million in 1900 – obviously helped but so did the demand created by the cocoa manufacturers and their aggressive marketing – conservative Rowntree excepted. Nevertheless, they were not out of the woods: in 1878 only four of the firm's nineteen cocoa brands delivered a profit, although they did account for seventy per cent of sales.

From a personal point of view, Joseph may have realised he was at the point of no return career-wise. On his third child's birth certificate in 1875, he no longer described himself as a master grocer, but as a cocoa manufacturer. Until then, grocery was the trade in which he had spent all of his working life, but cocoa and chocolate were to be his life from now on, with many new challenges.

In 1876, Homoeopathic Cocoa was launched, riding on the popularity of the medicinal content ascribed to arrowroot. Other products included Iceland Moss, Hexagon Cocoa, Pearl Diamond Cocoa, Star Cocoa, Farinaceous Cocoa, Shield Chocolate, Shilling Eating Chocolate (launched in 1872); in 1873 de Sante Plain, Nonpareil chocolate drops, small creams and cream balls, Flake Cocoa, Chocolate Creams, Chocolate Balls, Chocolate Beans and Chocolate Drops; in 1876 Chocolate Cream Castles, chocolate cigars, chocolate rolls and oval fancy picture boxes of creams; in 1878–9 Queen Chocolate and Exhibition Creams. More diverse lines included a granular effervescent citrate of magnesia fruit sauce and the agency for Neaves' Farinaceous Infant Food – early competition for Nestlé products.

But things were, at last, about to change. The confectionery line which was to have the greatest impact upon the firm's fortunes was introduced in 1881 and was a major departure from cocoa products.

A serendipitous sales call by Claude Gaget in 1879 had a significant and lasting impact on Rowntree's. Gaget, at the time, was working in the London office of Compagnie Française des Chocolats et des Thés, Parisian confectioners specialising in gums and pastilles – imported sweets which, up until then, were the exclusive preserve of French manufacturers. His brief there was to develop a new line of sugar-based products. This he did and went out on the road to garner orders. Initially, Joseph Rowntree's conservatism and immovable insistence on unrivalled quality made him refuse Gaget's samples, apparently once telling him that his latest batch was fit only to be thrown in the Ouse, a rebuffal all the more stinging and graphic for Gaget as the river was visible from Joseph's office window.

Determined to land a Rowntree contract (and others, of course), Gaget returned to London and soon perfected his recipe. A subsequent sales call in York was much more promising. The samples he presented to Henry and Joseph that day resulted in the manufacture in 1881, after two years of anxious and frustrating perfecting and experimentation, of Rowntree's famous Crystallized Gum Pastilles. Joseph had obviously realised that anyone able to match the quality of these French pastilles at a lower price would gain a huge commercial advantage and thus break the French monopoly. Joseph Rowntree was determined to 'dissipate the mischievous supposition that the finest goods cannot be got in this country'. A swipe at the French who were still more or less dominant in the confectionery market.

Gaget got his order and was taken on board and put in charge of the newly created French Confectionery Department where he also perfected Almond Paste. Crystallized Gum Pastilles were indeed now consistent with the Rowntree's insistence on the highest quality, but sellable at a realistic retail price. They were turned out loose in 4lb unbranded wooden boxes at a penny per ounce. These iconic sweets were of course the precursors of Rowntree's Fruit Gums and Fruit Pastilles and satisfied the brothers' objective to make a quality product. 'Don't forget the fruit gums mum...'.

The pastilles saw Rowntree's through a perilous time and provided the capital for a much-needed expansion. In 1882, Henry and Joseph bought Simpson's flour mill in North Street adjacent to Tanner's Moat. By 1885, 4 tons were being produced every week.

During Henry's time as sole owner, the firm's income, from a starting point of around £3,000, increased annually by a negligible amount – just a few hundred pounds. During the first years of the partnership with Joseph, revenue was getting better due largely to economies and product range expansion: £7,387 in 1870, £10,860 in 1873, £12,506 in 1874, £44,000 in 1880. By 1883, sales revenue was £55,547 and £99,000 by 1889 – caused by more new lines coming to market, and there was a noticeable jump when the gum pastilles hit the streets – in short, the Claude Gaget effect. Net profits were initially pegged but eventually increased fivefold from an average of around £372 (0.85 per cent) between 1872 and 1879 to £1,649 (1.67 per cent) in 1889 – better, but still lamentably poor.

The firm's average profit between 1870 and 1879 was £372, but losses were booked in 1873 (-£544) and in 1876 (-£280). Family members, as expected, chipped in by lending capital; £1,500 from brother John, £1,000 from their mother Sarah while Joseph's wife contributed £1,069. Joseph's part of the working capital equalled the amount of the mortgages and bank overdraft with which the partnership was saddled. Henry's 'private balance sheet' showed a steady increase in 'sum owing,' from £539 in 1871 to £3,858 in 1883.

However, with this came a concomitant rise in costs. Theirs was a labour-intensive business and staff numbers inevitably grew: from a payroll of thirty in 1872 to forty in 1874, 100 in 1880 and 200 in 1883. In 1869–70 the weekly wage bill was £7.2s. but by 1883 it had mushroomed to £85.10s.163.

First thing every Monday morning, a little bit of theatre was enacted at Tanner's Moat when samples of the cocoa beans that were to be offered at the next day's London auction were ceremoniously roasted and tasted using a small two-cylinder gas roaster. They could have been Trinidad, Grenada or Caracas deemed best for Prize Medal Rock, or Homoeopathic, or chocolate powder, or some other product or other. Decisions made, a telegram was despatched before 1 pm telling the agents which beans to buy.

When Gaget settled in York he lived in a house in Queen Street, next door to Rowntree's; this was one of those premises bought by Rowntree and demolished to make way for extensions to the factory. G. Wright, a Rowntree's contemporary to Gaget, described him as 'an exceedingly clever confectioner, passionately devoted to his work. He, with the help of Joseph Rowntree, brought many novelties in gums to perfection.'

Auguste Claude Gaget died at his sister's house, 9 Dewsbury Terrace in York, on 14 July 1906 aged 62. He had retired from Rowntree's through ill health in 1895 after sixteen years' service. Research by Colin Lea has revealed that before going into confectionery, Gaget was a soldier in the French Army and was taken prisoner by the Germans at Strasbourg in the Franco-Prussian War. His obituary in *Cocoa Works Magazine* remembers him thus:

> Mr Gaget introduced several kinds of sweets, notably Almond Paste, the sale for which has developed largely during recent years, and he also devoted a considerable amount of time to the introduction of Clear Gums. As a workman he was most painstaking, and always insisted on the work from his department being turned out in the best possible manner.

Sadly, he suffered the undeserved indignity of a burial in a pauper's grave with eleven others. This is not a reflection of any mean-spiritedness or ingratitude on the part of Rowntree's; after all three Rowntree's managers represented the company at his funeral and Joseph Rowntree sent a wreath. It was more of an illustration of Quaker protocol that funerals be unassuming, low-key affairs. To repeat, because it deserves repeating, ninety-five years later, on 21 May 2001, the *York Evening Press* said: 'It seems a great shame that the man who started it all is forgotten. Perhaps we should raise a monument to Auguste Claude Gaget. Or maybe remember the Frenchman with an annual Pastille Day.'

Pastilles highlighted another hugely important issue at Tanner's Moat, which continued to act as a drag on the firm until it was finally resolved. Pastille production entailed the purchase of boiling pans which were much, much cheaper than a vital Van Houten press. The brothers may have derived some solace from, and congratulated themselves on, the significant saving here but they both remained naively unaware of just how important that press was in the confectionery market and of how Cadbury, who had already purchased a machine and was already reaping the rewards in terms of – ironically for the Rowntree brothers – quality of product and by rising sales and margins.

Maybe Joseph was now taking a more circumspect and long-term, less conservative view of the market and began again to weigh up the benefits of acquiring the expensive Van Houten press needed to produce pure, market-leading cocoa essence.

Whatever, Joseph finally stopped prevaricating, buoyed by the success of his pastille sales, unnerved by Fry's launch of Pure Concentrated Cocoa to compete with his cocoa essence in 1883, and the prevailing view that essence was the future. The eventual investment in a Van Houten press paved the way for the production and launch in 1880 of cocoa essence Rowntree's Elect, 'more than a drink, a food' and made from top quality cocoa.

The name Elect was borrowed from the apothecary trade, where it signified a particularly efficacious drug. Rowntree's Elect was described as 'an extremely light powder, the essential product of the cocoa bean after it had been roasted and ground and the fat (cocoa butter) taken out by hydraulic pressure.' But despite the new technology and increased demand, output remained low. In 1893 Elect still only accounted for six per cent of sales and two and a half per cent of output. Company profits were unimpressive at two and a half per cent of turnover in 1888.

The pastille-driven success manifested itself in a number of ways. For example, before pastilles the day's output could easily be transported in a small cart, but in 1887 a horse-drawn lorry was required to deliver the daily production, averaging 4 tons of cocoa, chocolate and sugar confectionery, to the station.

We have seen how the per capita consumption of cocoa expanded dramatically during this decade. This was reflected in Rowntree's sales: between 1870 and 1890 they grew from £7,384 to £114,529 increasing to £463,199 in 1900. The comparative figures for Cadbury's were £54,790 to £515,371 and £1,226,552; and for Fry's, £143,750 to £761,969 and £1,326,312. In 1870, Rowntree's had four per cent of the UK market, increasing to fifteen per cent by 1900, and Cadbury's were at twenty-seven per cent in 1870, rising to forty-one per cent in 1900. All this was at the expense of Fry's, whose share declined from seventy per cent to forty-four per cent over the same period.

The success of fruit pastilles enabled Joseph to invest in more property and to refurbish or extend existing properties including the North Street flour mill and the Tanner's Moat cottages. Crucially, it also allowed him to purchase new machinery in 1880: a long-awaited refrigerator and better machines for washing the beans and turning out the nibs.

Henry the man, his death and its aftermath

Henry, likeable, good-humoured and always seeing the comical side of a situation, was very popular with his staff. He was an incorrigible 'glass half full' man. The archives are full of warm anecdotes and examples of his good humour. He once ran a steam pipe from the boiler house to the stable so that the donkey could have a weekly Turkish bath. He installed a parrot in the girls' workroom and taught it to squawk 'Now lasses, get on with your work!' When travelling to and from Scarborough by train Henry would generally ride in a non-smoker but would sometimes change to a smoking compartment, although he did not smoke. When asked why, he replied that he always changed when he had a good cigar to give away. He trusted staff implicitly as shown by this habit: when he needed something to be fetched from his home, he would provide the man with a plan of his house showing precisely where the articles were to be found.

After fifteen years of working as a team with Joseph, Henry Isaac died in 1883 from peritonitis after a short illness. He was 45 and left a 33-year-old widow, and three school-age children: Frank, born in 1868 and his two sisters Alice Mary, born 1870 and Ethel, born 1873. Henry had married their mother Harriet Selina Osborn fifteen years earlier in 1868 when she was 19 and he 30. He died in debt to the company; the family were supported by a bequest from his mother, Sarah, and an annual allowance of £150 from Joseph. They continued to live at Top House. The Quaker family rallied round as might be expected but Selina must have felt terribly vulnerable in spite of this: her father had died in 1875, her mother now lived in Scarborough and her only sister Frances was now married as Mrs Windsor Thorp and living in Leeds.

Reputedly a happy, humorous and optimistic man, it is likely that Henry would have been much missed at home and at work. In April 1882, he did us a service by writing to Claude (1882–1959), the newborn son of his third cousin Allan Rowntree and, in welcoming him to the world, enumerated, tongue in cheek to some extent, the various qualities that go to make a Rowntree:

> Humility, Self-abnegation, a willingness to be guided by others, Reticence, Suavity of manner, an entire absence of a critical or satirical spirit … don't keep thy mother awake at nights. Hate alcoholism, toryism, priestcraft, and all other concrete forms of sin … believe me, dear Claude, to be now and ever (unless thou turned tory) thy affectionate cousin.

Staff employed at Tanner's Moat at the time of Henry's death comprised nine office staff, eight travellers, two foremen, fourteen keymen, eighty male workers and ninety female. Henry's death coincided with another fall in the price of cocoa, and pressing annual mortgage repayments of £12,000 on recently bought premises in Foss Islands and North Street.

Henry Isaac Rowntree was a fine man manager and rescuer of drunkards, but he certainly had his shortcomings as a businessman. However, he was the son and brother who, for whatever reason, crucially decided not to stay on at the Pavement shop. He was the man who made the decision to buy the Tuke business and in doing so, through Quakerly brotherliness manifested by a desperate commercial situation, drew Joseph to Tanner's Moat and paved the way for him and then his nephew Seebohm to lay the foundations of one of the world's most successful confectionery companies. Joseph praised his fight for temperance and declared that this work here was a greater gift than any ability to make money. It is quite impossible to tell how far all this in turn was directly responsible for the social welfare which manifested itself in Joseph's trusts, the enlightened labour relations, the stunning pipeline of globally successful, stellar confectionery brands, the ergonomic, eco-and worker-friendly factory in Haxby Road, the clean, sociable and salubrious garden village at New Earswick and the diligently researched and enduring work on poverty, social welfare, education, workers' pensions and workers' rights rigorously conducted by Joseph and Seebohm, which helped form the basis of our welfare state. Without Henry Isaac Rowntree, many things in our world today might be very different and it's a lot more than just being able to take a break and have a KitKat.

Joseph arranged the Quaker funeral and burial at the Friends' Burial Ground in the grounds of The Retreat. As we have seen, Sarah Rowntree had no hesitation in offering Selena a home at 38 St Mary's and this remained at Selina's disposal after Sarah's death in 1888, when Joseph bought the property from his mother's estate. Frank was 14, Alice 13, and Ethel 10 when their father died: the girls attended The Mount School and Frank, who had been at the Friends School, Sidcot, in Somerset, was brought back to finish his schooling at Oliver's Mount School, Scarborough. A month after Henry's death, the house at 22 The Mount was empty and arrangements were proceeding to find a new occupant. The rent was £42 to cover mortgage repayments and the property included a stable at the bottom of the garden, which had been let out at £9 a year, and a Mrs Thorp would show prospective tenants round.

The dossiers relating to the estate included accounts for the girls' school fees, an invoice for repairs to the house and a Leak & Thorp invoice itemising Selina's dress requirements from 3 May to 9 June 1883, totalling £25.9s.11d. The thirty-three items include silk, ribbon, mantles, bonnet, gloves, buttons, cashmere, alpaca, braid, lining, frilling and £6.15s.10d for dressmaking – all probably mourning attire for Selina and her daughters. The probate valuation of furniture, linen, plate, china, books, clothes, jewels and ornaments amounted to £339.9s.180d.

Brothers John and Joseph were executors of Henry's will, which was made on 25 February 1868, three days before his marriage to Selina. It had never been updated. He left all personal and household effects to his wife; and bequeathed all his personal estate to his two brothers, upon trust to pay all the income arising therefrom to his wife during her lifetime, and thereafter to hold it on trust for any children. He empowered his executors to sell any of his estate at their discretion and to invest the proceeds in their own names, in any stocks, shares, mortgages or other securities, as they might think fit. They should be at liberty to carry on his business of cocoa manufacturer, or to sell and relinquish the business as they might think fit so to do. He also left any 'real estate ... as trustee or mortgagee' to John and Joseph. In other words, Henry entrusted all his business and financial affairs to his brothers, confident, no doubt, that they would take care of the interests of his wife and family. Significantly, no alterations had been made when the partnership with Joseph was agreed.

The probate figures showed the gross amount of personal estate as £7,537, with debts and funeral expenses of £4,963 deducted, leaving a net estate of £2,574.181. The half-year accounts for the firm for 1883 show that Henry still owed more than £1,400 of capital; so he must have still been paying back with interest the advance of £2,000 from his father's will. His personal folio ledger showed he owed £3,858 to the business. When Joseph joined the firm, he had 'insisted that Henry should have the first £150 made and that they should only divide anything above' that amount. The sum of £150 continued to be paid to Selina every year after Henry's death.

Henry must have been taking a proportion of the annual profits, which averaged out at £693 between 1870 and his death. We know that Selina did not get a share of subsequent revenues because she wrote to Joseph in November 1890 requesting 'a little more than £150 from the business'. She had received a £100 legacy from Sarah Rowntree's will in 1888, but she was no doubt aware how much more profitable her late husband's business had become by then: the net profit for 1890 was £9,008. Joseph retorted angrily with the correspondence referred to above, in which he rails at Selina about the sacrifices he had made financially and personally for Henry and the firm and how he had saved it from certain ruin.

Joseph did, however, ensure that Henry's son Frank got a good education which equipped him for the valuable role he subsequently played in the company. Like his father, he was entranced by mechanics and machines, and at 18 took an engineering course at Owens College, Manchester followed by technical training at the food machinery makers Joseph Baker & Sons at Willesden. In 1893, he joined Rowntree's in the engineering department, working with James Archer, and remained in this role until the fitting out of the new factory at Haxby Road was completed. In 1897, when the firm became a limited company, he was one of the first directors and was given 500 £10 shares by Joseph. Like his father he was a talented public speaker and enthusiastic teacher and organiser of the Layerthorpe Adult School.

Henry and Selina's younger daughter Ethel married the artist Harry S. Banks in 1902, settling in Somerset. In 1904, Alice married Alfred Oppenheim, an Austrian violinist and music professor, frequently travelling abroad with her husband. Census returns reveal Selina to be 'living on her own means'. In 1891, she was listed at Seamer Road, Scarborough, with Alice, schoolteacher and Frank, an engineering student. In 1911 her address was Ford Cottage, Clifton, York, which suggests that when Joseph moved from 38 St Mary's to Clifton Lodge in 1905, Selina went to live near Frank and his family on Water End. She later moved to Weston-super-Mare after Frank's death in 1918 to be closer to Ethel and Harry. She died there on 23 November 1919.

Chapter 11

Joseph Rowntree II (1836–1925): From Bootham School to Pavement to Tanner's Moat

J oseph Rowntree, second son of Joseph Rowntree senior and Sarah Stephenson, was born on 24 May 1836 in the family rooms above the gardenless shop in the buzzing and vibrant York street that was Pavement. His arrival could only have contributed further to what we have described as a noisy, hectic, almost commune-style domestic set-up where family shared living space, meals and opinions with up to twelve apprentices and a procession of Quaker visitors.

Joseph started at Bootham School in 1847, when he was 11, joining the forty or so pupils studying there at the time. If Joseph's time at Bootham would later prove influential, the trip he took to Ireland during this time, as described above, had probably the biggest impact. Joseph senior would be only too aware how seeing at first hand the lamentable conditions that were '*an Gorta Mór*', or the 'Great Hunger', would affect his boys.

Other influences on Joseph Rowntree junior

A visit to London later in 1855 was also to have a profound and lasting effect on Joseph. His visit was to attend the Society of Friends' Yearly Meeting with his father and brother, John. This trip, no doubt, had a significant effect on the two boys from both a religious and commercial standpoint. Exposed for the first time to the beating heart of Quakerism and the frenetic activity of City trade and business, the boys would have gone home to York somewhat wiser for, and inspired by, their experience.

As with Bootham and Ireland, Joseph would have taken experiences back home which would have influenced and informed his attitudes to life, people and work which re-emerged at Pavement, Tanner's Moat and Haxby Road. Joseph was soon to return to the capital to work as a grocer's apprentice for three months near Fenchurch Street from 1857. Apart from honing the usual, but challenging, grocer's skills of tea tasting and coffee grinding, he benefited from visits to bonded warehouses, docks, banks, customs offices, sugar refiners and a first-class grocer in the West End. But it was not long before his father summoned him back to York on the pretext, perhaps, that there was a stocktake waiting to be done. John Stephenson was despatched to ensure his prompt return.

The Pavement shop was to give Joseph Rowntree a sound and invaluable seventeen-year apprenticeship in retail and business management, particularly in relation to the grocery business. This, and his time in Fenchurch Street, provided a priceless foundation for the next stage of his career when he joined his brother at the cocoa works in Tanner's Moat.

We have already quoted from the uncompromisingly business-like memorandum Joseph Rowntree senior visited on his young charges; further details of shop life give more of the atmosphere and conditions there. Apprentices (including John and Joseph presumably) were allowed out until 10 pm in the summer and until 8.45 pm in the winter months; they had leave to attend weekday Meetings every fortnight; those who came from far away could go home once a year; they each had a separate lodging room for washing and there was no smoking or firearms. It concludes with, 'it is my earnest desire that the household may in all respects maintain those habits and practices in regard to dress, language etc which distinguish the religious Society of Friends.'

The younger Joseph would have enjoyed the camaraderie engendered by the Bond of Brothers – the club established by his father in 1849 to enhance the sense of belonging and community with his apprentices. The only rules, in 1860 at least, were to come to the reunion and meet on the steps of the minster at noon on 13 June; and to write before that date describing what had happened in the year so far. This would be collated by the president and circulated to all. Belonging and comradeship were other features he was at pains to inculcate at the Tanner's Moat and Haxby Road factories.

Another influence, later imported in a modified form in Rowntree's, was Joseph's visit to Sibford School in Sibford Ferris, west of Banbury, north Oxfordshire, in April 1857. This showed him how valuable a role practical instruction played in the curriculum: 'the union of manual and mental labour was advantageous'. Sibford School was founded in 1842 as a co-educational boarding school for the children of 'disowned' Quakers – those who had married outside the Society of Friends – as their children were barred from entering Ackworth School. The boys worked part time on the farm while the girls did household duties. Thus, it was possible to reduce fees to parents, which varied according to means.

He obviously enjoyed his visit to Peter Bedford (1780–1864), the Spitalfields' Quaker silk merchant and philanthropist who was doing much good work with convicted thieves and lobbying to reduce the number of crimes punishable by death. Bedford held levées of up to thirty Coldstream Guards in his home, feeding them 'plum cake and coffee' while he read out passages from the Bible. Today the Bedford Institute Association, which was founded in 1867, continues its original purpose to commemorate the life and continue the work of Peter Bedford, with its eight branches across East and South London working to nurture healthy citizens. They became places of refuge from the slums of East End streets, offering activities, summer camps, and outings for unemployed men and women with children.

Back in Pavement, Joseph appears to have resumed his duties with characteristic verve and enthusiasm. He is described as 'pensive and serious' but also industrious and always in the thick of it. On market days, according to one apprentice, 'he was all activity and "go", head thrown back, chin up, and his voice ringing out over all the others as he called out his orders.' He showed tact and consideration towards his colleagues. On Saturdays Joseph would delight in reading out articles from the *Manchester Examiner and Times* to the apprentices over tea.

Within six months of his return, aged 21, he was sharing the teaching of reading and writing at the adult school in Lady Peckett's Yard with his brother John. John took class 'A', Joseph 'B'. As noted above, John's strategy was to win his pupils over with plum cake and proceeded to read right through the Bible, starting with Genesis. Joseph was somewhat more eclectic, painstakingly preparing his Sunday lessons and imbuing them with an appropriate message and theme – and that is essentially how he approached his teaching for the next forty years or so. In addition to the Sunday morning lessons, Joseph took it upon himself to provide home tuition in students' houses, a practice which allowed him to see for himself the abject poverty in which many of his students lived. It also demonstrated a sincere belief in universal and ecumenical education: to the Rowntrees a man or woman deserved an education regardless of their creed or station. Indeed, his work as a teacher in the adult schools had a profound and lasting effect on him. He later described his experiences here as one of the most powerful influences on his life, seeing his role as a 'great blessing ... to have the opportunity of meeting week after week with a number of men seeking to improve themselves mentally and spiritually ... it brings the teacher face to face with many of the facts of life.' His educational works also included setting up a reading room and library in 1862, specifically for shop and office workers, which was the forerunner of the Albert Library he established in the Clifford Street Meeting House. This, in turn, spawned the York Friends' Library and Debating Society and was the impetus for the library and further education he established at the Haxby Road factory.

All of these experiences and influences had a profound effect not just on Joseph Rowntree the Quaker, but they also informed the way he managed and behaved as a businessman and employer and manager of men and women.

Joseph was 23 when his father died in November 1859, leaving him and John to run the Pavement business, and support their widowed mother and sister and John's wife, Elizabeth.

He took a holiday with his cousin Joshua in Switzerland, a country which would come to feature often in the course of his life. Indeed, travel was to be a constant in his life: 'money spent on travel is never wasted'. In 1877, he went to the Netherlands on a business trip, probably to find out more about the Van Houten press; in 1880 he visited Germany with the family and, later in the year, to Switzerland with friends.

Around the time of his father's death, he began to develop his passionate interest in urban poverty – the seeds of which were sown on that visit to Ireland and the home visits to his students from the adult school. His methodology was, like his father's, based on statistics, a relatively young discipline that had been growing in use from the beginning of the century.

Joseph and statistics

The science of statistics grew out of what was called 'political arithmetic' in the seventeenth century. Starting as a description of the collection of demographic information, political arithmetic evolved during the next century, first into the investigation of social problems by governments and individuals (the 'statistical movement'), and then as a description of social conditions as a part of social reform or 'ameliorism'. Finally, it came to describe the collection of data through direct observation. In 1797 the *Encyclopedia Britannica* defined statistics as 'a word lately introduced to express a word or survey of any kingdom, county or parish'. This conflation of demographics with a 'survey' led to the introduction of the national population census in the United Kingdom. In 1834, the London Statistical Society was founded by Thomas Malthus amongst others, with a view to 'procuring, arranging and publishing Facts calculated to illustrate the Conditions and Prospects of Society'. Through members such as Edwin Chadwick working on the Poor Law Report of 1834, for which he produced the Report on the Sanitary Condition of the Labouring Population, and William Farr who made statistical analyses on the link between cholera and density of population, the work of the society moved closer towards morally driven social investigation.

Joseph's meticulous and painstaking research took in the poor laws over the past half century, spending on armaments and education, the number of paupers over the last twelve years, numbers of illiterate men and women (from marriage registers and the numerous 'x's used for signatures), crime figures for 1805–1860, population figures, trade figures and the national spend. According to the Customs and Excise, the population was classified as one million 'upper and wealthy'; nine million 'merchants' clerks, shopkeepers etc'; eighteen million 'mechanics and operatives' and one million 'poor'. From all of this Joseph was able to see an inextricable link between poverty, illiteracy and crime. His disturbing findings were collected in *British Civilisation: In What it Consists and in What it Does Not Consist* and were intended to be read at adult school conferences.

Agonising over advertising

If Quakerism was in part responsible for philanthropy and enlightened industrial relations within the industry (Bryant & May and Huntley & Palmers were to some extent exceptions within the faith) and a paternalistic approach towards employees, it was by no means a cohesive force when it came to advertising. While others in the industry – such as rivals Fry and Cadbury – were embracing marketing and advertising, Joseph was very uncomfortable with anything so ostentatious and shallow, which is how he viewed product line promotion. As we know, he preferred to let the quality of his cocoa speak for itself, delivering goods to wholesalers and retailers unbranded with just a formal sales letter and, indeed, supplying labels bearing the name of the customer, which tended to give the impression that the customer was the producer rather than Rowntree's. For example, shop X in Malton would sell Rowntree's Rock Cocoa as X's Rock Cocoa; shop Y in Strensall would sell Rowntree's Elect as Y's Elect. Branding in reverse. The Rowntrees believed that a grocer was someone to look up to, that he was respected and merited a 'reverential air', that he was highly skilled and dignified, serving customers who were comfortably off with some rather special, exclusive lines. With a customer base like that, who needed the 'puffery' of advertising? The products would speak for, and sell, themselves … reputation was everything.

We know that Joseph would rather delay an order than send out substandard goods to his customers. When Seebohm, his son, once pointed out the sorry plight of a wholesaler who had been waiting six weeks for an order, Joseph responded by saying the delay was due to a manufacturing fault and that a further fortnight's delay was possible, 'but when he does get it, it will be what he ordered'. A letter from the mid 1870s shows just how unequivocal Joseph was:

> As we do not advertise we are enabled to give greater value for money than those firms whose sales depend on advertisements. We prefer to trust to quality ... steadily increasing sales strengthens our opinion that this is a sound method of doing business.

Joseph Fry had been advertising in the press since the 1830s – Fry's marketing spend in 1866 was about £2,000. The introduction of wrappers, of course, facilitated and boosted branding. Before that, up to the end of the nineteenth century, chocolates were sold loose in wooden boxes. One of the earliest examples of successful wrapper branding was Fry's Five Boys launched in 1886 for Fry's Milk Chocolate. It shows a range of emotions excited by eating Fry's chocolate: 'Desperation, Pacification, Expectation, Acclamation and the Realization it's Fry's'. A matching poster appeared in 1905 telling us that 'The "Five Girls" want Fry's "Five Boys" Milk Chocolate and will have no other'. To make Desperation appear tearful, ammonia was sprayed close to his face.

At the same time, these advertisements and wrappers demonstrated another universal and enduring theme – that chocolate is quite simply exceedingly good, and fun, to eat. 'Pascall Chocolate Eggs are good to eat, Pascall Novelties complete the treat' delivered the message. A 1927 Cadbury's poster tells us that their chocolate has 'tastes that thrill'. Terry's took no prisoners when they launched their Theobroma – the food of the gods assortment. Theobroma was the highest authority available since it was the Linnaean classification name for the cacao tree. 'Mars are marvellous' and Fry's Caramets were 'sweet bliss'. Bounty was 'far and away the most exotic chocolate treat'. Crunchie 'makes exciting biting!'; Everybody was a (Cadbury's) 'fruit and nut case'. Rowntree's Milk Chocolate contained 'delight in every bite' in 1928. Cellophane was introduced in the 1920s which, to some extent, took over from paper wrappers and provided much the same opportunities for pithy slogans and powerful branding.

Chocolate boxes too, for assortments, offered another vehicle for branding and eye-catching graphics. From 1862, Fry's and Cadbury were selling chocolates in boxes, Easter and Christmas selections were particularly popular; in 1882 Rowntree's had no fewer than 150 different boxes on offer. Sentimentality was the order of the day in artwork, and the boxes themselves were extremely popular. Apart from their primary, immediate use as a chocolate box, they were often a long-term repository for odds and ends, photographs, postcards and other keepsakes – long fuse, slow drip advertising. Cadbury's, indeed, produced some very lavish boxes, plush-lined with silk and satin and designed to hold jewellery, handkerchiefs or gloves long after the chocolates were eaten. Tins followed and these, too, produced vivid and colourful designs with immediate and long-term functions, to which many a cupboard and loft will attest.

Eminent artists were often deployed to great effect: Caley's, Bovril Chocolate and Fry's used John Hassall – most famous for *The Jolly Fisherman* poster he created in 1908 for the Great Northern Railway. Fry's also commissioned Tom Browne, one of the best of the British comic postcard artists at the beginning of the twentieth century, and Chas Pears, a prolific poster artist for the London Underground and an official war artist in both world wars. Alfred Leete drew Rowntree's Mr York in 1928; before that he had produced *Your Country Needs You* in 1914 – probably the best-known war poster of all time. Mackintosh used Jean d'Ylen, celebrated French poster artist, for their Toffee de Luxe in 1929, as well as Heath Robinson, cartoonist and illustrator – best known for his drawings of crazy machines – and Mabel Lucie Attwell, book and magazine illustrator, for Toffee Town, as used in national newspaper advertisements. Raymond Peynet, creator of the famous *Les Amoureux*, worked on Dairy Box and Sir Alfred Mullins, celebrated painter of horses, drew Caley's famous *Marquee* and *Lady* posters. G. M. Elwood designed some of their chocolate boxes around 1922. Richard Cadbury, an accomplished artist in his own right, worked on some of his own chocolate boxes.

To Joseph, as with others in the trade, being a grocer was a dignified and skilled business catering for the better off in society. He would not sell down to the mass market which was beginning to emerge and which slowly, but surely, formed the ever-growing core market for his business. To Joseph, as with some other Quakers, and to some extent shopkeeper manufacturers generally, advertising and attractive, alluring shop windows smacked of disingenuousness and implied a masquerading of substandard goods. This scepticism was partly fuelled by the extensive use of advertising by companies selling patent, 'quack' remedies and medicines – a massive £2 million was spent by this sector in 1914 – and the distrust, before 1890, of advertising agencies, which were largely seen as being concerned solely with cynically selling space in newspapers, with none of the associated expertise in design and copywriting, sales projections or even circulation or readership figures.

The unfortunate and inevitable consequence of not advertising was that all of Rowntree's lines were undersold and none was particularly successful as a result. Although between 1870 and 1879 sales rose from £7,384 to £30,890, margins remained tight and losses were recorded.

Chocolate and health

Advertising, apart from attracting the attention of a rapidly growing consumer market to the product, also enabled the manufacturer to parade and promote other qualities, often to the disadvantage of the competition. Alleged health benefits were a factor in the high nutritional values afforded by rich, pure milk content. This, of course, chimed with the traditional claims surrounding so-called medicinal confectionery; lozenges, voice jujubes and barley sugar, for example, had all boasted medical benefits, as indeed did Mackintosh's Toffee – good for sore throats. Posters and adverts were frequently populated with healthy, rubescent children. Cadbury's Dairy Milk Chocolate was 'rich in cream'. 'Overflowing with goodness' was trotted out by both Mackintosh and Nestlé while Pascall's Ambrosia Devonshire Chocolate was 'the glory of Devon in a packet'. Fry's famous churn-shaped showcard from 1925 announced that their milk chocolate contained 'full cream milk from west of England farms'.

Cadbury's actively promoted their Essence as pure, safe and compliant under the terms of the 1872 and 1875 Adultertion of Food Acts (whereby all ingredients in cocoa had to be revealed), thus tapping into a growing public awareness of food safety and purity, or, put another way, adulteration. By contrast, Rowntree's denied themselves this window of opportunity by being much more conservative, sticking with their Rock Cocoa and largely refraining from advertising and branding. There has been a glass-and-a-half of milk in every bar of Cadbury's Dairy Milk since 1928. *The British Medical Journal* of 26 December 1891 endorsed Bovril Chocolate – Bovril Caramels contained ten per cent Bovril; Oxo Chocolate was manufactured on a similar basis – 'a stand-by between meals'. Bovril's claim was that 'it contained 300 per cent more actual nourishment than any other chocolate extant'. It was particularly suitable for children and the sick, as well as being good for sportsmen and travellers: 'a food by the way'; 'a perfect food in itself.' Oxo also marketed Oxo Toffee (containing fluid beef and fresh cream milk) as did Boots – Vitamalt Toffee – while Horlicks produced a malted milk toffee. Terry's Snack was ideal for walkers as it contained raisins and 'nutritive'.

Invaluable support also came from the British Food and Drugs Act of 1860 and the Adulteration of Food Acts in 1872 and 1875. Sales of Cadbury's unadulterated Cocoa Essence were to increase by 114 per cent in the 1870s. Perception too was crucial: Cadbury's were able to take the higher moral ground when they disbanded all their adulterated lines – all still quite legal and providing good turnover – and put all their resources behind the pure Cocoa Essence. In doing so Cadbury's earned an unrivalled and unimpeachable reputation for purity and honesty in production. This not only chimed with the tenets of their Quaker faith but set the bar for cocoa and chocolate quality from the 1870s onwards. In many ways Cadbury's never really looked back. Van Houten published a *Report on the Van Houten's Cocoa* (for the medical profession only) by Professor Attfield FRS, Professor of Practical Chemistry to the Pharmaceutical Society of Great Britain, and other key opinion leaders. The introduction, by C. J. van Houten, tells us:

Now that medical men are deprecating the habitual use of alcoholic liquors, and even tea and coffee are found too exciting for many a temperament – to say nothing of the growing cases of nervous disorder in this age of hot haste and feverish anxiety – the question of what beverage may be recommended, as at once refreshing and innocuous is assuming the highest importance. Cocoa has long been known as a useful article or diet ... unlike tea or coffee, it is not only a stimulant but a nourisher.

Attfield went on to endorse the use of alkalis in Van Houten's cocoa – soda or potash – adding 'not only does it not spoil but very greatly improves the cocoa'. This must be one of the first examples of medical education aimed at the profession by key opinion formers working on behalf of commercial companies.

In 1870, some eight years after Henry bought his business, Rowntree's had about five per cent of the chocolate and cocoa market attributable to the three main companies; Cadbury's had ten per cent or so, and Fry's the rest at eighty-five per cent. By the end of the decade this had shifted to ten, twenty-eight and sixty-two per cent respectively.

Adulteration in cocoa and chocolate

Closely associated with healthiness were the themes of quality and purity, key elements in chocolate production, particularly amongst the perfectionist Quaker manufacturers. Fry's early adverts were described as 'venerable announcements', which had a 'certain coy primness about them'; Cadbury's end-of-century slogan was 'Absolutely Pure, Therefore Best'. To the Methodist Mackintosh's it was all very simple: 'always quality first, publicity second, as advertising alone can only sell a poor article once'. For their Quality Street, the slogan for shopkeepers was, 'Put your shop in Quality Street by putting Quality Street in your shop'. Linking healthiness, quality and purity is adulteration, or the avoidance thereof.

An adulterant is a hostile substance found in substances such as food, cosmetics, pharmaceuticals, fuel or other chemicals that compromises the safety or effectiveness of that substance.

There are few, if any, foodstuffs or beverages which have escaped the blight of adulteration. Short changing on ingredients and supplementing them with additives and rubbish – some of it toxic – has always been an easy way to increase profits. Some manufacturers introduced bright colours in sweets by illegally adding toxins: green (chromium oxide and copper acetate), red (lead oxide and mercury sulphide), yellow (lead chromate) and white (chalk, arsenic trioxide) have all found their way into your sweet packet or chocolate bar, and into your and your children's stomachs.

In an 1885 cover cartoon for *Puck*, Joseph Keppler famously satirised the dangers of additives in sweets by depicting the 'mutual friendship' between striped candy, doctors, and gravediggers. Research into the dangers of additives, exposés of the food industry, and public pressure led to the passage of the 1860 Adulteration of Food and Drink Bill to regulate food and drugs, including sweets.

We have the mediaeval guilds to thank for early attempts to regulate quality standards but these were intended to protect the market rather than the customer or consumer. Moreover, the guilds only operated in towns and cities, so adulteration in the countryside remained unregulated.

As soon as the distinction between consumer and manufacturer became more apparent, the opportunities for systematic food fraud were seized upon by the less scrupulous. By the eighteenth century there was adulteration on an industrial scale. Bakers were at it: they used chalk and alum, more commonly found today in deodorants and medications for the treatment of piles, to whiten bread. Potatoes, plaster of Paris, clay and sawdust helped to bulk up their buns and loaves. Brewers were at it:

apart from the time-honoured use of water as a dilutant, poisons such as strychnine – rat poison – were introduced to give that lovely hoppy bitter taste, and to reduce the hop bill. Cocoa manufacturers mixed in arrowroot, potato starch, sago flour and powdered seashells to reduce the required cocoa content; iron rust, red lead or brick dust were used to give that rich brown colour and to ensure a good night's sleep. Grocers coloured their cheeses with lead. The list goes on and includes spirits, olive oil, cheese, pickles, anchovies, mustard and confectionery – all found to be adulterated and often in ways which had a serious and adverse impact on health. The use, for example, of copper was widespread and anchovies were dyed red with lead oxide. A twelve-year study published in 1848 concerning the adulteration of food found not a single loaf of bread subjected to analysis that was unadulterated. Anthony Wohl gives us an interesting list of the adulterants in his 1983 book *Endangered Lives: Public Health in Victorian Britain*:

> The list of poisonous additives reads like the stock list of some mad and malevolent chemist: strychnine, cocculus inculus (both are hallucinogens) and copper as in rum and beer; sulphate of copper in pickles, bottled fruit, wine, and preserves; lead chromate in mustard and snuff; sulphate of iron in tea and beer; ferric ferrocyanide, lime sulphate, and turmeric in chinese tea; copper carbonate, lead sulphate, bisulphate of mercury, and Venetian lead in sugar confectionery and chocolate; lead in wine and cider; all were extensively used and were accumulative in effect, resulting, over a long period, in chronic gastritis, and, indeed, often fatal food poisoning. Red lead gave Gloucester cheese its 'healthy' red hue, flour and arrowroot a rich thickness to cream, and tea leaves were 'dried, dyed, and recycled again'.
>
> As late as 1877 the Local Government Board found that approximately a quarter of the milk it examined contained excessive water, or chalk, and ten per cent of all the butter, over eight per cent of the bread, and 50 per cent of the gin had copper in them to heighten the colour.

Not everyone minded, it seems. In 1771, Tobias Smollet reported in *The Expedition of Humphrey Clinker* that London bread was:

> a deleterious paste, mixed up with … bone ashes, insipid to the taste and destructive to the constitution. The good people are not

ignorant of this adulteration; but they prefer it to wholesome bread, because it is whiter than the meal of corn. Thus they sacrifice their taste and their health.

Nevertheless, scientific investigation was developing apace as were scientific analysis and the detection of adulteration.

In 1820 it took Frederick Accum, a visiting German chemist and laboratory assistant to Sir Humphry Davy, to do anything about it: he identified numerous toxic additives in many foods and drinks. The title page of his best-selling book, *The Treatise on Adulterations of Food and Culinary Poisons* featured a skull and an ominous quotation from the *Old Testament*: 'there is death in the pot'. Accum's argument, quite reasonably, was that, 'The man who robs a fellow subject of a few shillings on the highway is sentenced to death but he who distributes a slow poison to the whole community escapes unpunished.'

It is hard to say how far the realisation that most foods were being systematically polluted and poisoned, the conclusive findings of Accum and Dr Hassall with his *Lancet*-published 'Hassall Reports', or even the fatalities in the Bradford Humbug scandal (when sweets made with arsenic caused twenty deaths and made 200 ill) provided the impetus for legislation. What we can say with greater confidence is that Britain's reputation with regard to exports was suffering, and that is a more likely reason why adulteration legislation was finally passed. All the while, in the background, factory and mill owners the length and breadth of the country were growing more and more annoyed by a surge in absenteeism blamed largely on the consumption of adulterated foods and drink. Money spoke loudest.

Adulteration was eventually made illegal under The Adulteration of Food and Drugs Act 1860 and The Adulteration of Food Acts 1872 and 1875. As mentioned above, one of the issues which gave impetus to this was the publication of a *Lancet* study in 1850 by Hassall, in which over half of all chocolate he sampled was found to contain brick dust. He and his editor, Thomas Wakley, surgeon and MP, had also identified gamboge, a violent purgative and irritant, lead, copper and mercury in various sweets; even the brightly coloured wrappers were polluted with the same toxins. Hassall sampled 2,500 products, making use of the microscope for food analysis for the first time, publishing his findings first in *The Lancet* and later in a book, naming and shaming, like Accum, the 'adulterers'. Hassall and Wakley catalogued each of the vendors, locations, dates and products purchased. Each food and drink item was analysed and the results were published with the conclusion that food adulteration was a lot more common than was believed and that many of the adulterated foods were actually poisonous. Chocolate products exposed by this research included oatmeal chocolate, acorn chocolate, Icelandic moss and barley chocolate. In France 'ferruginous chocolate' was considered 'so beneficial to women who are out of order, or have the green sickness' and was made from dissolving good chocolate in rusty water. Chicory, itself an adulterant, was often polluted by roasted carrots and turnips, for the aroma, with a sprinkling of 'black jack' (burnt sugar) to give it a rich coffee colour.

The chocolate cartel

The friendship forged between George Cadbury and Joseph Rowntree during their Pavement apprenticeship, and of course the bond created by Cadbury, Rowntree and Fry as Quakers, were the two driving forces responsible for the agreements the three companies made in 1872, 1889, 1895 and 1900, coordinating prices on chocolate and other confectioneries, but not on cocoa – the main product at that time. The cartel also limited trade discounts and shop point of sale in order to maintain decent margins for all the companies (but not the retailers). In 1918, the triumvirate signed what became known as the Cheltenham Agreements. Non-Quaker Caley in Norwich was also involved in some of these arrangements, as were Clarke, Nickolls and Coombs (Clarnico) of London. In 1935, neighbours Terry and then Nestlé joined to form a Five Firm Agreement for chocolate.

Joseph Rowntree and industrial espionage

But it was cocoa essence production, successfully pioneered by Cadbury, which, albeit indirectly, eventually led Fry, Cadbury and Rowntree out of their respective difficult times.

Confectionery companies – being private companies, and, more importantly, because confectionery recipes are not patentable – were extraordinarily secretive in order to stop competitors from stealing their bestselling products, rebranding and selling them as their own. For example, Mounds is a chocolate bar created in 1920 as a single piece for five cents. In 1929, the Peter Paul Candy Manufacturing Company purchased the line and began production. It is now made by The Hershey Company, consisting of a shredded coconut filling coated in dark chocolate. Sound familiar? Forrest Mars senior, patriarch of the Mars empire, pinched the idea from Mounds in the 1950s and launched it in Britain, calling his version Bounty. Bounty remains a bestseller today while few British chocolate aficionados have ever heard of Mounds.

Espionage became so pervasive that European confectionery makers began employing 'detectives' as a matter of course to keep an eye on workers. Commercially sensitive manufacturing processes were off-limits to all workers except on a need-to-know basis and outside contractors had to sign strict, highly punitive confidentiality agreements.

For example, when Nestlé first figured out how to successfully blend milk and chocolate, only a handful of Nestlé executives knew how the complete milk chocolate-making process worked. Apparently, the company also conducted employee background checks and put 'suspicious' workers under surveillance. At Hershey's, an elite few are privy to the proper mix of cocoa beans required to produce Hershey's distinct chocolate flavour. And Mars supposedly blindfold outside contractors when it's necessary to escort them through their factories.

Britain's two biggest chocolate firms, Cadbury's and Rowntree's, sent many a mole to work in competitors' factories. Desperate situations required desperate measures. In March, April and May 1872, Joseph Rowntree embarked on a voyage of blatant industrial espionage, taking in London, Paris, the Netherlands, Cologne, Bristol and Bournville, bribing employees of Fry's, Taylor's, Cadbury's, Dunn & Hewitt, the Quaker Stollwerck in Cologne, and Chocolat Menier in Paris to divulge their firms' production processes and recipes. This is an example of one of his advertisements in the *Clerkenwell News*:

To cocoa and chocolate makers. Wanted immediately, a Foreman who thoroughly understands the manufacture of Rock and other Cocoas, confection and other chocolates. Also several workmen. Good hands will be liberally dealt with.

Flyers were also produced (250 copies for 5s 6d) and distributed. Taylor's of London – 'the most extensive manufacturer in Europe of cocoa and chocolate, mustard and chicory' – suffered most. Joseph hired their foreman mixer, James French, on a trial basis for 20 shillings per week plus a gratuity of £5 for his recipes and £1 for his fare to York. If, after three months he wished to return to London, he would qualify for a further £1. His colleague, Robert Pearce, was taken on for 17 shillings per week after 'imparting all his knowledge'.

He manufactured all the Taylor's chocolate, apart from the finest, for such accounts as Hans Sloane's. William Garrett was recruited because he 'had the receipt of Unsworth's Cream Cocoas', and a register of all his workmates. Henry Thomson, a Taylor's man for twelve years and understudy to a superior with three times that experience, was made an offer of 30 shillings per week and 'a lump sum of £10 for all his receipts and knowledge'. Thomson never made it to York – perhaps his conscience got the better of him. Nevertheless, it seems that Joseph came away with a fairly complete picture of Taylor's recipes, plant, customers, wages paid and their production techniques. After subsequent visits, he was privy to their costs, budgets, sales and margins; later, a Thomas Neal furnished a detailed engineering report. The insidious question, 'has he any special knowledge of value?', became a standard question before Rowntree's job interviews. Similar raids took place on Compagnie Française who were in the Bermondsey New Road and Chocolat Menier in Southwark Street. 'Research' was carried out on other competitors, which included Quaker colleagues Cadbury's, Neave's Foods for Infants and Invalids of Fordingbridge, Chocolat Lombard and Maison Guérin-Boutron, both of Paris, Philippe Suchard of Neuchâtel and the English Condensed Milk Company of Leadenhall Street. How far this is a convenient and hypocritical abnegation of Quaker principles and of ethical practice in business generally is hard to tell – the practice of eliciting privileged commercial information from competitors for money may have been more acceptable then than it is today.

Nevertheless, most commentators have swerved around the episode; only Walvin (in 1998) and I (in 2017) have confronted it head on. Walvin says, 'it is curious that those commentators on the man and the company have simply overlooked this remarkable episode.' Borthwick Institute, at the University of York, has advertisements, notes and drawings gleaned from these interviews.

Joseph visited the Cadburys in 1875, the Netherlands twice in 1877, and spent his holidays with the Cadburys in Switzerland. None of these destinations can have been entirely coincidental, or just for the scenery.

The curious case of Cornelius Hollander, Dutchman and double agent

Agonising over a purchase of a Van Houten press was not Joseph's only Dutch dilemma. A Dutchman, Cornelius Hollander, was hired in 1885 at £5 per week because he supposedly knew the Van Houten cocoa recipe and Joseph hoped that this might be adapted to perfect his failing Elect. Unfortunately, the secretive and 'difficult' Hollander was not as useful as had been anticipated. Things did not start well with some unseemly haggling over the contract and remuneration, with the matter made more fraught as no translator of Dutch could be found in York and Hollander insisted on corresponding in Dutch. The deal was that Hollander would come to the factory and make the much-desired cocoa powder privately on his own <u>with ingredients he brought from the Netherlands </u>(Joseph's underlining). Eventually he was suspected of fiddling his expenses and was dismissed. Hollander's North Street laboratory, which was always locked, was broken into, revealing that he knew next to nothing about the Van Houten product. Police raided the Dutchman's house and retrieved items of Rowntree property and drawings of equipment.

Hollander was the chocolate industry's first double agent. He successfully sued Rowntree's for breach of contract. On Hollander's dismissal, James Archer, the company engineer, took over the Elect Department. Elect was re-launched in 1887.

Chapter 12

The Haxby Road Years (1890–1925)

Joseph's 'philanthropy' was never entirely altruistic – it was driven by an enlightened but acute business vision in which he identified and cultivated the benefits afforded by a contented workforce working in a reasonably pleasant environment. This came to fruition in 1890 when Joseph bought a 20-acre site to the north of the city centre on Haxby Road, with a view to building a more efficient and ergonomic factory which would enable the firm to improve production techniques and transportation, and meet the growing demand for their products. And all in a pleasant working environment. In Joseph's own words he wanted a workplace where his workers could 'develop all that is best and worthy in themselves … healthful conditions of labour are not luxuries to be adopted or dispensed at will. They are conditions necessary for success.' Tanner's Moat was inadequate in every way. We have already noted how Seebohm Rowntree declared 'Tanner's Moat was Hell.'

The new factory would be an efficient and congenial place of work – and so it transpired. For example, the offices were lit by electricity powered by a generator and the factory had its own North Eastern Railway goods branch line and halt – to expedite transportation and commuting.

Correspondence of 10 October 1890 gives a breakdown of the anticipated costs:

1 boiler	£400
1 second hand boiler	£120
Setting 2 boilers	£150
Economiser and setting	£150
Chimney	£550
Tank and tank tower	£170
Engine and fixing	£150
Pump	£100
NE Railway 270 yards	£400
Own line 800 yards	£1000
Drain and pipes	£310

Refrigerator   £500
Cubic feet of brickwork 1,096,00 @2 ½ d   £11,416
TOTAL   **£15,416**
Excludes shafting, steam pipes, gas and all fillings
+ £1,660 for the fruit installation

The decision to move to the Haxby Road site was not taken lightly or without anxiety. Joseph knew that this was very likely the turning point, the point of no return which may well lead to 'great wealth'. He had no desire for this and agonised over the effect it may have on his children, possibly leading them into 'self-indulgent and self-considering lives'. Nevertheless, he also recognised that the wealth would invest in him the power to use it to the greater good of his employees and society in general. This, of course, led to the establishment of the Joseph Rowntree trusts.

The manufacture of clear gums began in 1893, permitted by the extra space in Haxby Road. The fruit room and gums were first to transfer, and by 1898, all production was on the new site.

Two more members of the family joined the firm. First in 1892, came Arnold, a son of Joseph's brother John, then a year later Henry Isaac's son Frank. This reinforced the Quaker tendency to populate the higher echelons of their companies with their own, thus ensuring a degree of continuity and consolidation at the top. The number of employees in 1884 was 182; by 1899 this had risen to 1,613, and by 1902 it stood at over 2,000, doubling by 1908. Fry's and Cadbury's had seen equally dramatic staff increases from 250 to 4,500 and 230 to 2,683 over a similar period.

John Wilhelm and Seebohm (who came on board in 1888 after a university chemistry course at Owens College, Manchester) spent their early years working in the different departments to make them 'thoroughly acquainted with the practical side of the business' in a form of work experience. Two years after he joined, John Wilhelm was earning £30 per year. In 1891, Theodore Hotham Rowntree joined to do the accounts and statistics; J. B. Morrell started that same year in the Cake Chocolate Department, moving on to raw materials in 1898, a function which took him to the West Indies to purchase plantations in Jamaica and Dominica. In 1896, John Wilhelm Rowntree urged his colleagues to buy overseas estates to fend against speculators, keep their beans unsullied by allegations of 'slave grown cocoa' and harvest better quality beans. Estates were duly acquired in 1899 in Jamaica, Trinidad and Dominica but were 'a commercial failure: plagued by mismanagement, they were unprofitable from the outset'. In the end, the estates delivered Rowntree's eight per cent of their needs; they sold them off in 1914.

Mr Crooks' box-making company in North Street initially supplied all the packaging, but this was taken in-house in 1898. From 1877, William Laycock carted the finished goods to the railway station and brought back supplies and raw materials; he was an employee of the Eastern Railway Company. When he started, one journey per day sufficed; by 1905 three journeys plus 'specials' was the norm. Seebohm Rowntree made an immediate impact when he hired the company's first chemist in 1896 – the Quaker Samuel H. Davies who set up a laboratory – to expand the range and improve the purity of the products.

Wages were probably about average for the industry although care would have to be taken with rates for comparable jobs at nearby Terry's and Craven. In 1886 a fitter was on £22 for a sixty-hour week; boys were on £6 per week; men £18; joiners 6 ½d per hour. In 1887, girls of 14 were started on £3 6d per week. Joseph insisted on good handwriting and some applicants were sent back to school until their writing was of a sufficiently improved standard. One way to get a rise was to be proficient in shorthand.

A number of fires at North Street had led to the establishment of a fire brigade. The alarm was raised by an errand boy who went around knocking on the doors of all the firemen. One story tells of a worker falling into a tub of glucose when a fire was announced.

As we have seen, the payroll increased significantly over the years; here are the numbers:

1872, 30
1874, 40
1880, 100
1883, 200
1894, 893
1899, 1,613
1904, 3,564
1909, 4,066
1924, 6,932

Staff benefits and welfare came thick and fast with social clubs such as singing, angling and football, although debating was never as popular as it had been at Pavement. Joseph opened two savings banks and instigated a committee to look into a staff pension scheme – groundbreaking stuff in

the history of industrial relations. Two years later it was up and running
– the first of its kind and with no template or precedent to follow; it
predated the state pension by two years. This was a huge corporate risk as
there was no data to help and no idea, of course, of how it might perform
in terms of future liabilities. The pensions were inflation linked, 'money
value' and aligned to wages. The fund was gifted by the company to the
tune of £9,000, while Joseph contributed £10,000 of his own money into
the scheme. The firm paid in 30 shillings for every 20 shillings paid in
by the men and up to 60 shillings for every 20 shilling contribution from
the women. The uptake was good with ninety-eight per cent of eligible
employees joining the scheme in the first year. Security in older age was
the name of the game and Joseph's cutting-edge scheme had banished
at a stroke the sceptre of destitution and the worry of the workhouse for
so many.

Employees approaching retirement age at the opening of the scheme
were also accommodated so that they too benefitted in equal measure; the
initial investments allowed the scheme to proceed on a profitable basis
from the start. It later also provided for widows whose husbands were
killed in action in the First World War. A fund had been started in 1911 to
compensate widows with £50 on the death of their husbands and this was
doubled in later years. The Widows Benefit Fund was established during
the war to allow a pension to widows aged 50 or over (later changed to
45) on the death of their husbands. Joseph Rowntree was determined
to see these measures through, as shown by the minutes of a board
meeting: 'I am so much impressed with the need and value to our people
of the proposed arrangement that I ask the Board to accept the principle
before discussing the cost.' Counter-intuitive as it may have been to the
financially meticulous Joseph, it demonstrates very clearly to us, as it
must have to the board that day, just how passionately he believed in this
benefit. The inspector of taxes declared that the company's contribution
was not allowable as a business expense but Joseph challenged this
decision – and won.

The irrepressible Miss Wood and a liquid trip to Whitby

The tenets of Quakerism were imbued in Joseph, as they had been in
Henry before him; an undimmed respect for his fellow men, fellow men
who included the people who worked for him. Not only did this result
in a fair and considerate management style but it was also responsible
for his belief in fair and honest trading. Henry and Joseph always took

time to feel at one with their workers, solicitous of their welfare and well-being. Conflict – be it in relation to workers or commercial rivals – was anathema to them. The personal touch, mutual loyalty and respect, and familiarity were the watchwords.

However, the increasing size of the company had its downsides and one of these was that Joseph's personal relationship with his workers was, by necessity, starting to diminish. He was determined to not let this happen and set about compensating for his increasing distance by creating what might be seen as extensions of himself. A girl's welfare officer, Miss Wood, was appointed in 1891 to look after the health, moral upbringing and behaviour of female staff, some of whom were as young as 13. This was something of a pioneering move in British industry, even though an 1864 factory inspector's report had recommended that firms which employed a large number of females should 'take on a married female of mature age to act as an "onlooker"' – exactly what Joseph did in hiring Miss Wood. One of the problems Joseph Rowntree had identified was that there were few, if any, women in the firm of any maturity, as his female workforce left at a relatively young age to get married, start families – and never returned because at this point married women, as in most industries, were not employed.

Miss Wood, among other things, instituted a sober dress code of black dresses and no skirts or blouses. This was provoked when one young lady presented for work in a blouse which left her throat exposed; the reaction of the outraged Rowntree's 'onlooker' was to exclaim that such immodesty 'might easily draw a man's attention to you'. Miss Wood was alarmed by the prospect of naked throats but had no problem with girls turning up for work with their hair festooned with heavy metal curlers. Notwithstanding, the appointment of Miss Wood was obviously a success as within a year an assistant 'onlooker' was hired. The 'other things' she was paid to do included running the library and getting the right sort of books for the clientele, tracking down absentees, and generally acting as an agony aunt and nurse.

A work's outing to Whitby was even more shocking than the bare-throat episode. Some of the party left the specially chartered train at Goathland on the North York Moors, planning to walk the rest of the way and meet the main group for an afternoon stroll on the beach at their destination. A rain storm intervened and diverted the walkers into a public house for shelter. When they finally emerged, many of them were so drunk that they had to be escorted to the station by the Whitby police. There were no more outings for a number of years. Joseph, nevertheless, did continue with the regular 'concerts' – lavish meals in the Bootham Exhibition Buildings to which the whole workforce was invited – a rare treat for most in those days. Office staff (the equivalent of management) were frequently invited to Joseph's house for 'social evenings'.

Miss Wood's department took over the hiring of girls. Day one started with the supervisor meeting with the girl's mother to assure her that her daughter's welfare was paramount, and every girl was given a 'companion' or mentor to train her on the job. Often the homes of applicants of both sexes were visited to confirm that they were 'clean and respectable'. Girls and boys and men and women were, of course, segregated as far as possible with separate dining rooms and women-only corridors. Boys were a constant problem due to their high turnover and the negative effects this had on production, and so it was in 1900 that D. S. Crichton, a Congregationalist minister, was taken on to look after the boys' pastoral care. Many young men had to leave when they reached 21 as the jobs they were doing would only be cost-effective if Rowntree paid child rather than adult rates of pay. Crichton tried to minimise this by strategically placing boys in jobs where there was a likelihood of ongoing work.

Outside the firm, Joseph continued his work in social reform. He was a co-founder of the Temperance Legislation League with Lord Peel and committee chairman until his death. A Yorkshire Quarterly Meeting in 1889 stung him into action when he heard Friends claiming that poverty was accountable solely to 'the drink', in other words, self-inflicted. Joseph believed that 'the drink' was a cause but only a contributory cause. Accordingly, he proceeded to set the record straight. With Arthur Sherwell, he researched the issue in some detail and in 1899 published the influential 800-page book, *The Temperance Problem and Social Reform* – a veritable bestseller which sold 70,000 copies in ten editions. *The London Times* said of it: 'here is an invaluable compendium of authentic information'. This book was followed by *Public Control of the Liquor Trade* in 1903 and *The Taxation of the Liquor Trade* in 1906. The latter included supporting research from the United States, which took many painstaking years to acquire by Sherwell and others. Joseph accompanied Sherwell to Scandinavia on one occasion to research the Gothenburg Public House System. It seems likely that by this time he himself had become a total abstainer; records show that in 1867 he had shipped forty-eight bottles of wine from Hamburg to York and wine and beer feature in his annual domestic accounts until 1880. In 1874 he took delivery of twelve bottles of champagne.

The Gothenburg Public House System was a successful attempt by the Swedish authorities to curb excessive drinking. Every Swedish householder had the right to distil their own spirits until 1855 when a law was passed outlawing domestic distillation. Local authorities now had the power to grant licences. The city of Gothenburg awarded the retail spirits licences to only one company, which would be run as a trust and would control bars, restaurants and off-licences. Premises were purposely unattractive and unwelcoming in order to discourage drinking; shareholders received a maximum return of five per cent annually while all other profits were to be used to provide libraries, museums, parks and other public amenities.

Joseph persisted with his enlightened attitude towards his workforce, and in 1885 stocked and opened a library for his staff. He put in £10 of his own money, a sum that was matched by a grant from the company's Pure Literature Society. One penny was deducted from the weekly wages of all employees – a not inconsiderable amount for someone earning the average wage of £1 per week.

Cocoa Works Magazine (*CWM*) was launched in 1902 as a vehicle to maintain communication and impart company and employee news at all levels. This was an important plank in Joseph's intention to maintain a high level of communication at all but the most commercially sensitive of levels and was one of the UK's first company magazines.

Quaker thinking on such issues as temperance and gambling naturally permeated the company and came to bear on many other, non-welfare related aspects of factory life. Gambling, for example, was rife until it was banned in 1904, and the company never knowingly employed anyone who had a liquor licence. Mothers of children born out of wedlock were likewise excluded, and any man who 'got a girl into trouble' was denied the usual three-day break for honeymoon on marriage. Sick pay was not paid to anyone absent from work due to a sexually transmitted infection, and indeed, many sufferers were dismissed as a precaution against contagion amongst the workforce. The popular York Races were always problematic and requests for time off to attend were routinely turned down. Things came to a head in 1914, when 1,200 staff protested en masse, with 754 men voting to have time off, 619 voting not to and 188 abstaining. Amongst the women, 283 voted in favour, 666 not and 150 abstained. Seebohm Rowntree relented and agreed to take requests for time off. In all, 2,477 workers – or forty-nine per cent of the workforce – applied, but only the men were permitted leave of absence for a half day at the May and August meetings.

Haxby Road and the increasing headcount coincided with a necessary change in industrial relations. As we have noted, the opportunities for familiarity and personal contact with staff were receding. It was now increasingly necessary to introduce rules and regulations more appropriate to a large company, and that is what happened from 1892.

The time system was tightened up with doors opening at 6 am. Anyone not inside by 6.05 am was excluded until 8.25 am by which time a quarter of a day's pay would have been lost. Two 'lates' in one week was punished with a week's unpaid suspension. Late-coming after breakfast and dinner was also not tolerated. Inventory controls were set up to minimise wastage and improve requisitioning. Later, the working week was reduced to forty-eight hours, and the working day was changed from 7.30 am to 5 pm with an hour for dinner. There was no reduction in pay. The later start also obviated the need to provide breakfast. Latecomers were now docked half a day's pay.

Staff catering was a major challenge as the number of staff continued to grow. From a 1912 edition of *CWM* we learn that the following prodigious amounts of food were sold in 1911: 59,009 1d buns and pastries; 108,124 ½d cups of tea; 10,743 plates of sausage and mash; 25,978 plates of peas; 19,315 portions of fish; 8,395 pies, 31,072 glasses of milk and a (disappointing) 9,522 ½d cups of cocoa.

Joseph, in what can only be described as a thoroughly modern act of management, immersed himself in all aspects of the company's business. A good example of this, and at the same time, of his empathetic attitude to his staff, is shown when he assumed the role of sales manager. In November 1892, he took himself on a sales trip with one of the Yorkshire travellers, a Mr Tasker. It was a trip which allowed him to meet his customers, understand their problems, see the competition at first hand and how his products were received in the marketplace. In Batley Carr we meet a Mr Thackray:

a pleasant and friendly disposed man who expressed himself as highly pleased at the attention on calling on him; he does little with Elect but is much taken with our new Homoeo … and thinks it equal to Epps's. Oddy's was less impressive as Leak & Thorp's for frontage, where we have a good sale of … Rock and Rock Powder and recently some Elect. The manager, Mr Scaife, is well pleased with our things and says they won't have any rubbish at their store. As an instance of what was rubbish he mentioned the Co-op's Nutritional Homoeo. In Pudsey, George Rankin is 'a well-stocked little shop.

> Speaks enthusiastically of Elect and brought his mother in to tell us
> what she thought of it. They think it's so good that they will do all
> they can to push it, for which purpose I can send samples etc.

By any standards these, and the many other, call reports are exemplary.
They are meticulous in their detail and show a man ready to learn from
and listen to his traveller and his customers – lending sales support and
encouragement where required. The reports are, properly, summarised
by some general remarks on the representative and his market which give
an insight into travelling salesmanship in those days. He writes, 'It is
clearly a difficult district to work. There is a great deal of rough walking,
along turnpikes and footpaths and across fields ... railway communication
is often very awkward.' As an example Joseph cites the 44-mile journey
from Fulneck to Morley 'up and down hills, foggy and slippery', leaving
them no option but to take the train, or rather four trains and a journey of
an hour and three quarters. 'As regards Tasker ... there was not a single
[call] when he seemed to be otherwise than cordially received ... I was
able to tell Tasker on parting that I had spent two exceedingly pleasant
and satisfactory days.' In addition, Joseph notes Tasker's personal
circumstances, his house, two servants and the like and makes allowances
for his dress on account of the conditions in some of his patch. For their
part, the travellers are professionals, they each submit lists of customers
by town with details of turnover and population.

In 1897 Rowntree's became a limited company and the name changed
to Rowntree & Co Ltd. It nevertheless remained very much a family
concern with Joseph chairman of the board and sons John Wilhelm and
Seebohm and nephews Arnold and Frank and J. Bowes Morrell, directors.
Arnold's brother, Theodore, was company secretary. Joseph apart, these
men were all under 30 years of age. Morrell, fellow Quaker and Bootham
School old boy, was the first outsider to gain entry to the upper echelons
of the firm as finance director. He was the son of the owner of the York
City and County Bank which provided some of the finance for Haxby
Road.

Marketing, again

Advertising remained minimal and suspect, despite the fact that it
was increasingly apparent that the other players in the market – Fry's,
Cadbury's, Van Houten and Cailler's – were all advertising their products
aggressively. John Wilhelm and his cousin, Arnold Stephenson Rowntree,

were both rather more enthusiastic about advertising than Joseph. They succeeded in doubling the advertising budget in 1892 to £4,000, largely spent on Elect, and grandiloquently announced this in a letter to the travellers:

> In connection with our Advertising, we are considering the question of an important forward mover in the coming year, and of entering upon National Advertisements, as distinguished from the localised advertisements, which are all we have hitherto attempted.

The adverts in national newspapers featured a 1d voucher and coupon, which could be redeemed for a sample of Elect. The slogan read, 'A cup of cocoa and your morning paper for nothing'. Unfortunately, this tentative foray into the dangerous world of advertising was short-lived, although in 1893 the first steps towards branding took place with the registering of the famous Rowntree and Co signature. This was the very signature that decorated the foot of the letter quoted above. But it was not until 1897 that Rowntree's embarked on a cohesive and properly resourced marketing campaign for Elect Cocoa, championed by John Wilhelm. Space was taken in two quality magazines, *Tit-Bits* and *Answers* at roughly £35 a page.

The importance of Elect, even if not reflected in actual sales, can be seen by the fact that Elect staff now numbered 240 and output was at 26 tons per week. Advertising staff, though, still only amounted to one solitary man in 1899.

Surprisingly, two eye-catching advertising stunts came in the late 1890s – surprising if you consider Joseph's antipathy – when his nephew Arnold organised one of those new-fangled motor cars to tour the country with a giant 9 foot Elect Cocoa tin lashed on the back. On windy days it was shipped to its destination by train. The car replaced a pony pulling a delivery cart. Nothing could have been more uncharacteristic from a company whose chairman was so implacably opposed to advertising. But, unsurprisingly, it had its desired effect – despite breaking down at one point in Sheffield city centre in a blaze of publicity, with the driver escaping prosecution on condition that he drove at a maximum speed of 3 mph. Arnold later went on to have a barge covered in Elect posters towed by a brace of mechanical swans cross the Thames on the course of the 1897 Oxford and Cambridge Boat Race. From this bizarre, but no doubt extremely effective stunt, samples of Elect were generously distributed.

More conventional marketing came with the pivotal appointment of S. H. Benson as advertising agent, a man noted for his integrity and values. This was important to Joseph because he believed most marketing people to be charlatans. Benson embarked on a campaign to heighten the profile of Elect in the marketplace and to make it easier for the Rowntree travellers to get that all important foot in the door. It was called *The Daily Telegraph* scheme and was conducted largely through sampling. Coupons were placed in *The Daily Telegraph* which were redeemable for a 1d stamp and a tin of Elect. This led to the opening of thousands of new trade accounts to meet the demand. Elect adverts appeared on London buses with appropriately attired conductors and women readers of the *Daily Mail* were invited to hop on board and receive a tin of Elect. 'Have you had your ride on a Rowntree Bus?' *The Daily Mail* demanded. So successful was the campaign that the police were on the point of halting the exercise to preserve public order. One way or another, 20,000 samples were given away at the end of 1897. In addition to this, 20,000 boxes of chocolates were shared between everyone who introduced six new Elect customers, and 1898 calendars were free of charge with a tin of Elect.

The health-giving qualities of Elect were emphasised, particularly its alleged benefits to the nervous system and as a cure for anaemia. The great advantage of Benson's innovative campaigns was that, by sampling, the consumer could actually taste (and smell) the product for themselves, rather than just see a picture of it on the page and be obliged to believe the advertiser's claims. In 1902, 500,000 tins of cake chocolate were donated to London's poor as part of the coronation celebrations, as well as 60,000 additional tins for the stewards serving the meal, 'as they would be of greater importance to us socially than the 500,000 poor'. Benson was also responsible for commissioning the world-famous but commercially unsuccessful Beggarstaff J. & W. posters in 1896.

At the same time the company, independent of Benson, sampled the chocolate on a door-to-door basis and organised tasting exhibitions. Elect tins were couponed – redeemable for a box of chocolates – and a trade stocking discount was introduced. Nevertheless, Joseph was unimpressed, particularly by Benson's efforts, and cut the budget in 1899. By 1901 his scepticism regarding marketing – 'a speculative quantity' – was as acute as ever and he resorted to his conviction that quality alone sold the product in the long term. Rowntree board minutes reveal, bizarrely, that Rowntree's advertising 'was done quietly, in such a way as not to incite competition on the part of others'. Product quality remained 'the best advertising agency'.

Chapter 13

The Cocoa and Chocolate Competition at the Start of the Twentieth Century

What were Joseph and his colleagues up against in those early Haxby Road days in terms of the marketplace and the competition? Joseph's greatest commercial challenge in the late 1890s, and in the early years of the twentieth century, was to ease the company from the restrictions of Tanner's Moat into the expansive commercial potential offered by Haxby Road. In doing so he might break the stranglehold foreign manufacturers operating in the UK had on the domestic market, particularly in the increasingly popular milk chocolate market. He might compete successfully with Cadbury's, Fry's, Caley's and others. Van Houten now had sales agencies in London, Leeds, Liverpool, Edinburgh, Glasgow and Dublin for its alkalised essence and Cailler was the leader in milk chocolate. Chocolat Menier established a factory in Southwark in 1870 and by 1873 was turning out 500 tons a year.

At the end of the nineteenth century, Swiss companies were selling 30 tons of milk chocolate a week in the UK while Cadbury's, for example sold barely one. In 1911 over half the chocolate eaten in the world was still made in Switzerland. Pralines (invented by one of the chefs employed by the French Maréchal du Plessis Praslin in the seventeenth century) came over from Brussels in 1912 through Jean Neuhaus and paved the way for Leonidas (founded 1910) and Godiva (1912). They were usually packed in posh chocolate boxes called *ballotins*. The French were still importing their gums on a large scale and they were also the market leaders in chocolate assortments or creams. Cadbury's Dairy Milk was making inroads on Cailler's, Nestlé's and on Lindt's market share from 1906 but Rowntree's never really competed in this increasingly lucrative market. Their first attempt at a milk chocolate block in 1899 – Swiss Milk Chocolate – failed, largely because it was made from powdered milk and not condensed milk in the best Swiss style. Another factor was Joseph Rowntree's misguided belief that the 'rage' for milk chocolate was no more than a 'passing phase'. The Swiss hold on the market tightened yet further in 1904 when Nestlé started importing Kohler and Cailler milk chocolate brands.

Joseph did, nevertheless, see the real need to ramp up the company's sales force. He consulted Reckitt's for advice – the Quaker chemical company based in Hull – and a sales manager, J. Bromilow, was appointed in 1892. The important Co-operative Society accounts were made the responsibility of one traveller, a Mr S. Cartwright, effectively now a corporate sales manager. Between 1890 and 1897 the sales force grew from fourteen to thirty-three under the management of John Wilhelm and Arnold Stephenson Rowntree.

Product development, though, remained decidedly haphazard and unscientific, with approval usually based on tastings held at directors' conferences. The number of lines just kept increasing with no significant single sales successes. Further attempts at milk chocolate were made from 1904 to 1910 but Mountain Milk Chocolate, Alpine Milk Chocolate (a copy of a Cailler brand) and Malted Milk Chocolate all failed to impress the market. Bulgarian Soured Milk Chocolates were developed to cash in on the vogue for chocolates containing supposedly life-extending microbes; these were much in demand from apothecaries as well as grocers and confectioners.

The market generally continued to expand, as, inevitably, did sales. During the period 1900 to 1913, cocoa sales increased from £2.5 million to £3.5 million peaking at £3.8 million in 1906; eating chocolate increased from £1.1 million to £3.3 million while sugar confectionery went up from £6.1 million to £11 million; Cadbury's sales increased to £2.2 million, Rowntree's from £0.5 million to £1.5 million.

Mars Food UK Limited, Slough

Strictly speaking Mars were not competitors to Rowntree's until they established their Slough factory in 1932. However, it is useful to know their history as, from the 1930s, they were major players in the chocolate-making industry and, as such, became major competitors to Rowntree's.

Franklin Clarence Mars (1883–1934) was the son of a gristmill operator. He went into the wholesale confectionery business in Tacoma, Washington, from 1910. Franklin's mother Elva started it all: she taught him to hand dip candy with the result that he was selling candy by the time he was 19. He established the Mars Candy Factory in 1911 with Ethel V. Mars, his second wife, in Tacoma. This factory produced and sold fresh candy wholesale, but ultimately the venture failed due to the presence of a better established business, Brown & Haley, also operating in Tacoma. By 1920, Mars had gone home to Minnesota, where the earliest incarnation of the present-day Mars company was founded that year as Mar-O-Bar in Minneapolis and later established there as Mars, Incorporated. Frank C. Mars launched the Mar-O-Bar in 1922 and initially it was not a great success, mainly on account of its fragility. Mars' Milky Way followed in 1923 – an immediate hit promoted as 'chocolate malted milk in a candy bar'. In 1929 the company moved to Chicago and Frank's son, Forrest E. Mars senior, joined the company. The Snickers bar was launched in 1930.

Forrest arrived in England in 1932 with £5,000 and set up Mars Ltd in a rented factory in Slough with twelve staff. He launched the Mars Bar as a sweeter version of the US Milky Way, which itself is quite different from the European market Milky Way.

The US variety of Mars Bar is again quite different from its European counterpart. Initially the bars were coated in chocolate supplied by Cadbury's ('Why ever did we do that?' Sir Adrian Cadbury wryly asked recently) and they were such a success that staff increased from twelve to over 100 within a year.

Mars Ltd are incredibly secretive. A 1993 *Washington Post Magazine* article momentarily took the lid off, as the reporter was able to see the 'M's being applied to the M&M's, something that 'no out-sider had ever before been invited to observe'. Moreover, in 1999, for example, the company did not acknowledge that Forrest Mars senior had died or that he had even worked for the company.

Despite this commercial paranoia, Mars demonstrated many of the philanthropic industrial welfare initiatives pioneered by our indigenous Quaker companies: they included a pension plan, an in-house doctor, a cafeteria and a company newsletter. Mars paid well and in return demanded long hours and the highest quality in their products. This arrangement is enshrined in their *Principles in Action* communication published in September 2011, which traces the history of Mars, their legacy as a business committed to their Five Principles, and the company's goal of putting the principles into action to make a difference to people and the planet through performance. It embraces health and nutrition, supply chain, operations, products, and working at Mars. It also describes its businesses, including Petcare, Chocolate, Wrigley, Food, Drinks, and Symbioscience.

Over two million Mars Bars are produced every day in Britain alone. Maltesers appeared in 1935 and Mars Bars were supplied in 1940 for the troops and for prisoners of war in Germany. In 1960 the unforgettable slogan, 'A Mars a day helps you work, rest and play', was heard for the first time. That same year Galaxy hit the streets in competition to Dairy

Milk with the UK's biggest ever TV advertising campaign. In 1982 M&M's were the first sweets to be taken into outer space when the crew of the first space shuttle included them in their food packs; three million Mars Bars were taken with the task force to the Falklands.

M&M's (named after the company's founders) had been launched in the US in 1941 as a cheaper alternative to Smarties. Forrest Mars senior got the idea when he saw soldiers in the Spanish Civil War eating chocolate pellets with a hard shell of tempered chocolate surrounding the inside, preventing the candies from melting. A black 'M' first appeared on each sweet in 1950, later changed to white in 1954. The two-bar Bounty was launched in 1951, Treets in 1955, Galaxy in 1958, Topic in 1962 and, in 1967 Twix, Revels and Marathon, later reverting to Snickers in 1990 in the UK, France, Germany and the Netherlands. Chocolate and peanut M&M's were introduced in 1990.

Apart from the Milky Way–Mars Bar–Milky Way mid-Atlantic triangle confusion mentioned above, there is much more opportunity for disorientation. Milky Way in Europe and worldwide is known as the 3 Musketeers in the US; Galaxy in the Middle East is known as Dove in America and worldwide; and Starburst was known in the UK and Ireland as Opal Fruits until 1998.

Nestlé, Switzerland

As we have noted Henri Nestlé was born in Frankfurt in 1814. In 1875, thirty-two years after moving to Vevey on Lake Geneva in 1843, the chemist started making *farine lactée*, a baby food (*Kindermehl*) made from Alpine milk in powder form and ground cereal. Henri Nestlé and Daniel Peter with Jean-Jacques Kohler, his chocolate-manufacturing neighbours, then went on to develop the first real milk chocolate when the two businessmen combined their products to produce Chocolat au Lait Gala Peter – 'The Original Milk Chocolate' – in 1874.

Sales were boosted by Nestlé's extensive use of the new-fangled vending machines which were springing up everywhere and which, in this case, dispensed 1d chocolate bars. In 1904 they made an agreement with Kohler & Cailler to import their chocolate product and thus strengthened their position in the UK market. In 1913, chocolate production began at Hayes. The white chocolate Milky Bar was launched in 1937 and soon gained a reputation for being good for children because it contained only cocoa butter, sugar and milk. It is made entirely from natural ingredients without artificial colours or flavours. Nearly half a pint of milk is poured into every 100g of chocolate.

Thorntons, Sheffield

Joseph William Thornton left his job as a sales representative for the Don Confectionery Company in 1911 and opened his first Thorntons Chocolate Kabin shop on the corner of Norfolk Street and Howard Street in Sheffield. Products included Violet Cachous, Sweet-Lips, Phul-Nanas and the curiously named Curiously Strong Mints. Chocolate production began in 1913 in the back room of their second shop on The Moor. Easter eggs and Thorntons Special Toffee were the main lines until the 1950s when the Continental Chocolates range was launched.

In 1948 the company moved to Belper and in 1954, Walter Willen, a Swiss confectioner, joined and created Swiss Assortment – a range of handmade confectionery. The firm was forced to change the name to Continental Assortment after complaints from the Swiss Embassy.

Epps, London

Dr John Epps (1805–1869) was the son of a Calvinist London merchant and one of the pioneers of homoeopathy in Britain. He established premises at Great Russell Street, Bloomsbury, and was joined by his brother James (1821–1907) from 1837.

Epps's Cocoa was first sold in 1839 for the use of patients who were unable to tolerate tea and coffee. It was an instant cocoa drink, made simply by adding hot water or milk to the powder. When the prohibitive duty on cocoa was slashed in 1832, the market grew exponentially. Easily prepared cocoa had been difficult to procure, and the fat in the raw material was undrinkable to many. Dr John Epps discovered a way to make it more appetising, mixing the cocoa with twenty per cent West Indies arrowroot and thirteen per cent sugar.

James Epps introduced the product to the mass market. He aggressively advertised Epps's Cocoa, and introduced a memorable slogan, 'grateful and comforting' by 1855. Epps's Cocoa was initially produced under contract by Daniel Dunn of Pentonville Road, who had invented instant cocoa powder in 1819. James Epps established his own factory at 398 Euston Road, London in 1863, where he installed his nephew, Hahnemann Epps (1843–1916), as manager.

A new steam-powered works was introduced at Holland Street, Blackfriars from 1878. At this time Epps was the largest cocoa powder producer in Britain, with an output of nearly £5 million (2.3 million kg) a year. At its peak, the family firm processed half of all cocoa imports into Britain.

But by 1898 Epps's Cocoa had been overtaken in sales by Dr Tibbles' Vi-Cocoa and Rowntree's. James Epps died in 1907 and his gross estate was valued at £735,387. This was larger than contemporaries in the food industry, such as the mustard magnate Jeremiah James Colman (1830–1898), instant custard producer Alfred Bird (1811–1878) and James Horlick (1844–1921).

Taylor Brothers Ltd, a London cocoa manufacturer, was acquired in 1907. Epps's Cocoa powder had been reformulated to include forty-four per cent sugar, forty per cent cocoa and sixteen per cent West Indies arrowroot by 1924. Rowntree's acquired James Epps & Co for £70,000 in 1926.

The Epps factory was closed in 1930, and the manufacture of Epps products was transferred to Whitefields Ltd of Plaistow.

Henry Thorne, Leeds

Like others in the confectionery industry, Henry Thorne was a Quaker. His first shop in Briggate around 1837 sold mustard and chicory but this quickly grew into one of the country's bigger confectionery companies. They embraced new technology, notably steam power, and pioneered the use of photography on their tins. By the 1960s Thorne's (their slogan was 'The World's Premier Toffee') was producing over two million pieces of confectionery a day. In 1971 the business moved into the premises of their sister company C. W. Mattock, confectioners and 'toffery' of Sowerby Bridge, and the factory in Lady Lane, was closed and demolished.

Taylor Brothers Ltd, London

Taylor Brothers Ltd were cocoa and chocolate manufacturers based at Brick Lane in the East End of London, where the company had a mustard and cocoa mill. They were established by Henry Taylor, William Taylor, and John Taylor.

Around 1880 they were claiming to be 'the largest manufacturer of cocoa in Europe'. Their most successful product was Maravilla Cocoa, which was sold in tin-lined packets. The company also made Taylor

Brothers' Original Homoeopathic Cocoa and Soluble Chocolate as well as Challenge Mustard, which was 'celebrated for its pungency and purity of its flavour'.

As we have noted, in 1907 the company was sold to James Epps and Co Ltd, who continued the business under the original name.

Dr Tibbles' Vi-Cocoa, Leicester

This brand was a popular energy restorative and could be regarded as the Lucozade or Gatorade of its time. At its height, it was one of the highest-selling cocoa-based drinks in Britain.

William Tibbles (1834–1912) was born into an impoverished family in Leicester; the 1851 census reports that they were living in the local workhouse. Tibbles described his occupation as a frame work knitter and medical practitioner in the 1861 census. No evidence survives to suggest that Tibbles ever underwent any formal medical training.

Tibbles claimed that botanicals had cured him of consumption in 1867. He began to sell coca and its concentrated extract, cocaine, as a general cure for debility and consumption from 1871. In 1876, he was advertising Tibbles Concentrated Essence of Composition and Cocaine. Tibbles later invented Vi-Cocoa, a mixture of malt, hops, kola and cocoa. He licensed the recipe and naming rights to Dr Tibbles' Vi-Cocoa Ltd, a company formed to sell his product. Advertisements for Vi-Cocoa first appeared from 1893.

The company was renamed as Dr Tibbles' Vi-Cocoa Ltd in 1898 with a capital of £400,000. Tibbles retired soon afterwards. The company was renamed the Watford Manufacturing Company in 1907 and by 1914, more than 1,000 people were employed. Vi-Cocoa and Delecta chocolate were the principal products.

Construction of a large new factory began in 1918–19, but was never completed due to liquidity issues. The company had benefited from healthy sales during the First World War, supported by military contracts. The Watford Manufacturing Company went into liquidation in 1922 and Lord Leverhulme purchased the company assets for £543,000 in cash. The Watford factory was employing 400 workers by 1929 but was sold off in 1930, and production was absorbed into Unilever. Vi-Cocoa was still being advertised as late as 1945.

Daniel Dunn, London

Daniel Dunn invented instant cocoa powder: Dunn & Hewett became one of the largest cocoa manufacturers in Britain.

Daniel Dunn (1773–1862) was born at Netherton, Dudley into a poor family. His blacksmith father taught him the value of honesty, and his mother instilled in him a strong work ethic. Dunn was forced to earn a living from the age of 10. He joined the Swedenborgian Church in 1796, and remained a keen member throughout his life. The church was founded in England on the belief that God explained the spiritual meaning of the Bible to scientist and Swedish Lutheran theologian Emanuel Swedenborg to reveal the truth of the Second Coming of Jesus Christ.

Dunn was an inventive and creative youth and this materialised in the eleven patents he was granted over time. When his horse nail manufacturing business failed in 1800, he turned to making instant coffee and instant tea from a factory at Bartlett's Buildings, Holborn from around 1800. Expanding trade allowed him relocate to a larger factory at Pentonville ten years later.

Dunn invented instant cocoa powder in 1820. His method was to add sugar and arrowroot to cocoa to create a soluble powder. Hot instant cocoa could be made in one minute by adding boiling water, whereas previously chocolate had to be boiled for an hour or more.

Charles Hewett (1819–1869), also from Dudley, had been apprenticed to Dunn from 1841. Hewett joined Dunn in partnership in 1857, and the business henceforth traded as Dunn & Hewett.

Iceland Moss Cocoa was introduced in 1859, made from cocoa, moss, farina and sugar. The moss was believed to have highly nutritious qualities. Competitors such as Rowntree's and Fry's would later introduce their own competing Iceland Moss Cocoa products.

Dunn employed forty-seven people in 1861: twenty-three men, fourteen girls and ten boys. He was a generous philanthropist throughout his life. When he died in 1862, his entire estate went to his third wife, Mary Dunn (1810–1885).

Management of Dunn & Hewett then fell to Charles Hewett. Dunn & Hewett employed sixty to seventy workers in 1864. Hewett was as good a philanthropist as his former partner: for example, a workman would be presented with a sovereign coin on the birth of a child. The firm organised an annual excursion or dinner for their workers. A company-funded brass band was established from 1864. Charles Hewett died in

1869 when management of the firm passed to Mary Dunn and two of Daniel's adopted sons, Arthur Day (1843–1918) and John Holm (1840–1897), a trained chemist.

By 1871 Dunn & Hewett were employing sixty-five people: thirty-six men, twenty-two women, four boys and three girls. Dunn & Hewett ranked among the largest cocoa manufacturers in Britain in 1876. The firm employed seventy workers in 1881. Mary Dunn died in 1885.

H. J. Packer, Bristol

The largest low-cost chocolate manufacturer in the world at one time. Edward Packer (1848–1887) was a Quaker who worked for J. S Fry & Sons in the 1870s. Packer left Fry's to set up on his own as a chocolate manufacturer in 1881. He worked from his house at 11 Armory Square and was assisted by his wife. Soon he was employing eight staff.

Packer went into partnership with Henry John Burrows (born 1853). Unfortunately, trade immediately declined and all employees, other than members of the Packer family, were let go. Burrows acquired full control of the business from 1884, adding his own initials to the company name, and began trading as H. J. Packer & Co.

Caleb Bruce Cole (1862–1912) was a confectionery salesman in Bristol. He was impressed during his contact with H. J Packer & Co, and borrowed £1,000 from his father to acquire the business in 1886. Around nine people were employed. The business began to grow from around 1889. Cole identified a gap in the market, and began to manufacture high-quality chocolate at an affordable price that was even in the range of what children could afford.

Cole disrupted the widely held belief that low-cost food production meant sacrificing standards of cleanliness or benefits for the workforce. In 1896 Cole was joined by his brother Horace; William John Mansfield (1846–1912) was taken on as general manager.

They opened a new factory at Greenbank, Bristol in 1903. It covered 4 acres and was at the time the largest low-cost chocolate factory in the world with 450 people on the payroll. Greenbank benefitted from access to a major railway line.

H. J. Packer & Co became a limited company from 1908 and four years later they acquired Carson's Ltd of Glasgow, with a share capital of £50,000. Trading at the top end of the chocolate market, Carson's had been the first company to introduce tray chocolates.

H. J. Packer & Co were employing 1,000 people in 1912 when they headed upmarket with a new top-end subsidiary company, Charles Bond Ltd based in London. The new range was an instant success and Charles Bond, or Bonds, survived until the 1960s. In 1914 a dedicated Carson's chocolate factory was established in Shortwood, Bristol to supply the south and west of England markets..

Packer were the fourth largest chocolate manufacturer in Britain by 1922, and the largest manufacturer of low-cost chocolate in the world. The company name was changed to Carson's Ltd from 1962. The Carson's brand became well known as Britain's largest producer of chocolate liqueurs, filled with some of the world's leading brand names of spirits, liqueurs and fortified wines such as Harveys Bristol Cream and Hennessey cognac. Elizabeth Shaw, an upmarket chocolate manufacturer, was acquired in 1968.

Cailler, Vevey

This Swiss chocolate brand was founded by François-Louis Cailler in 1819 and bought by Nestlé in 1931. Francois-Louis Cailler was born in Vevey, Switzerland in 1796 and with Abram L. C. Cusin, he opened a grocery shop in Vevey in 1818 before starting to produce chocolate on a larger scale.

Records show that in 1806 Vevey was already home to seven chocolate factories, making it a veritable hub of chocolate production.

In 1821, François-Louis Cailler and Abram L. C. Cusin dissolved the partnership, so Cailler continued to run the business on his own. After a bankruptcy in 1826, Cailler's wife took control of the business until Cailler was once again allowed to manage it himself. In 1830, Charles-Amédée Kohler (1790–1874) bought a mill in Lausanne to establish a chocolate factory. In 1832 Cailler purchased two new factories in Corsier-sur-Vevey and Vevey; both were on the Canal de la Monneresse and were water powered.

François-Louis Cailler died in 1852 and his wife continued to run the business together with their two sons, Auguste and Alexandre. In 1867, Daniel Peter, François-Louis Cailler's son-in-law, started producing chocolate under the name Peter-Cailler. In 1875, Daniel Peter invented milk chocolate, followed by Cailler pralines in 1890.

In 1898, Alexandre-Louis Cailler opened a new factory in Broc and began producing milk and hazelnut chocolate on a large scale. In 1904, Daniel Peter and Charles-Amédée Kohler became partners and founded the company Société Générale Suisse de Chocolats Peter et Kohler Réunis. Cailler began to produce their own Branches. The original Branche was first mentioned in Kohler's recipe books in 1896.

Under an agreement with Peter and Kohler in 1905, Nestlé launched their own milk chocolate produced by Peter and Kohler. Before the start of the First World War, Cailler expanded their range of chocolates by introducing Fémina, an extra-fine mix of pralines sold in a gift box.

In 1911, with the chocolate industry resurgent, the companies managed by Daniel Peter and Kohler, which were already partners, merged with Cailler. They joined forces in order to introduce high-quality Swiss chocolate, whose reputation rested on the invention of both milk and fondant chocolates, to a larger global audience. The name of the new company was Peter, Cailler, Kohler, Chocolats Suisses S. A.

Alexandre-Louis Cailler developed a very different process for the manufacture of milk chocolate than that adopted by Peter. The process, which is still used today, allows for the production of chocolate that is creamier and has a richer milky flavour. To make this chocolate, Alexandre-Louis Cailler used condensed milk made from the Alpine Gruyère region. To this day, Cailler are the only Swiss chocolate manufacturers that use condensed instead of powdered milk to produce their milk chocolate.

In 1920, Kohler launched Chocmel brand chocolate with honey and almond slivers. In 1923 Cailler launched Frigor, which was developed by Cailler confectioner Charles Panchaud. In 1929, Peter, Cailler, Kohler and Chocolats Suisses S. A. all merged with the Nestlé group.

H.C. Boisselier, Watford

The Boisselier Chocolate Company was founded by Henri Conrad Boisselier who in 1900 was working for the Watford Vi-Cocoa Company. He later bought the company and renamed it Boisselier's Chocolates.

Leonidas, Brussels

Born in 1882 in 'Nigdi, Greece, a politically and economically unstable region, Anatolia Leonidas Georges Kestekides made a living by selling 'granitas' – a kind of sorbet – and other sweets with his brother, Avraam. In 1900, he decided to move to the United States where he became a confectioner.

In 1910, Leonidas exhibited at the World Fair in Brussels with the Greek delegation where he won the bronze medal. While in Brussels, he met Joanna Emelia Teerlinck. Together, they moved to Ghent, where the International Exhibition was held in 1913. Here he won the gold medal and opened his first tearoom at 34 Veldstraat.

From 1922 onwards, members of Leonidas' family joined him in Belgium to work alongside him. When Ghent started to get too small Leonidas left to open the Pâtisserie Centrale Leonidas in Brussels, on rue Paul Delvaux, and left the management of the Ghent tearoom to the rest of his family.

Lindt & Sprüngli, Zurich

The origins of the company date back to 1836 when David Sprüngli-Schwarz and his son Rudolf Sprüngli-Ammann bought a small confectionery shop in Zürich, producing chocolates under the name David Sprüngli & Son. Before they moved to Paradeplatz in 1845, they established a small factory where they produced their chocolate in solidified form in 1838.

When Rudolf Sprüngli-Ammann retired in 1892, he gave two equal parts of the business to his sons. The younger brother David Robert received two confectionery shops known as Confiserie Sprüngli. The elder brother Johann Rudolf got the chocolate factory. To raise the necessary finances for his expansion plans, Johann Rudolf then converted his private company into Chocolat Sprüngli AG in 1899. In that same year, he acquired the chocolate factory of Rodolphe Lindt in Bern, and the company changed its name to Aktiengesellschaft Vereinigte Berner und Züricher Chocoladefabriken Lindt & Sprüngli.

Stollwerck GmbH, Köln

Stollwerck GmbH were German Quaker chocolate manufacturers, which expanded in Europe and America to become the second largest producer of chocolate in the United States by 1900.

It all started in 1839 when baker Franz Stollwerck opened a business in Cologne. He diversified into chocolate and other sweets, enjoying particular success with his cough drops. In 1845, local pharmacists protested and requested that he be prevented from selling medicinal items, but this got nowhere. His business flourished and he also opened two coffee houses in Cologne. One of these was briefly converted into a music hall before becoming a chocolate and confectionery factory in the 1860s. In 1871 his sons registered a separate company, Gebrüder

Stollwerck, which merged back into the original company in 1876, after the death of Franz Stollwerck.

Stollwerck's five sons expanded the business into a multinational corporation with plants in Europe and America. The second youngest of the brothers, Ludwig Stollwerck, was instrumental in introducing new technology, including the first vending machines in 1887. These were initially used to sell small samples of chocolate, but their immediate popularity meant they were soon selling whole chocolate bars. By 1893, Stollwerck were selling their chocolate in 15,000 vending machines. They set up separate companies in various territories to manufacture vending machines to sell not just chocolate, but cigarettes, matches, chewing gum and soap products. By 1890 their Cologne works alone had 1,500 staff.

Stollwerck then turned their attention to the export market and subsidiaries opened in England, Belgium and Austria-Hungary. In 1894, Stollwerck founded Volkmann, Stollwerck & Company in the USA, in partnership with German businessman John Volkmann, to produce vending machines in their factory in New York. By the early 1890s there were over 4,000 of their vending machines on New York train stations. They also became a leading manufacturer of cinematographs. In 1902 the company went public, but the First World War brought Stollwerck's rapid expansion to a halt.

Costly acquisitions and the Great Depression were the ruin of Stollwerck. They were rescued by Deutsche Bank in the 1930s, which marked the end of the family ownership.

Lazenby & Son (York) Ltd

And then there was Lazenby & Son (York) Ltd on the Hull Road which, despite the 200 employees on its books, seems to have vanished into a York industrial history black hole. In 1915, Percy Lazenby set up as a fifty-fifty partner with confectioner Harold Needler in Hull. However, Needler ploughed more equity into the business and so a financially diluted Percy left and the business became part of Needler's. Percy's appointment as head of the Chocolate Department had coincided with Needler's decision to invest in and expand chocolate confectionery to complement the lower margin sugar confectionery already up and running.

According to Raymond Needler in his definitive *The Needlers of Hull* (1993), the minute book of February 1915 tells how Percy had been headhunted from Carson's of Shortwood near Bristol.

In 1927, Percy moved on to York where he built his own factory on the Hull Road called The Works, and established his own chocolate manufacturing company complete with all the modern machinery, including massive conches. A conche is a surface-scraping mixer and agitator that evenly distributes cocoa butter within chocolate; it also enhances flavour development through frictional heat and its release of volatiles and acids, and oxidation. The conche is named after the shell whose shape it resembles. Richard Lazenby joined his father in the early 1940s, along with Percy's wife, Lottie Lazenby, as directors.

At their height, Lazenby employed 200 or so people. They produced couverture for food and biscuit makers. Couverture is chocolate made with extra cocoa butter to give a high gloss. The company also traded under the name of Ellanson Couverture. Contracts were won with Carr's, MacFarlane, Fox's, Huntley & Palmers and Craven's as well as supplying liquid couverture to Rowntree's.

During the Second World War the company produced and stored tens of thousands of block couverture – an essential foodstuff which was issued to the Royal and Merchant navies to provision their lifeboats on the Arctic convoys. The Lazenby engineering shops were busy making tensioners for British Army tank tracks.

Given the contract supply nature of the business, it was not appropriate for Lazenby to advertise or brand their products. So, for example, the fleet of Commer vans they used were simply sprayed chocolate brown, with no distinguishing corporate branding.

Lazenby started appearing in the commercial trade directories in the early 1930s. *Kelly's* 1933 directory lists them as Lazenby & Son, Lawrence Street under chocolate manufacturers. They are in good company – the usual suspects Rowntree's, Terry's and Backhouse & Co, Clementhorpe are all listed. Confectionery manufacturers listed are these three again, along with Craven, M. at the Ebor Confectionery Works in Coppergate and Stanley Brothers (York Ltd) in North Street, F. Maynard Ltd in Toft Green and, from 1933, Stanley's Winter Nips in Clementhorpe. In 1949, Dorothy Chocolates (York) Ltd arrived on the scene at Lead Mill Lane and Ridgewells at 21 Back Swinegate as chocolate makers.

In 1953, Lazenby started appearing under a new heading in the directory: 'Chocolate Couverture Manufacturers' was the listing – exclusive to Lazenby. The address is Hull Road, telephone number 545547; they also retained their listing under chocolate manufacturers. In 1955 the telegram address is given as 'Chocolate York' – stealing a march on Rowntree's and Terry's in much the same way as domain names are sought after and coveted by companies today. Lazenby were still listed exclusively under the 'Couverture' heading in 1963. They fail to appear again after that date.

Interestingly there were 150 or so 'confectioners' (sweet shops, grocers, tea rooms and the like) listed in the 1920s and this had shrunk to about seventy-five in 1959 – thanks, no doubt to the inexorable rise of the supermarket. It seems likely too that 'big chocolate', not least in York, was producing its own couverture, thus accelerating the demise of Lazenby.

As mentioned above, it is quite astonishing that such a large company and employer have left so little trace of their thirty-year operation. The Borthwick and York Explore Archive both drew a blank as did the extensive *York Press* archive.

Much of the scant, yet fascinating, information above was provided by John Lazenby, grandson of Percy, to whom we all must be grateful for filling a gap in our industrial history which few knew even existed.

Lipton's, London

Lipton's, most famous for their tea, established a chocolate factory in London in 1895. In 1914, *Whitakers Red Book* describes them as:

Tea growers and merchants, provision merchants, naval and military contractors. Specialities: tea, coffee, cocoa, chocolate, preserves (jams, marmalade, bottled fruits etc.), provisions of every description, poultry, game etc. Employees 10,000.

At the 1922 British Industries Fair they advertised as the:

'Largest Manufacturers and Distributors of Food Products in the World'. Lipton's are the Actual Manufacturers of: Biscuits, Cocoa, Chocolate, Confectionery, Pickles, Sauces, Jams and Jellies, Marmalade, Sausages, Potted Meats, Coffee Essence, Cornflour, Farinaceous Preparations. By appointment to H. M. King of Spain; H. M. King George V; T. M. King and Queen of Italy. (Stand No. B.7.)

The competition for England's premier chocolate companies, including Rowntree's was, then, many and various. And despite the obvious strengths inherent in Fry's, Cadbury's and Rowntree's, they were to a great extent always playing catch up in the early years of the twentieth century. They were still bombarded by foreign imports and not helped at all when, in 1911, the Liberal government reduced the import duty on chocolate, taxing only the raw materials used in its manufacture. The Dutch remained supreme in the provision of alkalised drinking chocolate until Cadbury's came up with a rival brand in 1906. Likewise, Swiss milk chocolate was unchallenged until 1905 when Cadbury's again brought a version to market but Cailler's and Kohler's lines continued to sell well under the distribution of Nestlé. Suchard and Lindt were dominant in plain chocolate for baking and Menier's selections continued to corner the market. Ironically, the only real relief came with the start of the First World War, when imports from Germany and Austria-Hungary dried up. In 1895 there had been 178 German companies processing cocoa beans.

Chapter 14

Cocoa Works Magazine

Today, the company magazine or newsletter is an accepted, and expected, part of inter and intra corporate communication. In the early twentieth century, however, it was unheard of, until, that is, the launch of *Cocoa Works Magazine*.

The inaugural issue of *Cocoa Works Magazine*, or *CWM*, was published in March 1902 and the last issue was in May 1986. Over that time, it provided a fascinating and detailed record of life at Rowntree's from the board to the shop floor. Its subtitle was, 'A Journal in the Interest of the Employees of Rowntree & Co Ltd, York'.

The aim and scope of its up to forty pages per issue was quite simply to provide a means of communication within the company to keep all staff informed about what was going on at all levels. Joseph Rowntree and his colleagues on the board could no longer maintain the personal, one-to-one communication he in particular had nurtured as there were just too many people now. *CWM* was seen as one way in which the company could mitigate for the loss of that personal touch. Joseph Rowntree says as much in his letter to D. S. Crichton in the inaugural issue, explaining the impossibility of keeping up a personal acquaintance with the staff, particularly as there were now three factories on different sites: Haxby Road, Tanner's Moat and North Street, and the company was becoming increasingly departmentalised with self-contained units.

Joseph wanted 'the entire body of workers to be animated by a common aim' and the magazine to be 'a periodical devoted to matters of common interest'. It also featured a suggestion scheme, unique at the time, for which prizes would be given for anything:

'no matter how small' that was adopted to improve manufacturing or packing goods, for improvement in the quality of goods; for quicker or more economical methods of manufacture, or of carrying on any work undertaken by the Firm; for improvements in machinery etc, for improvements in the conditions under which work is conducted; any other matters which affect the welfare of the Firm and of the Employees.

In the first edition, Joseph Rowntree also drew attention to the new bowling green and rose garden, and took the opportunity to warn 'some of the young people' not to allow their rooms (such as the men's new dining room) 'to get into a dirty and slatternly condition'; otherwise 'there is little inducement to add to what has already been done.'

The first *CWM* also featured a gripping account of the explosion on the Royal Mail Steamer *Para* by John Wilhelm Rowntree, when he and his wife had the misfortune to be on board the vessel which was bringing cocoa back from Trinidad and Granada:

> There was an appalling roar, a momentary flash followed by blinding darkness. Mrs R and myself found ourselves hurled into the air ... ship's officers and crew behaved as Englishmen should ... the captain, while in the air, shouted for the Fire Brigade. The explosion was caused by an experimental shipment of bananas. One of the parties on board was attempting to see if, by extracting oxygen from the containers holding the bananas, deterioration could be avoided or minimized. The result was catastrophic with three dead and others injured, one of whom was 'in delirium'.

Issue one also included a list of new books added to the staff library which now contained 1,200 volumes, 400 of which were in circulation at any one time. The librarian, Mr M. E. Woods, added some book reviews. Garden Notes were provided by Roughway; news was given of the progress of the Hospital Fund, the Savings Fund, the Funeral Club Benefit Club and the Medical Aid Society, along with company financials. Reports were published from the singing class (thirty members); the angling club (forty members); the bowling club (recruiting) and the football team, which had reached the semi-final of the Faber Cup and was still in with a chance of winning the York and District League. We are reminded that Miss Wood engages girls every Tuesday and Friday at 10 am at Tanner's Moat, while Mr Crichton does likewise for boys on Mondays and Thursdays at 9.30 am. The girls' gymnastic class is 7.30 pm every Monday evening and members 'are expected to wear a very becoming costume of dark blue and red, about 5 shillings ... any overstrain is carefully guarded against.' At the dressmaking class the penny fee per night 'is paid whether the member is present or not'. Commons sketches also featured.

Issue two finds Roughway describing how to cultivate kale, mint and gladiolus; births, deaths and marriages are introduced – the most high-profile of the marriages being between board member J. B. Morrell and

Bertha Spence Watson. Presents to Mr Morrell included Green's *Short History of the English People,* Grote's *History of Greece* and Gibbon's *Decline and Fall of the Roman Empire. An Ostrich Story* was written for the children, and the Fur and Feather Society, and the Boating and Swimming Society both reported.

The third issue had an article on the Rowntree-owned Jamaica Cocoa Curing Station at Dover, Jamaica, with a photograph of Mr Lewis (second in charge at Dover) with his bride, the daughter of Mr Supersangsingh, owner of the Dover estate. There was 'much music and jollity' at the wedding. Cookery Notes included recipes for milk soup, hot pot and feather buns. In the next issue the focus was on 'Invalid Cooking' with advice on beef tea to the effect that 'the most juicy and inferior parts of the buttock yield the richest tea, not the leg or shins'. Other recipes for the invalid included beef jelly and canary pudding. The Girls' Temperance Society and the Drum and Fife Band both made their first appearances; small ads for items for sale and exchange started, and information was given on the company holidays for the year.

In 1910, Captain Robert Falcon Scott visited nearby Bootham School to give a talk prior to the ill-fated British Antarctic expedition's attempt at the South Pole. This was reported in *CWM* along with an announcement that a fund had been established to pay for a Rowntree's sledge for the expedition.

The Rowntrees' concern over the health and well-being of their workers, and Joseph's and Seebohm's personal interest in the impact of poverty, were reflected in the pages of *CWM*. Every year the Medical Officer of Health's report on the state of health in York was covered. In 1908, Dr Edmund Smith announced the comparative death rates in different parts of the city: in salubrious Bootham it was 9.9 per thousand while in poor Walmgate it was 15.2 per thousand, with many of these deaths being children under 1 year of age. Things were much improved from 1860 when the city average was 24.1 per thousand but there was still much work to be done. Smith also revealed the dangers of enteric fever, or typhoid, citing one of the main causes in a place such as York was ice cream made from infected water: 'the sale of ice cream in the public streets is an abomination and should be abolished by Act of Parliament'.

In a 1909 edition we learn that of the 2,067 children born in York in 1908, ten per cent died before their first birthday. The medical inspection of children at school, which was statutory from 1907, revealed that thirty per cent had four or more defective teeth. Following a tuberculosis exhibition in the city in 1910 an article called 'Consumption and Teeth' was published, alerting staff to the need for good dental hygiene as dental cavities were a notorious reservoir for mycobacterium tuberculosis, the bacterium which causes TB. In 1912 Joseph, who was a lifelong non-smoker, spearheaded a campaign in *CWM*, 'Down with the Cigarettes', against the increase in smoking in his factory. Supported by medical experts, it concluded that smoking made 'boys feeble and dim-witted'.

We have already covered the April 1914 report on the 'very dangerous practice of wearing unprotected hat-pins'. Wet feet were a constant problem with the girls and, to minimise the ill effects of wearing damp shoes all day, each department had a supply of spares which could be worn on site; the girls' own footwear was dried, ready for the journey home.

In June that year, there was a report on the visit from Siberia of a group of peasant farmers – delegates from the Union of Siberian Co-operative Association representing 550 butter-making associations and 640 butter-buying shops which, between them, were responsible for 40,000 tons of Russian butter exports. Dr Tchaykovsky was in charge and was the interpreter. The final issue of the year reported Sir Robert Baden Powell's visit to the works, and published his morale-boosting message. During the First World War, casualty reports became a sad regular feature. Perhaps the most memorable of these was the death of L. E. Rowntree, son of John Wilhelm, reported in the December 1917 issue.

CWM surely achieved its aim and, as best it could, fulfilled the role which Joseph hoped it would. What it also does is illustrate, quite vividly, what a social company Rowntree's was – celebrating the ethos and ambience which Joseph and his co-directors wanted to instil in the firm. It also shows the firm – to employees and outsiders alike – to be an international company, and its executives to be very well connected locally and in the industry.

The February 1904 edition of *CWM* gives a detailed breakdown of the staff at Rowntree's and, in doing so, provides a picture of the internal structure of the company and how it had developed and was developing. Here are the details:

Cream, chocolate confectionery: 520 male, 1107 female;
Cake chocolate and cocoa: 299, 306; Packing and despatch: 48 male;
Box making: 97, 82; Mechanics, joiners and bricklayers 157 male;
    timekeepers, gardeners etc 63 male;
Department managers 8 male; Social Workers 3 male, 4 female;
Depot Packers 35, 9; Clerks 185 male, 51 female; Engineers 9 male;

Lab workers 4 male, clerks of Works 5 male – making a total in York of 1395 men and 1550 women.

In addition there were 55 travellers covering England with a further 17 for Scotland, Wales and Ireland; there were 13 overseas representatives and 40 permanent advertising staff – all male. In Jamaica, Dominica and the West Indies there were 9 white managers and overseers; 75 male East Indian coolies and 25 female; 165 male Negro cultivators and 178 female.

These numbers compare with headcounts in 1894 and 1899 of 892 and 1,613 respectively.

Chapter 15

Out Of The Slums:
New Earswick Garden Village

rguably, one of the pinnacles of Joseph Rowntree's ongoing programme of social reform lay in the trusts he established and in the garden village that was New Earswick. In 1904, he emulated the Cadburys when he inaugurated the three trusts that live on and thrive today: the Social Service Trust, the Charitable Trust and the Village Trust. While the first two are, and always have been, of incalculable value on so many different levels, it is the third which concerns us most as the Village Trust had a direct effect on part of the workforce just down the road in the Haxby Road factory. Joseph was one of the first industrialists to realise that a happy workforce was usually a productive workforce. Coming to work after a night spent in an insanitary, cramped, overcrowded and damp hovel was never going to get the best out of a workforce. What if the opposite were true? What if the man and woman clocking on and off at Rowntree's lived in a roomy, heated, sanitary, sunny house in a leafy, semi-rural village with a friendly community and a buzzing social life with an ergonomic and enlightened school for the children?

The trusts were always intended to be dynamic in that the work they did moved with, and adapted to, the changing times. In Joseph's words: 'I hope that … these trusts may be living bodies, free to adapt themselves to the ever-changing necessities of the nation.' The beneficiary of the Village Trust was the model garden village that was to become New Earswick, or 'The New Estate' as it was often known. The social services and charitable trusts were concerned with supporting social research and surveys, adult education and Quaker-related work – in effect, ensuring the endurance of the social work to which Joseph had devoted much of his life thus far.

In setting up the trusts, Joseph Rowntree effectively handed over half of his personal fortune by giving the trusts almost fifty-two and a half per cent of voting shares in Rowntree's. As a Quaker, Joseph believed that money was best used in life when you could do something constructive with it – that 'wealth and property beyond the needs of the individual should be used for the common good'. His philosophy and aspirations relating to the trusts are laid out in the 1904 *Founding Memorandum*.

The simple aim of the Village Trust was to provide the average worker on a wage of about 25 shillings per week with a new type of house that was 'artistic in appearance', clean, sanitary, and ergonomically designed in an environmentally friendly village with social, religious and educational amenities. In other words, a decent place to live with a vibrant community ethos which was not a Hungate or a Walmgate slum. At least ten per cent of the village was to be made up of parks or recreation areas; houses would only take up twenty-five per cent of the land and there would be strips of grass between the roads and footpaths. Small but vitally important details.

Many factors would have conspired in Joseph Rowntree's mind to power the establishment of New Earswick on a site just minutes away from the Haxby Road factory between York and the village of Haxby. These include his deep concern for the welfare of his workers; the research findings and solutions exposed by Seebohm concerning local poverty and the plight of the urban poor published in his groundbreaking *Poverty: A Study of Town Life*; his own Quaker beliefs; Cadbury's monumental achievements at Bournville and Robert Owen's and David Dale's 1786 village New Lanark. There was also the pioneering work on garden cities by Ebenezer Howard, manifested in the shape of Letchworth in 1903 (Britain's first garden city), Saltaire – Titus Salt's 1851 model village – James Reckitt's Quaker garden village in Hull later in 1908, and in later aspects of William Lever's Port Sunlight.

By 1924 the population of New Earswick was about 2,000 and 850 of these people worked for Rowntree's. New Earswick featured a variety of house types: some were in groups of seven with an access passage between the third and fourth houses. Gardens were about 350 square yards and came with two fruit trees – just enough for 'a man to properly cultivate by spade labour in his leisure time'. They cost £318.7s.11d to build and rent was 6s 3d per week. The architects were Raymond Unwin and Barry Parker, whose challenging brief was to design and build high-quality housing at affordable rents with adequate living space within restricted floor space. The building programme was: 1902 – 123 houses; 1902–1904 – 28; 1904–1919 – 229; 1919–1936 – 259. Total spend on land, houses and services was £450,000.

In fulfilling his brief, Unwin used indoor floor space as a bicycle store and a coal store, thus obviating the need for outhouses, reducing costs and releasing upstairs space for a third bedroom. The flushing toilet was downstairs and the bath was in the kitchen under a hinged table flap. A black range was installed, with a pantry, fitted cupboards and a copper 'fitted with a steam exhaust which prevents the steam from penetrating into the rooms on washing day'. Gas and water was on tap. The first houses had earth closets, which were replaced in 1906 with a water system. By 1948, ninety-three per cent of the 530 houses had three bedrooms; one had two and the rest had four or five. Separate bathrooms were a feature of thirty new houses built in 1954. The living room was always situated to capture maximum sunlight and very often looked out to the back to effect this. Floors in New Earswick were typically linoleum and red quarry tiles while taps and door knobs were all brass. Twelve bungalows were built for older residents; these featured a large room usable either as a living room-cum-bedroom, or as two separate rooms. This versatility gave obvious social advantages and financial benefits on heating costs and they were fitted with alarm bells for emergencies, connected to a qualified nurse's rent-free residence.

Socially and environmentally, New Earswick was simply decades ahead of its time. And how very different it was from the squalor, damp and crowded conditions endured around Walmgate. There were shops for the residents: in the 1930s these included Howard's haberdashery, Mrs Farrell's sweet shop, Ernie Wood's chemist, Fred Wiley the cobbler, the Co-op butchers, Burrell's bakers and Coning's wet fish shop. The houses in Chestnut Avenue were built in 1917 in blocks of four with a central passageway for access. Chestnut Avenue then epitomised the ethos of the village: tree-lined, virtually traffic-free avenues which were, and still are, pleasant to live and play in. Cost to build was £309.15s.7d and rent was 6s per week if the bath was in the scullery; if it was upstairs it was 6s 8d. A library and a savings bank were opened. Pig sties were erected in 1905. White Rose Dairy began production in 1904 – the inspiration of Seebohm Rowntree – to provide pure milk to residents; Seebohm was aware from his research for *Poverty* that contaminated milk was a factor in the high infant mortality rate. He hired a Dane, Wilfred Sorensen, known (geographically inaccurately) as 'Oslo', from the Manchester Pure Milk Co, and bought some land for him to build a farm on and to raise a herd. High levels of hygiene were adopted: all milk was filtered and cooled to destroy bacteria.

New Earswick's busy social life was centered on the Folk Hall built in 1907. Its main purpose was to provide a venue for societies and clubs and to run activities which reflected the interests of the residents. Amongst the first to be formed were the Women's Guild and the Horticultural

Society. In a liberal and liberating move that was revolutionary in those days, Joseph Rowntree urged and encouraged women to get out of the home and use the many facilities offered in the Folk Hall: 'In this country it seems to be the thought that women do not need recreation,' he said, citing the example of Germany where it was, and still is today, the norm for families to go out together with their children. During the First World War, the hall was used to shelter Belgian refugees. The village library opened in here in 1908, with the first 100 books donated by Joseph Rowntree.

Another function of the hall was as a place of worship – for all faiths. In time, though, a separate Wesleyan Chapel and a place for Anglican worship were established. The Society of Friends and Roman Catholics continued to use the hall; in 1917 it was given Quaker Meeting status; a Sunday school followed in 1918.

The New Earswick Musical Society was a frequent user. The society was founded in 1914 (out of the 1912 Choral Society) as the New Earswick Dramatic Society and 106 years later still performs two shows every year, now in the Joseph Rowntree Theatre in Haxby Road. In 1933 the Society had 260 active members and performed a staggering twenty-four productions – Gilbert and Sullivan plays and operas – one every two weeks. In 1935 its success helped drive through a new hall with seating for 450, a well-lit stage and dressing rooms.

Seebohm Rowntree's opening speech revealed the range of societies and organisations using the hall then: the Library Committee, the Women's Guild, the Orchestral Society, the Village Council, the Rose Carnival, the Children's Welfare Centre, the Musical Society, the Men's Social Club, as well as all the sports societies. The first football club was formed in the early 1900s, soon to be followed by the cricket club; initially both played on the green opposite the shops in Hawthorne Terrace. However, Westfield Beck proved a hazard and the shop windows were too often a target for the eager batsmen. So, from 1923, both teams were able to play on pitches on the newly developed 16 acre sports fields. There were also tennis courts, a bowling green and a sports pavilion.

In the late 1940s the hall took 1,075 lettings in one year, bringing in £710 with highly profitable Saturday night dances proving particularly popular. The adult education courses encouraged by the Rowntrees were also held at Folk Hall.

As stated, in developing New Earswick, Joseph Rowntree was influenced not only by Cadbury's Bournville, but also, and principally, by Ebenezer Howard's (1850–1928) vision of a kind of utopian, but achievable, city where citizens lived in harmony with nature, as described in his 1898 *Tomorrow: A Peaceful Path to Real Reform*, retitled *Garden Cities of Tomorrow* in 1902. Howard's towns were to be slum free and managed and financed by the residents who were offered a financial interest. They combined the best of town and country life. Equal opportunity, good wages, entertainment, low rents, beauty and fresh air were the aim. We recognise all of these elements in Joseph Rowntree's New Earswick. Joseph saw the benefits of a semi-rural lifestyle and environment as enjoyed at Fry's Somerdale Factory and at Cadbury's Bournville self-contained semi-rural village and 'factory in a garden'; and he wanted the same for New Earswick. At the same time, he hoped to imbue a sense of civic pride and responsibility (avoiding the 'stultifying paternalism' of Lever's Port Sunlight) by empowering the residents to be actively involved in the running of the village and its amenities.

Joseph was also concerned about the schism which he saw widening between town and country life. As 'the residence of town workers in the country', New Earswick, would, at least for York, 'help to bridge the gulf between town and country interests'. The Folk Hall was thus named to evoke a bucolic air reinforced by, amongst many other things, its country dances.

Howard's humanistic ideal and progressive vision was influential in other countries too, not least in Germany where the German Garden City Association – '*unseren Deustschen Vettern*', 'our German cousins' as the people of New Earswick welcomed them on their visit in 1909 – flourished. The 200-strong delegation was met by the lord mayor, the sheriff, the town clerk, the chief constable and Seebohm and Arnold Rowntree; Mrs Joseph Rowntree entertained them at lunch in the De Grey Rooms. Letters of apology were received from King Edward, Prime Minister Asquith and the Archbishop of York. The delegation included engineers, mayors, doctors, factory inspectors and barristers from Germany, Austria, Poland and Russia. Joseph Rowntree's speech, translated into and delivered in German, extolled not only the philosophy behind New Earswick but also the German system of pensions, invalidity support and nationwide education, as evidenced by a recent deputation. The party moved on to New Earswick in a procession of fifty vehicles, entering through the splendid archway built by the residents.

There is, however, a sinister side to the story. Theodor Fritsch (1852–1933), German publisher, noted anti-Semite and writer, claimed to be the originator of the garden city concept, anticipating Howard in his 1896 *Die Stadt der Zukunft (The City of the Future)* – the 1912 second edition was subtitled *Gartenstad (Garden City)* – which became a blueprint of the German garden city movement as adopted by Völkisch circles. Völkisch was a German ethnic and nationalist movement active from the late nineteenth century until the Nazi era. In 1893, Fritsch published his most notorious work, *The Handbook of the Jewish Question*, which levelled a number of conspiratorial charges at European Jews and called upon Germans to stop intermingling with them. Hugely popular, the book was in its forty-ninth edition by 1944, having sold 330,000 copies, and counting Adolf Hitler among the many it influenced.

Fritsch took a highly racist perspective – totally at odds with Howard's – which later became part of Nazi ideology and made Fritsch something of a Nazi prophet. His other work, largely published in his journal, *The Hammer: Pages for German Sense (1902–1940)*, was anti-Semitic and supremacist. Even though German eugenicists were sitting on the board of the German Garden City Association in 1910, and the long tradition of town planning and architecture had been hijacked in the name of ethnic cleansing and eugenics, the association rejected Fritsch. This did not, however, stop their work leading to, for example, the establishment in Bremen of a *Siedlung* under the Third Reich: part garden city, part half-open prison, part eugenicistic selection centre.

The first New Earswick 'school' opened in the Folk Hall in 1909 after pressure from the trust on a dilatory local authority to act; it catered for twenty-five infants. The first permanent school was built in 1912 for 352 5 to 14 year olds, to save them the trek to Haxby Road School about a mile away. New Earswick School (later New Earswick Elementary School) or the 'Open Air School' as it became known, was another model of enlightenment. Boys and girls were taught the same subjects – science, for example, had usually been the preserve of boys – and there were no high windows as the full-length windows faced south, folded open to an extent of 18 feet and were at head level to maximise natural daylight. Each child had 15 square feet of floor area affording ample space in between desks – fifty per cent more than was stipulated by the Board of Education then. Class sizes were limited to thirty pupils although, at the time in York, classes of between fifty and sixty were the norm; the trustees paid for an extra teacher to facilitate this. As the school neared completion, the influential magazine *Building News* waxed lyrical, highlighting all its features.

Interestingly, it is the school that is at the heart of the village, not, as might be expected, the social and religious centre, Folk Hall. In his opening address, Joseph's views on the prevailing 'corrupting system in which schools received payment by test result based on a narrow and limiting state curriculum' – what we now call teaching to test – have an eerily modern ring:

> this mechanical system ... its general effect was to turn out children who perhaps might pass examinations but whose mental activity was stunted, and who had little capacity for meeting the demands of daily life.

The importance of attracting the very best teachers was never underestimated:

> The most potent influence will no doubt come from the teachers, this will make itself felt in many ways. New Earswick School is coeducational throughout, sewing and cooking will not be neglected for the girls, we want the girls when they grow up to be able to enter marriage with intelligent understanding so that they may be true and helpful companions to their husbands and able wisely to guide the minds of children.

To cater for those children who might benefit from a secondary education, scholarships were established at a nearby grammar school. These included a grant for books and, where necessary, a maintenance allowance for their parents. Children benefitted from this over the years, sixty of whom went on to join one of the professions. Discipline was never compromised as two extracts from the Punishment Book show:

> 28th February 1927: L. Smith age 10 – running home (twice warned) 2 strokes – hand;
> 12th December 1938: N. Peacock 11 – stealing 3 shillings – 3 strokes – hand at mother's request.

The impressive clock on the cupola, with its weather vane in the form of a Quaker reading to two children, was donated by Joseph Stephenson Rowntree.

The Village Trust, which gave birth to and administered New Earswick, was one of the three charitable trusts set up by Joseph Rowntree in 1904. The other two were the Social Service Trust and the Charitable Trust. The aim of the latter was to provide funds for projects close to the hearts of the Rowntree family: for example, Seebohm's sociological research and quest to expose and address the causes of poverty, and John Wilhelm's work in education. This general remit extended to include grants for such projects as Woodbrooke permanent settlement, school improvements and teacher recruitment, scholarships, Quaker history teaching and teacher training, the promotion of temperance, the causes of poverty, peace studies, the effects of unemployment and the training of the unemployed, public park provision, and the acquisition and publishing of relevant publications. Joseph himself said in the *Founding Memorandum*: 'The soup kitchen in York never has difficulty in obtaining adequate financial aid, but an enquiry into the extent and causes of poverty would enlist little support,' – a statement defining the difficulty of raising money to investigate the underlying causes of poverty, an invisible cause.

The trusts were also a manifestation of Joseph's fervent belief that philanthropy needed careful planning and management: the trusts would have this, they would not be spontaneous, arbitrary or random in any way. Again, from the *Memorandum*: 'If the enormous volume of the philanthropy of the present day were wisely directed, it would, I believe, in the course of a few years, change the face of England.' What was needed was 'wise direction' of charitable and philanthropic giving.

Chapter 16

Early Twentieth-Century Rowntree's

The new century saw Rowntree's evolve rapidly into a global company as one of the market leaders in confectionery manufacturing. Joseph's eldest son, John Wilhelm (1868–1905) opened up the company's first plantation in what was then the West Indies and key markets were established in Australia, New Zealand, Canada and the USA.

John Wilhelm had the vision to see that rivals such as Cadbury's, as well as American or German companies, might monopolise the market. He saw a future in which Rowntree & Co became a multinational enterprise with their own plantations and branches in the United States, Canada and Australia. In 1898, he sailed to the West Indies to explore such an eventuality and to find a location for a plantation project. In 1899, he persuaded the board to buy estates in Trinidad, Grenada, Jamaica, the Gold Coast and Western Samoa, though his father harboured doubts about the project and the resources it required. By the 1900s, as we have noted, Rowntree & Co were selling their products in Australia and New Zealand, soon to be joined by Canada and the United States. Things were slowly starting to change on the sales and marketing front. In 1906, forty men were working in the advertising department and there were eighty-five or so travelling salesmen.

Rowntree's and slavery

Around 1903, Rowntree had found itself implicated by association in what the Tory press called the 'cocoa scandal'. Quaker opposition to slavery had always been fervent, and is well recorded. In 1657, George Fox was vocal in denunciation, travelling in 1671 to the West Indies and America to see the situation for himself. In 1736, Benjamin Lay summed up the Quaker position when he called it 'hellish practice ... a filthy sin ... the greatest sin in the world ... [slavery is] of the very nature of Hell itself and is the belly of Hell'. Quakers made up the majority of the 1787 Abolition Society and were responsible in part for The British Slave Trade Act of 1807 and the Slavery Abolition Act of 1833; they formed the Anti-Slavery Society in 1823.

The Cadburys were particularly active, especially William, a Cadbury buyer and George Cadbury's nephew. At the time Cadbury's sourced forty-five per cent of their high-quality cocoa beans from Príncipe and São Thomé – Portuguese colonies off the West African coast in the Gulf of Guinea. Rumour had it that the workers there were slaves and this was confirmed in a sale notice for a São Thomé plantation which included 'two hundred black labourers worth £3,555'. William Cadbury's investigations confirmed the worst: outlawed slavery was rife in São Thomé, under the aegis of the Portuguese government. A fact-finding mission under Joseph Burtt was despatched to Príncipe and São Tomé, commissioned by Cadbury's, Fry's, Rowntree's and Stollwerck.

Some years previously, *Harper's Monthly Magazine* had hired an English journalist, Henry Nevinson, to investigate the story from Angola where he eventually found indisputable evidence of a slave trade – shackles and skeletons and allegations of witchcraft. The hub of 'this deed of pitiless hypocrisy' was Benguala where the captured natives were press-ganged into becoming 'voluntary workers' (*serviçais* in Portuguese) over on São Thomé for five years. This contracted labour was slavery by a different name. Nevinson visited the islands and saw 30,000 slaves on São Thomé and 3,000 more on Príncipe. Twenty per cent of the *serviçais* died each year in '*okalunga*' – hell on earth, 'their dead bodies lashed to poles and carried out to be flung away in the forest'. Nevinson's findings were serialised in *Harper's* and published in a book, *A Modern Slavery*, which exposed the sordid and shameful working conditions there for contracted workers as just that – modern slavery; the Cadbury – Rowntree – Fry – Stollwerck research in 1907 confirmed the situation. Burtt convinced the Rowntree's board on 2 May 1907 'beyond all doubt'. Attempts to enlist the Foreign Office to take action against the Portuguese resulted in little more than a Foreign Office cover-up to protect Portuguese labour contracts in South African mines. All the while, though, the chocolate companies were facing increasing criticism and accusations of hypocrisy, led by the London's *Standard* of 26 September 1908 exposing 'that monstrous trade in human flesh ... the very islands which feed the mills and presses of Bournville.' The outcome was a boycott of cocoa from São Tomé and Príncipe in March 1909 by the Quaker companies and a protracted libel case, Cadbury Brothers Ltd vs the Standard Newspaper Ltd, which began in November that year.

In 1911 the highest civic honour possible was bestowed on Joseph Rowntree. He was made an Honorary Freeman of the City of York; only twenty-three other men had received the honour since 1876 and he was the first businessman to be honoured with it – predecessors were from the church, military, professions or aristocracy. His acceptance speech did not disappoint. Joseph used it to thank the city for the honour and its progress in local education, health and sanitation; then he spoilt the party for some when he reminded the great and good of York about the urban poverty which cast a shadow on many of their streets, raising the question, *what are you doing about it?*

Two fascinating Rowntree exhibits from the early twentieth century can be seen in the Castle Museum in York. The first is an advertisement for Elect in the form of a smirking red cat with a green bow tie covered in Rowntree 'R's. The second is a Rowntree's cocoa tin which Ernest Shackleton took to the Antarctic with him on his 1908–1909 Nimrod expedition. Unused, it was brought back to England with other supplies when Shackleton and three colleagues got within 97 miles of the South Pole before turning back. The cocoa tin was donated to the museum by a woman from Sydenham who had been given it by one of Shackleton's sisters. The handwritten label on the tin reads, 'This tin of cocoa is one of the unused stores brought back by Sir Ernest Shackleton's expedition from the Antarctic'. It was privileged to have been chosen as one of the top museum objects from the North Yorkshire region as part of the BBC's History of the World project.

Chapter 17

Rowntree's at War, and After

The history of the part chocolate has played in war is as old as the history of chocolate. Chocolate has often played an important role in more recent wars – either as a ration for servicemen, as a gift to liberated civilians, or as a peace offering to the vanquished. As we know, in 1780 Fry's were commissioned to supply the Royal Navy with a ration of chocolate in cocoa slab form for its sailors, to replace rum and to provide them with something a little more nutritious to go with their ship's biscuit. In the 1850s Fry's tins were sent to the troops fighting in the Crimean War. Chocolate played a role during the Boer War when Queen Victoria instructed George Cadbury to send 120,000 tins of chocolate to the troops in 1900. At first he refused, citing his Quakerly aversion to war but the Queen responded by pointing out that this was not a request but a royal command. The issue was resolved by sharing the order with Fry's and Rowntree's, and the tins were sent out unbranded to obscure their origin: each tin contained a half block of vanilla chocolate. George Cadbury then salved his conscience by producing and distributing over one million anti-war pamphlets. Rowntree's shelved an idea to celebrate their royal warrant with Queen's Gift Tins in 1899 because the gesture may have been misconstrued as 'pandering to some degree to the present war fever'.

The new-found military importance of chocolate was highlighted by the 1905 issue of *War Office Times and Naval Review:* 'Now chocolate is ... the sweetmeat of the Services: on the march, at manoeuvres, or on any special occasion where staying power is needed.' Chocolate was now War Office material; chocolate was now official; chocolate would be regular issue from now on.

In 1914 attitudes had changed to some degree and Joseph Rowntree, again with Fry and Cadbury, sent tins of confectionery to the troops in the trenches. They contained sweets, chocolates and, in a compartment at the base of Rowntree's tins, a set of postcards. For a time at least, the drop in demand caused by the privations of the First World War had little impact on sales and profits – amply compensated as they were by War Office orders for chocolate rations and the virtual elimination of foreign competition from the continent. Even though tariffs on cocoa and sugar were increased and freight charges and general taxation had risen, the naval blockade by German submarines served to focus the government's mind on the provision of essential foods such as milk and cocoa and this too helped the chocolate companies. Sugar shortages, though, led to the suspension of many brands and recipe changes for others and crippling manpower depletions occurred as men left for the front. At Rowntree's, 193 men left to take up their roles as Territorial Army reservists – just when the company needed them most to meet increasing demand.

Needless to say Rowntree's did not, for obvious reasons, initially endorse or comply with the general policy of dismissing conscientious objectors. In 1916 the company compromised, as it were, by not employing objectors; this was to stem the ill feeling they caused amongst the rest of the workforce. Pension contributions of workers on active service were paid in full by the company and, as we have seen, provision was made for war widows. By May 1915, 750 Rowntree men had signed up, with further 'losses' due to trained fitters and turners moving into the armaments industry under the terms of the Munitions Act. Indeed, Rowntree's would have closed had not the Ministry of Works conferred reserved occupation status on those workers remaining.

In a bid to grow the depleted workforce, the company rescinded their policy of not hiring men aged over 35. Belgian refugees were taken on, although Hindus, quite astonishingly, were rejected on the racist grounds that 'it would not do to employ [them] in any of the general rooms, or where there were girls'. Between April 1916 and March 1917, the number of male employees fell from 2,644 to 1,855 while the number of women declined from 3,341 to 2,655 over the same period.

Elsewhere, Cadbury's provided books and clothing for the troops and Caley's Marching Chocolate was issued to British troops under the name of Marcho. Special wrappers were produced showing soldiers presenting arms (but unfortunately the rifles were drawn on the wrong shoulder). After the war it was marketed at, and became popular with, sportsmen and outdoor enthusiasts, receiving plaudits from such popular heroes as Jack Hobbs, the Surrey and England batsman.

One amazing story published in *CWM* in 1915 was headlined 'Elect Cocoa Saves a Soldier's Life' and was sent in by Sergeant T. J. Williams of the 5th King's Own Lancashire Regiment. His letter began, 'to inform you what good service one of your tins cocoa did for me,' and went on to relate how, during the Battle of St Julien, he received a 1 lb tin of Elect, which he duly put in his emergency ration pack along with a tin of tea and sugar:

> Advancing under heavy fire and now and again dropping flat on the ground a bullet entered my valise. [It] had gone through the tin containing the tea and sugar, the tin of Rowntrees had been penetrated on one side and not the other. What luck! If it had gone through it would have penetrated my back. It speaks well as to the strength of the tin but more so for the strength of the cocoa. Ha! Ha!

Less happily, *CWM* published a litany of casualty announcements and photographs throughout the war including Lawrence, John Wilhelm's only son, who was killed in action in 1917. At the outbreak of the First World War, Lawrence Rowntree was a conscientious objector. He nevertheless served his country as a volunteer orderly and driver for ten months in the Friends' Ambulance Unit at Dunkirk and in Belgium; Lawrence was one of the first forty to be deployed in October 1914. He then returned to England and worked at the military hospital in Haxby Road (the Cocoa Block requisitioned from Rowntree's). When conscription was introduced, Lawrence had a change of heart and first enlisted into the Royal Field Artillery as a gunner, via the Medium Machine Gun School at Coventry on 23 May 1916. He saw action at Ancre, the first tank battle, as a crew member in HMLS *Crème de Menthe*: all of the forty-nine tanks in the British Army being deployed there in November 1916 in what was to be the final battle in the Somme offensive. *Crème de Menthe* had its tail wheel blown off; Lawrence was injured and repatriated to Edinburgh where he made a full recovery. He was later commissioned into the Royal Artillery and redeployed to the Western Front in July 1917 where he fought in the Ypres salient throughout the 3rd Battle of Ypres. Four months later on 25 November 1917, Lawrence was killed in action.

This is how he is honoured in the York Casualty Role of Honour:

> Rowntree, Lawrence Edmund Second Lieutenant 'A' Bty. 26th Bde., Royal Field Artillery. Killed in action 25th November 1917. Aged 22. Son of Constance Margaret Rowntree, of Low Hall, Scalby, Scarborough, and the late John Wilhelm Rowntree. Buried Vlamertinge New Military Cemetery, Ieper, West-Vlaanderen, Belgium, XI. B. 5. Commemorated in The King's Book.

As stated, the dining room in the Cocoa Block was requisitioned as billets for the 1,000 or so men of the 8th Battalion, the West Yorkshire Regiment (Territorials); in 1915, the Leeds Rifles came and went to be replaced by men of the King's Own Yorkshire Light Infantry; the block was later converted into a temporary military hospital. Belgian refugees accommodated in New Earswick gave French lessons to local residents. A fund was set up for 1d per head to support the refugees, described as 'innocent sufferers of Prussian brutality' and nine houses were hastily furnished and provided rent free for nine families. Joseph Rowntree announced in the Christmas 1914 edition of *CWM* that 500 men had joined up, with two killed; all 500 were dignified by being listed by name and by department. By 1917, 1,739 regular staff and 985 temporary staff were on Army or Navy service.

One of the oddest, yet inevitable, developments during the war was the establishment of the Ration Department in 1917. Commercially counter-intuitive, it was described as 'a department for cutting down orders' in the *CWM* of December 1917. Twenty girls from across the company were employed to score out lines from travellers' orders and to stamp them 'rationed' before they were sent to Packing, all to ensure compliance with the government sugar restrictions, which limited the amount of chocolate sold to any one customer. The sugar restrictions were obviously very punishing as two thirds of UK imports would normally come from Germany and Austria-Hungary. To compensate, syrups were used and in 1915 Rowntree's established Confectionery Ingredients Ltd in King's Lynn with Strange & Graham, flavourings and essence makers, to develop vanillin, a cheap substitute for vanilla. There was research into saccharin as a sugar substitute and by 1917 it was being produced in bulk and sold to third parties at good margins. Nestlé, of course, were debarred from the UK, leaving the door open for Cadbury's, not Rowntree's, to fill the vital gap in the milk chocolate market. Now milk chocolate, synonymous with Cadbury's Dairy Milk, superseded cocoa as the main product of the chocolate industry.

By the end of the war Rowntree's had lost 179 employees, killed in action or missing. On 12 September 1920, Seebohm Rowntree unveiled an oak memorial to the fallen which cost £179.17s.5d and was funded by employee contributions; Joseph Rowntree donated the £800 recently collected for his and Emma Rowntree's golden wedding celebrations.

Embracing advertising – at last

After the war the company, by and large, languished in the doldrums. A lack of clear direction and policy, lots of short-run unprofitable lines, the failure to compete with Cadbury's Dairy Milk and the persistent suspicion of advertising and marketing all took their toll. Sales had increased by seventy per cent between 1918 and 1920 – the boom following the war – but the wage bill had exploded simultaneously – by nearly 300 per cent.

The company and the economy generally faced the inevitable bust: pay cuts followed, agreed between Rowntree's and Cadbury's-Fry's who between them employed fifty-six per cent of the nation's chocolate industry workers. Profits, such as they were, were fed back into the company to help reduce the price of chocolates in the shops. From 1918, Rowntree's faced increased competition from a merged Cadbury's-Fry's: a tripartite merger was considered by the Rowntree's board but quickly rejected.

Advertising was becoming less expensive and, indeed, essential if companies were to increase product awareness, combat the claims of competitors and establish brand recognition – the latter facilitated by the 1875 Trade Marks Act. Branding also allowed a company to differentiate its product in the market and this was largely responsible for the dichotomy which existed in the confectionery marketplace: high-quality proprietary brands versus low-quality nameless products. Advertising had been a powerful tool in convincing consumers that products were pure and unadulterated – an increasingly important issue in the minds of people who had put up with all manner of foul and toxic additives before the 1872 legislation. But increasingly, advertisements and posters were used to tell consumers how a product fitted effortlessly and essentially into their lives, and how it positively affected their lifestyle. This opened the way for pithy slogans and eye-catching pictures.

All of this, though, as we have repeatedly seen, was anathema to Joseph Rowntree and members of the board. In 1919 they agonised sniffily that the new type of advertising appealed to 'the cinema type of mind' rather than to the more cerebral customer, whom they still saw, unrealistically, as their target audience. The real need, of course, and ably demonstrated by Cadbury's, Caley's, Mackintosh and others, was to target the working-class customer who, due to rises in wages and money in his and her pockets, was now the socio-economic group responsible for the increases in consumption, and therefore, sales and, to some extent profits. Once again things had to change and they did, finally, in 1920 when the

Rowntree's board reluctantly accepted that the only way to change their fortunes was to advertise their way out of the crisis. They were behind Nestlé and Cadbury's in milk chocolate, behind Cadbury's in cocoa and behind neighbours Terry's in assortments. A marketing budget of £133,000 was approved for the first half of 1921, getting closer to, but still some way off, Cadbury's figure of £200,000.

This was set against a changing inter-war years market. Annual consumption of milk chocolate rose by sixty-six per cent, wages increased by over fifteen and a half per cent and consumer spend on food grew by forty per cent; at the same time food prices in the shops decreased by sixty-five per cent. These factors, in association with improved production techniques and economies of scale, coincided with a significant fall in the retail price of milk chocolate: from 4s 2d to 1s 4d per lb. From now on chocolate was no longer a semi-luxury, but a must-have purchase by the man, woman and child in the street. Weekly per capita confectionery consumption grew in 1920, 1930 and 1938 from 4.7 oz to 5.7 oz and 7.1 oz with chocolate accounting for roughly half of this.

Chapter 18

Benefits in the Workplace

T he earlier years of the century were a time of significantly improved, innovative and pioneering worker benefits at Rowntree's, benefits which frequently anticipated other firms and government legislation making them mandatory.

A company doctor was engaged in 1904, following Cadbury's example in 1902. Joseph was astute enough to appreciate the validity of *mens sana in corpore sano* ('a sound mind in a sound body') in his workforce. There had been a self-help medical club since the late 1890s but in 1904 Rowntree's appointed a company doctor to provide medical care, medical examinations for prospective employees and advice on health and safety in the workplace. Dr Peter MacDonald, Joseph's son-in-law, was the first to hold the post; he had married Agnes Julia (1870–1960), Joseph's elder daughter. Consultations were free; treatment was on 'equitable terms'; prescriptions were usually 6d a bottle, more for costlier medicines; eye tests and prescription spectacles were available, as were extractions for 'unsound teeth'.

One of MacDonald's early clinical observations was that a significant element of staff ill health was caused or exacerbated by poor dental health. He wrote to Joseph on the matter saying that not only a doctor but also a dentist was therefore needed and that the dentist should be the priority – a staff dentist was duly appointed, Herbert Ashley, who retired in 1917. In a 1905 issue of *CWM*, MacDonald explained his rationale in an article entitled 'Good Teeth Good Health'. He was obviously influenced by the Administration of State Insurance of German Workmen for sickness and old age who had been 'devoting increased attention to dentistry ... defective teeth often have a very deleterious influence on general health and, partly in its own interest has had the teeth of large numbers of workmen properly attended to.' Joseph Rowntree justified these important steps as follows: 'Healthful conditions of labour are not luxuries to be adopted or dispensed with at will; they are conditions necessary for success. In keen international competition the vigour and intelligence of the workmen are likely to be a determining factor.'

An optician was appointed in 1919 followed by a female doctor in 1925 and nurses, one of the first being Nurse Clayton in 1919 who had trained at Canterbury Hospital. Sick and funeral societies had been in place since the turn of the century. Dr MacDonald moved on in 1912 to be replaced by Dr Ferguson from York County Hospital.

Joseph and his colleagues on the board appreciated that the girls at Rowntree's spent most of their waking hours in their factory with little time left to prepare themselves for later life. Joseph accordingly set up a domestic school staffed with qualified teachers to train all girls joining the firm before age 17 in household management, home nursing, care of infants, needlework, upholstery and cookery – two hours per week in work time, paid. The thinking behind this was explained in *CWM*: 'the contention that factory life unfits a girl for home duties by allowing her neither time nor opportunity for learning what is necessary for the management of a home.' The school was government supervised and subject to regular inspection and, as to be expected, only the best qualified teachers were engaged. Miss Miller came from the Edinburgh School of Domestic Science to teach cookery; Miss Cashmoor from the Bristol School of Domestic Economy and girls' clubs in London to teach dressmaking and hygiene.

In 1921, a continuation school was set up in the city under the auspices of York Education Committee and after that, the focus at Rowntree's continuation schools moved to English, swimming, singing and gymnastics. This was initially led by a Miss E. A. Maunsell. For boys, from 1908, the Works School had provided Swedish physical education as well as classes in Mathematics, Woodwork, Experimental Physics, Chemistry and English. The Swedish Ling System of Gymnastics, to give it its proper name, took place in the new gym recently converted from the Cardboard Box Store. It was a special form of gymnastics where 'all the muscles of the body are systematically and harmoniously developed. There is no lop-sided development in Ling's System,' *CWM* assures us.

Clubs mushroomed with boating, angling, bowling, chess, football, cricket, tennis and photography, and there were mandolin and guitar, brass, and drum and fife bands. By 1904, one third of all male employees and over four fifths of females were enrolled in at least one club.

A greater say in the running of the firm and factory was afforded by the establishment of Works Councils – at departmental level in 1916, followed by a Central Works Council in 1918. The councils – one each for women and men – comprised equal numbers of administrative staff appointed by management and shop floor workers nominated by themselves through ballot. Here, Joseph Rowntree anticipated the government, in this case the Whitley Committee, which later recommended that such committees be set up industry-wide. Staff promptly voted for extended weekday working hours in lieu of working Saturdays. The payment of one week's paid holiday every year was introduced in 1918, nineteen years before it became obligatory for all employers to do likewise.

In 1921 the Rowntree's Appeals Committee was established, the first impartial industrial tribunal in the UK. In effect, this allowed workers the right of appeal against unjust disciplinary action or punishment for breaking works' rules. Workers could have their case heard before the committee – made up of two workers and two members appointed by the directors, with a chairman voted for by the other four. Of the thirty-one cases heard between 1921 and 1938, fifteen involved theft, ten of which were thrown out. Of the others, four had their penalties reduced and one had all charges dismissed. There were sixteen other appeals involving management decisions: seven were upheld, three had a penalty reduction and six found in favour of the appellant. Justice was done and, in the cases here, seven workers' lives were saved the enduring ignominy of being wrongly blighted. From 1923, workers were also given a say in who was to be their foreman or forewoman, approving the management nomination or disapproving it and suggesting an alternative.

Another of Joseph's pioneering innovations designed to improve communication was what is today called the company meeting. Every year, after the customary address to the shareholders, another meeting would be convened attended by all the workers. This would comprise a detailed survey of the year's developments, changes and results.

The long-awaited profit sharing scheme was finally introduced in 1923. Joseph had mooted a scheme for employees in 1907 but, because of the almost unanimous opposition within and without Rowntree's, it was shelved until 1916. Then, after much research, a scheme was established; although payouts were minimal until 1938, between 1943 and 1953 around £1.5 million was distributed.

On a wider, civic basis, New Yearsley Club Baths, the only Edwardian 50-yard pool in the north of England, opposite the factory, were built in 1909 by Rowntree & Co and gifted to the citizens of York. The cost was around £3,000; it held 226,890 gallons of water, measured 150 by 51 ft and was 6 ft 9 ins deep. Nestlé still supply steam to heat the pool, piped under Haxby Road. There were 100 dressing boxes on either side with slipper baths at the Haley's Terrace end. The architect was Fred Rowntree. Yearsley Baths replaced the open air, brick-bottomed old Yearsley Baths on the River Foss which opened in 1859 downstream from

Yearsley Bridge and York City Fever Hospital. They were never popular with girls or women as many of the men bathed naked there.

In 1919, Rowntree's bought 19 acres next to the River Ouse on what is now, ironically, Terry Avenue; the York Corporation bought five more, and architect Fred Rowntree set to work designing the public park that is still used and enjoyed today. His brief was to maximise the pleasure opportunities and to that end the original park comprised formal gardens, a tearoom, bowling greens, an ornamental lake, and a paddling pool. Rowntree Memorial Park opened on 16 July 1921 as a memorial to the 179 workers from the Rowntree's factory who had 'died or suffered' during the First World War. The citation on the plaque, written by Joseph, reads: 'A tribute to the memory of those members of the Company's staff who, at the cost of life or limb or health, and in the face of indescribable suffering and hardship, served their country in her hour of need.' He goes on to hope for 'the end of war ... an enduring peace ... the creation of a League of Nations will be a fitting crown ... and a true memorial to their endurance, heroism, comradeship and sacrifice.'

There are at least four versions of the legend surrounding 'Joseph Rowntree and the train journey'. They are all slightly different but draw the same picture of the man; what follows may be the genuine one, from Emily Spence (his great-great granddaughter):

> J. R. used to invite groups of workers out to the south of France every year. On one occasion, either on arrival or on their return from a day trip, they told him that they had paid for third class tickets, but travelled first. He said nothing, but the next day, took them back to the station, where they (and he) bought first class tickets, but travelled third. She also used to tell me that one man asked for some time off as he was getting married, and J. R. said that as this was so important, he wouldn't expect him in until the afternoon!

In February 1923, Joseph Rowntree retired as chairman of Rowntree & Co, handing over the reins to his son, Seebohm. John Wilhelm had retired through ill health in 1899; his brother Seebohm was the company's first labour director. Arnold Stephenson took charge of sales and advertising whilst J. B. Morrell became responsible for purchasing raw materials. Theodore Hotham Rowntree was appointed the first company secretary and T. H. Appleton the factory manager. These developments coincided with a doubling of cocoa consumption nationwide with the result that sales and profits increased.

When Seebohm Rowntree succeeded his father as chairman of the company, there were root and branch internal investigations into all aspects of the company's operations, but despite this little actually changed, and most significantly little actually changed in marketing. And this at a time when sales of confectionery sold loose in grocer's shops and tobacconists were declining in the face of packaged sweets and chocolates with brightly branded wrappers and attractive containers.

The company was restructured in the 1920s into Finance, Technical, Production, Labour and Distribution divisions, each under the control of a director. During this period, the company began to engage both in product development and marketing in a systematic way. This was in face of intense competition from other chocolate manufacturers and the wider economic crisis. The mass market for cocoa was in decline and Rowntree's were compelled to place greater emphasis on the development and promotion of their chocolate bars.

Rowntree's bought the London-based Lockhart's with its six restaurants and thirty-nine shops, Fuller and Maynard's Black Boy shops, and bought into the Scottish company Gray, Dunn & Co, (boiled sweet and chocolate biscuit manufacturers) in 1924. The marketing inertia was relieved to some extent by two new products. In 1925, they launched Plain York Chocolate bar – promoted with the repetitious and alliterative slogan: 'Plain Mr York of York, Yorkshire'. Avuncular Mr York was a chip off the Sunny Jim Force cereal and Johnny Walker whisky blocks in the branding world; his intrinsic plainness reflected the chocolate's main quality – plainness and its pure and honest simplicity. The anything but plain fruit and nut block, Motoring, followed with its milk or plain chocolate variations containing almonds and raisins. Sold as a snack suitable for a long journey, it tapped in to the increasing popularity of motoring amongst a well-to-do sector of the market. Both Motoring and Plain York were advertised with scenes from everyday life to drive home the message that eating Rowntree's chocolate was now an inextricable feature in our daily lives. The Cocoa Nibs also saw the first light of day around this time and were very popular with children, particularly in the promotional games and models in which they regularly featured.

The death of Joseph Rowntree

Joseph Rowntree died at home in Clifton Lodge on 24 February 1925 at the age of 88. York, of course, came out in its thousands for his funeral; his simple grave is in the Quaker cemetery on Heslington Road in the grounds of The Retreat.

The day of his funeral saw a dignified 'farewell tribute of honour' held in the packed dining room at the Cocoa Works:

> Right to the end, according to private papers, he was puzzling over the question of poverty and whether, through rigorous scientific enquiry, it could be made a thing of the past [working on some notes on John Bright]. In York, as in Bournville, people mourned not just the passing of the man, but of everything he symbolised that had brought such unexpected good to the world of business, on such a large scale.

His legacy in social justice, social welfare, industrial reform, Quakerism and Liberalism, education and the making of cocoa and chocolate is as manifold, profound, extensive and enduring as it comes.

Trusts apart, there are two fitting postscripts to Joseph Rowntree's life. The first came in 1927 when the Joseph Rowntree Memorial Library was built in Haxby Road outside the factory. It was designed by Fred Rowntree and housed the company library, which was previously inside the factory. Some of the books were from Joseph's personal collection, presented to the firm by his children and the interior decorations were paid for by employees of the company. Then in 1955, Rowntree's donated the eighteenth-century iron entrance gates to Rowntree Park on Terry Avenue to remember those who fell in the Second World War, 'in thanks for the courage and steadfastness of the people of York'.

Epilogue: Epitaph

Joseph Rowntree, of course, was not without fault as a businessman – no businessman or woman is. His unshakeable Quaker beliefs dictated his decision-making at times, not least in his long-term antipathy towards advertising when it was clearly the thing to do, his procrastination on the acquisition of a Van Houten press, and his reluctance to expand in to export markets when they were there for the taking. His price fixing and his programme of industrial espionage seem unethical today but who can say that such activity was not more the norm, or that he was merely reciprocating similar practices from his many rivals? Nevertheless, these injudicious actions simply delayed the huge success his company had on the global stage and are massively outweighed by his successes and pioneering work in industrial relations, pensions, health and safety, profit sharing, the working week, paid holidays, a social programme beyond compare, and all the rest, to say nothing of the inventiveness and imagination which, over time are giving us some of the most famous, enduring and enjoyable brands in confectionery.

Anne Vernon opens her 1987 biography of Joseph Rowntree with the interesting observation that the 2 March 1925 edition of the *Daily Mirror* had, on its front page, a full-page photograph of crowds of people walking past a newly dug grave with the caption 'Funeral of Mr Joseph Rowntree at York'. In a small box at the top right of the page was the news: 'New York Shaken By Earthquake'. Joseph Rowntree was indeed the kind of man who could eclipse an earthquake. This is how the earthquake was reported locally: *The Buffalo Courier* of 1 March 1925 reported that:

> people, panicked and frightened, rushed into the streets as buildings swayed in Buffalo and other cities throughout the affected area. This quake was felt within a 2 million square mile area and registered VIII on the Modified Mercalli Scale.

The stamp Joseph Rowntree left on the city of his birth is inestimable, indelible and highly visible: you see it (and smell the comforting aroma emanating from it) in the Haxby Road factory, in the infant school and village of his dreams in New Earswick, in the recently rebuilt Joseph Rowntree School (Jo-Ro to students), in the thriving Joseph Rowntree Theatre, in the Yearsley Road swimming baths, in the park he bestowed and which bears his name, in the firm's library building, on the site of the Pavement shop, in Top House in Bootham, in Bootham School, in the three Joseph Rowntree trusts administered by the Joseph Rowntree Foundation, and in the Joseph Rowntree Society.

The only thing missing, the only thing you cannot see, is the statue to York's greatest benefactor – you cannot see it because it is yet to be conceived. In 2012, when a campaign was launched to have a Joseph Rowntree statue erected in the city centre, the lame and inadequate response regarding a proposed site from a York Council blithely ignorant of their own city's heritage was, 'We are still in the early stages of determining the future use of this site and if this will or will not include public art.' Eight years later the site remains undeveloped – and there is still no statue.

The Last Will and Testament of Henry Isaac Rowntree

This is the last will and testament of me Henry Isaac Rowntree of Tanner's Moat in the city of York, cocoa manufacturer, made this twenty fifth day of February one thousand eight hundred and sixty eight. I bequeath all the furniture plate linen china glass pictures books and other household effects which shall at my decease be in the dwelling house wherein we shall there reside to my wife Harriet Selina Rowntree absolutely. I devise and bequeath all my real and personal estate whatsoever and wheresoever (except as herein before mentioned) unto my brothers John Stephenson Rowntree and Joseph Rowntree both of the city of York aforesaid Grocers their heirs executors administrators and assigns to hold the same upon the trusts herein after contained, that is to say upon trust (after payment of my debts funeral and testamentary expenses) to pay all the income arising from such real and personal estate unto my said wife during her life and after her death to hold the said trust estate upon trust for all my children if any who being a son or sons shall live to attain the age of twenty one years or being a daughter or daughters shall attain that age or marry if more than one in equal shares as tenants in common and if there shall be only one such child then for him or her in entirety and if there shall be no child of mine living at my death who being a son shall attain the age of twenty one years or being a daughter shall attain that age or marry then from and after the death of my said wife and such default or failure of children upon trust for such of my said brothers John Stephenson Rowntree and Joseph Rowntree and my sister Hannah Elizabeth Gillett wife of George Gillett of Banbury in the county of Oxford Banker as shall then be living and the child or children of such of them as shall then be dead in equal shares as tenants in common such child or children taking the share or shares only to which their his or her deceased parent or parents would have been entitled if living. I declare and direct that my said executors shall have full power under this my will to sell the said real estate and convert into money my said personal estate when and as they shall in the exercise of their discretion think expedient so to do and shall invest the proceeds arising from any such sale or conversion as aforesaid in their own names in or upon any such stocks funds shares debentures mortgages or other securities as they shall think fit and shall be at liberty to carry on my business of a Cocoa Manufacturer and any other trade in which I may be then engaged or to sell and relinquish the same when and as they shall think fit so to do. I devise all the real estates which shall be rested in me as trustee or mortgagee at the time of my decease to the said John Stephenson and Joseph Rowntree their heirs executors administrators and assigns upon the trust and subject to the equities affecting the same respectively. Lastly I appoint the said John Stephenson and Joseph Rowntree Executors of this my will and I hereby revoke all former wills and codicils by me at any time heretofore made. In witness thereof I have hereunto set my hand the day and year firstly hereinbefore mentioned.

Signed by the said Testator Henry Isaac Rowntree as and for his last Will and Testament in the presence of us who at his request in his presence and in the presence of each other have subscribed our names as witnesses.

Henry Isaac Rowntree
William Osborn, 3 Bootham Terrace, York
Joshua Rowntree, Solr. Scarborough

Proved at York the twenty fifth day of May 1883 by the affirmations of John Stephenson and Joseph Rowntree the Brothers the Executors to whom administration was granted.

The Testator Henry Isaac Rowntree was late of Tanners Moat in the City of York and of 22 The Mount in the suburbs of the same city Cocoa Manufacturer and died on the second day of May 1883 at No. 22 The Mount aforesaid.

Gross amount of personal estate £7537..16..1 No Leasholds extracted by Drawbridge & Rowntree Solrs. Scarborough.

Appendix II

Rowntree's Ongoing Heritage

July 2011 saw the opening of a new Nestlé UK archive created at the Haxby Road site. The launch was attended by Giles Naish who works at Nestlé in York and is the great-great-grandson of Joseph Rowntree. Over time many of the items have been exhibited at various places and at various events in the city; more than 37,000 photographs and over 100 hours of film have been digitised.

Items include a 1920s robot advertisement, a stained-glass window from one of the earliest Haxby Road offices, and a tin of Rowntree's cocoa found with the bodies of Scott of the Antarctic and the two remaining members of his team when they perished in March 1912. There is also a library of over 300 Nestlé films recently discovered in a wall cavity at the company's HQ in Croydon, original 1930s artwork for Black Magic advertising campaigns, a unique collection of hundreds of 1920s chocolate moulds and countless photographs, issues of *Cocoa Works Magazine*, catalogues and other documents:

> The state-of-the-art facility has been built to preserve documents, films, artefacts and artworks from all of Nestlé's UK sites, with climate and humidity controls to preserve its contents, and specially fitted lights designed to filter out harmful UV rays.

In 2012, a two-million-pound project, York's Chocolate Story, a visitor attraction celebrating the city's heritage – and future – in the confectionery industry opened in King's Square. It allows visitors to see at first hand the story of York's chocolate industry, with a strong emphasis on hands-on activities, anecdotes and memories from former employees of Rowntree's, Terry's and Craven's: visitors can have a try at making their own chocolate.

Supported by Nestlé, Kraft and Tangerine Confectionery, the attraction also works closely with modern chocolatiers in the city, thus demonstrating another facet of York's contemporary chocolate industry. The attraction is on two floors and includes a shop and restaurant.

A Rowntree Family Tree

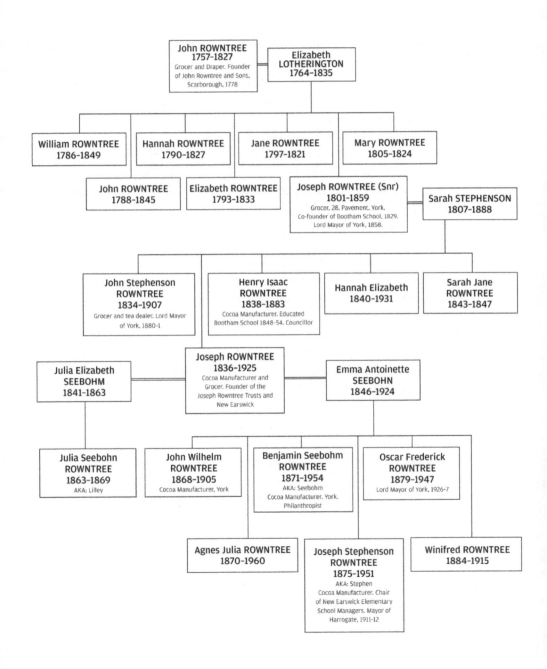

Appendix IV

A Rowntree Timeline

1725   Mary Tuke sets up her grocery business in York
1761   Joseph Fry establishes his cocoa business in Bristol
1778   John Rowntree (1757–1827) moves to Scarborough and opens a grocery shop
1779   Ackworth School, near Pontefract, opened
1796   William Tuke founds The Retreat
1801   **Joseph Rowntree I born**
1814   Joseph Rowntree I starts work in his father's grocery shop
1822   Joseph Rowntree I opens his grocer's shop at 28 Pavement, York
1824   John Cadbury opens his tea, coffee and chocolate shop in Birmingham
1826   Joseph Terry takes control of Terry & Berry in Bootham
1828   Casparus van Houten invents his hydraulic press and revolutionises chocolate making
1831   Joseph I elected improvement commissioner in York
Cholera epidemic arrives in York
Joseph establishes, with William Tuke, Bootham and the Mount schools
1832   Joseph marries Sarah Stephenson
Joseph founds the Friends' Provident Association with Samuel Tuke
1834   **John Stephenson Rowntree born**
1836   **Joseph Rowntree II born**
1838   **Henry Isaac Rowntree born**
1839   The railways come to York under George Hudson
1843   Thomas Craven establishes a confectionery business in York
1844   Joshua Rowntree born
1848   First day schools (later adult schools) opened by the Rowntrees in York
Joseph visits Ireland during the famine with sons Joseph II and John
1850   John Stephenson starts work at the shop in Pavement
1851   Joseph Terry employs 127 workers in St Helen's Square; Thomas Craven employs 123

1852   Joseph II starts at the Pavement shop
1854   George Cadbury apprentices at the Pavement shop
1855   Joseph I builds Penn House off Bootham
1859   **Joseph Rowntree I dies**
1862   Henry Isaac Rowntree buys the Tuke cocoa business
        Mary Ann Craven takes over the Craven family business
1864   Henry Isaac relocates his business to Tanner's Moat
        Joseph II begins a series of statistics-based studies on poverty
1867   Joseph Terry begins chocolate production at Clementhorpe
1868   John Wilhelm Rowntree born
1869   Joseph Rowntree II leaves Pavement and joins Henry Isaac at
        Tanner's Moat
1871   Benjamin Seebohm Rowntree born
1872   Arnold Stephenson Rowntree born
1873   Fry's produce the world's first Easter egg
1875   Henri Nestlé (a German) begins production of *farine lactée* in
        Switzerland
1876   Milk chocolate invented by Daniel Peter and Henri Nestlé
        Claude Gaget calls on Rowntree's, leading to the manufacture of
        fruit gums and pastilles
1880   Rowntree's buy a Van Houten press and launch Elect
1883   Henri Nestlé opens in London
        Henry Isaac Rowntree dies
1887   Joseph Rowntree II takes over at H. I. Rowntree
1888   Benjamin Seebohm Rowntree joins
1889   Charles Booth publishes *Life and Labour of the People in London*
1890   John and Violet Mackintosh start making toffees in Halifax
        Joseph buys land on the Haxby Road for the new factory
1896   Miss M. E. Wood appointed as girls' welfare officer
1897   Rowntree & Co Ltd formed
1898   Ebenezer Howard publishes what was to be renamed *Garden
        Cities of Tomorrow*
1899   Seebohm Rowntree publishes *Poverty: A Study of Town Life*
        Second Boer War starts
1900   Tins of chocolates sent to the troops in southern Africa by
        Rowntree's, Fry's and Cadbury's
1902   Work on New Earswick begins
        First issue of *Cocoa Works Magazine*
1903   Rowntree's implicated in the West Africa Cocoa Scandal

1904   Joseph Rowntree issues his *Memorandum* outlining the three Rowntree trusts
Rowntree's first doctor appointed
1905   Cadbury's launch *Dairy Milk*
Rowntree's launch workers' inflation-linked pension scheme
John Wilhelm Rowntree dies
1907   **John Stephenson Rowntree dies**
1908   The Rowntree trusts buy the *Northern Echo*
1909   Joseph Rowntree donates Yearsley swimming baths to the city
1911   Joseph made honorary freeman of the City of York
1915   Joshua Rowntree dies
1917   Lawrence Rowntree killed in action
1919   Milk chocolate bars supersede drinking chocolate as the main industry product
Cadbury's and Fry's merge
1921   Joseph Rowntree donates Rowntree Park to the city
1923   Seebohm succeeds Joseph as chairman
1925   **Joseph Rowntree II dies**
Mr York of York born

The Rowntrees and York Adult Schools

Members of the Rowntree family including Joseph and Henry, were, as we have seen, actively involved in setting up, helping run and teaching in the adult schools in York. Here are details of some of them. The thinking behind them – further education for the less well off – manifested itself again in Joseph's programme of free schools within the Haxby Road Rowntree's factory.

HOPE STREET FRIENDS SABBATH SCHOOL (1848–c.1869)

A Sabbath school for boys and young men aged 12 to 20 years of age, opened in Hope Street schoolroom in February 1848. Its founders were Richard Cadbury Barrow and Joseph Theobald. The surrounding area had already been canvassed for potential scholars and a number of local Friends volunteered as teachers. Its aim was 'to combine with secular education a practical knowledge of Scripture truth'. A library was initiated in 1848, a savings fund in 1850 and an annual tea held from 1851 onwards. Adult classes began around 1851 and in 1857 a separate adult school was formed in Lady Peckett's Yard. A Sabbath school for girls was established in 1856, with forty scholars on the register. By this point there were 140 on the register of the boys' school. The girls' school moved into its own premises in King's Staith in 1869.

YORK FRIENDS CENTRAL ADULT SCHOOL (1857–c.1927)

Adult classes, which began at the Sabbath school in Hope Street around 1851, broke away to form a separate adult school in November 1857. The school was set up in premises in Lady Peckett's Yard by John Stephenson Rowntree and his brother Joseph. It became known as the Central Adult School as more schools were opened in York from the 1890s onwards. There were thirty men on the register when it opened; by 1862 this had doubled to sixty. From the early 1870s, it was one of the largest schools in Yorkshire and averaged attendances of between 200 to 300. These figures include the branch schools at Leeman Road and Acomb, founded in 1891 and 1893 respectively.

York was one of the first schools to run a coffee cart company, from 1871. This was started by members of the Adult School Temperance Society on the initiative of Henry Isaac Rowntree (1838–1883). The school also had a library, a savings fund and a sick club (started in 1897). In 1875, a former Methodist Chapel in Lady Peckett's Yard was converted into new premises for the adult school. The property was owned by York Preparative Meeting. The school closed around 1927, when the property was let and York Friends Central Adult School Trust formed.

LEEMAN ROAD ADULT SCHOOL AND SOCIAL CLUB (1891)

Leeman Road was the site of the first branch school in York. A social club followed around 1895, and women's and children's classes a year later. In 1899, a sick club was also started for scholars. Its attendance figures were ninety-three men and thirty-four women in 1902. For the period 1908 to 1925, Quaker worship, with a full Preparative Meeting, was held at the school. The school closed around 1928 and its property was taken over by trustees. The premises suffered damage during the Second World War.

LAWRENCE STREET FRIENDS ADULT SCHOOL (1895–1977)

Set up by Friends in 1895, with thirty members, it was the third branch of the Central Adult School in the city. Women's and children's classes began the following year, and a sick fund was established in 1899. In 1903, it became part of the York and District Adult School Union.

BURTON LANE ADULT SCHOOL (1903–post 1930)

The Adult School in Burton Lane opened in 1903, after the formation of the York and District Adult School Union, and as part of its expansion drive in the city. The men's adult school closed in 1919, but classes for women continued until at least 1930.

YORK AND DISTRICT ADULT SCHOOL UNION (1903–post 1948)

Established in 1903 to bring together the four existing schools in York (Central, Leeman Road, Acomb and Lawrence Street) and to grow the adult school movement in the city. The union was a secular body and broke the direct links between the Society of Friends and the movement. However, many Friends continued to support it in a personal capacity and the union itself was presided over by Arnold Stephenson Rowntree (1872–1951). During 1903, new schools opened in Melbourne Terrace, Groves, Layerthorpe, South Bank and Northallerton and a school re-opened in Hope Street, site of the original Friends Sabbath School. The following year, new schools in Burton Lane and Hungate in York, Selby and Harrogate joined the union.

A sick club was also established. The expansion continued in 1905, with new schools in Bishophill and Holgate in York, and Cawood and Thirsk.

YORK AND DISTRICT ADULT SCHOOLS AND SOCIAL CLUBS LTD (1905–c.1985)
Formed in 1905 to administer the property of adult schools and their attached social clubs within the York and District Adult School Union. By now, the union included eighteen schools, twelve of which were in York itself. The first directors included Arnold Stephenson Rowntree, Theodore Hotham Rowntree and Francis Henry Rowntree.

NEW EARSWICK FRIENDS FIRST DAY SCHOOL (c.1917–c.1969)
A Friends first day school was set up soon after the Allowed Meeting was formalised in New Earswick in 1917 and had thirty-four members in 1918, rising to fifty-seven in 1929. Weekend lecture schools were held, addressed by such speakers as J. Edward Hodgkin and Edward Grubb, and study circles were held from 1918/19. The school was active until at least 1969.

YORK FRIENDS CENTRAL ADULT SCHOOL TRUST (1927–post 1949)
The trust was established in 1927 to manage the revenue from the property of the former Friends Central Adult School in York. The premises in Lady Peckett's Yard were let to Thomas Herd and the cottage to Frances West. The first trustees included Theodore Hotham Rowntree, Arnold Stephenson Rowntree and other local Friends. The trustees issued grants from the revenue, such as to York Preparative Meeting for the renovation of Bishophill Adult School. During the Second World War, the premises were requisitioned by the Army.

Other educational establishments associated with the Society of Friends in York include:

YORK FRIENDS BIBLICAL LIBRARY ASSOCIATION (1854–post 1946)
Following a conference held in York, a decision was taken in 1854 to create a Biblical library for the use of local Friends and a committee, comprising

Joseph Rowntree senior, John Ford and John Kitching, was appointed to acquire a set of recommended books from which the library developed. In 1985, a number of important seventeenth and eighteenth-century works from the library were donated to Leeds University Library to be added to the Birkbeck Library.

YORK BRITISH GIRLS' SCHOOL (1812–c.1891)

An elementary school for girls from poor families was set up in Newgate, York, in 1812 by a group of women Friends (Alice Horner, Priscilla Tuke, Mary Mildred, Martha Fletcher and Rebecca Fothergill). It was known as the British Girls' School and run on the Lancasterian system. It had around 100 pupils, who paid 1d per week to learn reading, writing and accounts. In 1816 the school moved to St Saviourgate. A new school to accommodate 150 girls was built on unused land on the site of the Friends' Burial Ground in Bishophill in 1829. Pupils from St Saviourgate moved to what became known as the Bishophill British Girls' School; it had only ninety pupils; this grew to 160 by 1844, but had declined to around 100 by 1870.

The school returned to Hope Street around this period and appears to have closed around 1891. The premises were retained by York Preparative Meeting.

I am grateful to Helen E. Roberts' *Researching Yorkshire Quaker History: A Guide to Sources* from which much of the above is taken. Compiled by Helen E. Roberts for the Yorkshire Quaker Heritage Project, it is published by The University of Hull Brynmor Jones Library (2003, updated 2007).

Further Reading

Allott, S., *John Wilhelm Rowntree 1868–1905*, York 1994.

Allott, S., *Friends in York – The Quaker Story in the Life of a Meeting*, York 1978.

Angell, S. W., (ed), *Quakers, Business and Industry Volume 4: Quakers and the Disciplines*, Longmeadow MA.

Armstrong, A., *Stability and Change in an English County Town – A Social Study of York 1801–51*, Cambridge 1974.

Backhouse, A., *The Worm-eaten Waistcoat*, York 2003.

Barker, P., (ed), *Founders of the Welfare State*, London 1984.

Batman, P., 'The Plight of Irish Potato Famine Migrants in Victorian Walmgate: A Study of Immigrants in Long Close Lane and Hope Street', *York Historian* Vol 36, 2019.

Bebb, P., *Shopping in Regency York*, York 1994.

Benson, G., *The City and County of the City of York* Vol 1, York 1911.

Bootham School Archive – Borthwick Institute of Historical Research, York.

Bootham School Register – Bootham Old Scholars Association, 2011.

Bradley, J., *Cadbury's Purple Reign*, Chichester 2008.

Brenner, J., *The Chocolate Wars: Inside the Secret Worlds of Mars and Hershey*, London 1999.

Brigend, J., *Topographical and Historical Description of the County of York*, London 1819.

Broadberry, S., 'The United Kingdom During World War I: Business as Usual?', www2.warwick.ac.uk, 2003.

Brown, S. K., *Bootham School York 1823–1973*, 1973.

Burg, J., *A Guide to the Rowntree and Mackintosh Company Archives 1862–1969*, York 1979.

Burkeman, S., *Pavement to Posterity – Joseph Rowntree and Why He Matters Now*, York 2001.

Butterill, C., 'The Temperance Movement in York 1830–1845', *York Historian* Vol 17, pp. 62–71, 2000.

Cadbury Bros Ltd., *Sweet-Shop Success: A Handbook for the Sweet Retailer*, Bournville.

Cadbury, D., *Chocolate Wars: From Cadbury to Kraft*, London 2010.

Cadbury Bros Ltd., *The Bournville Story*, Bournville.

Cann, J., *Rowntree Employees who Died in WWI*, York 2003.

Carr, C., *New Earswick Revisited*, York 2010.

Chamber., The Cravens, *The Chamber* Vol 8, pp. 2–4, 1980.

Chinn, C., *The Cadbury Story*, Studley 1998.

Chrystal, P., *Villages Around York Through Time*, Stroud 2010.

Chrystal, P., *York Then & Now*, Gloucester 2010.

Chrystal, P., *Chocolate: A History*, London 2011.

Chrystal, P., *York Industries Through Time*, Stroud 2012.

Chrystal, P., *A to Z of York History*, Stroud 2012.

Chrystal, P., *A History of Chocolate in York*, Barnsley 2012.

Chrystal, P., *Confectionery in Yorkshire Through Time*, Stroud 2012.

Chrystal, P., *Cadbury & Fry*, Stroud 2012.

Chrystal, P., 'The Rowntrees: Tales from a Chocolate Family' in Angell, S.W. pp. 169–189, 2017.

Chrystal, P., 'Lazenby & Son (York) Ltd – York's other confectionery company', *York Historian* Vol 36, 2019.

Chrystal, P., *A History of Sweets*, Barnsley 2020.

Clough, S. J., Girls' education in York in the nineteenth century, University of Hull, unpublished MA thesis, pp. 15, 44, 1986.

Coady, C., *The Chocolate Companion*, New York 1995.

Coe, S. D., *The True History of Chocolate*, London 1996.

Corley, T. A. B., 'How Quakers Coped with Business Success: Quaker Industrialists, 1860–1914', in D. J. Jeremy, (ed) , *Business and Religion in Britain*, Aldershot, 1988.

Dandelion, P., *The Quakers: A Very Short Introduction*, Oxford 2008.

Defoe, D., *A Tour Through the Whole Island of Great Britain*, London 1971.

Doncaster, P., *Memoir of John S. Rowntree*, London 1908.

Donnelly, J., *The Great Irish Potato Famine*, Gloucester 2002.

Drake, F., *Eboracum: or the Histories and Antiquities of the City of York*, York 1736.

Dronfield, E., 'Education in York' in Stacpoole, A., *The Noble City of York*, pp. 809–839, 1972.

Emden, P. H., *Quakers in commerce: a record of business achievement*, London 1939.

Evans, S., *Chocolate Unwrapped*, London 2010.

Feinstein, C. H., *York 1831–1981 – 150 Years of Scientific Endeavour and Social Change*, York 1981.

Feinstein, C. H., 'Populations, Occupations and Economic Development 1831–1981' in Feinstein.

Feuz, P., *Toblerone: 100 Years – The Story of a Swiss World Success*, Berne 2008.

Finnegan, F., *Poverty and Prostitution: A Study of Victorian Prostitutes in York*, Cambridge 1979.

Finnegan, F., *Poverty and Prejudice – A Study of Irish Immigrants in York*, Cork 1982.

Fitzgerald, R., 'Rowntree and Market Strategy, 1897–1939', *Business and Economic History*, Vol 18, pp. 45–58, 1989.

Fitzgerald, R., *Rowntree and the Marketing Revolution 1862–1969*, Cambridge 1995.

Freeman, M., *Quaker Extension c. 1905–1930: The Yorkshire 1905 Committee*, Borthwick Institute, University of York, 2008.

Freke, A., *J. S. Fry & Sons – A Rough Guide to the Family & The Firm*, Bristol 2010.

Fuller, L. K., *Chocolate Fads, Folklore and Fantasies*, Binghamton 1994.

Gillman, F. J., *The Story of The York Adult Schools from the Commencement to the Year 1907*, York 1907.

Goodall, F., 'Marketing Consumer Products before 1914: Rowntree's and Elect Cocoa', in R. P. T. Davenport-Hines, (ed), *Markets and Bagmen: Studies in the History of Marketing and British Industrial Performance 1830–1939*, London 1986.

Green, S. J. D., 'Social Science and the Discovery of a "Post-Protestant People": Rowntree's Surveys of York and their other Legacy', *Northern History* Vol 45, Issue 1, pp. 87–109, 2008.

Gumbley, E., *Bournville*, Market Drayton 1991.

Gutgemann, C., 'The Rowntree Family – On International Business and Contacts, Comparative Perspectives, and German Roots', www.rowntreesociety.org.uk

Hamish Fraser, W., *The Coming of the Mass Market 1850–1914*, London 1981.

Harrison, M., *Bournville: Model Village to Garden Suburb*, Chichester 1999.

Head, B., *The Food of the Gods*, London 1903.

Heer, J., *Nestlé 125 Years, 1866–1991*, Vevey 1991.

Hennock, E. P., 'Concepts of Poverty in the British Social Surveys from Charles Booth to Arthur Bowley' in M. Bulmer, *The Social Survey in Historical Perspective* pp. 189–216, 2011.

Henslowe, P., *Ninety Years On – An Account of the Bournville Village Trust*, Birmingham 1991.

Hillman, J., *The Bournville Hallmark – Housing People for 100 Years*, Studley 1994.

Hills, R., *The Inevitable March of Labour? Electoral Politics in York 1900–1914*, York 1996.

Hindley, D., *Advertising in Victorian England 1837–1901*, London 1972.

Howard, E. F., *Friends' Service in War-time*, London 1920.

Howard, E., *To-morrow – A Peaceful Path to Real Reform*, London 1898.

Jackson, E., Joseph Rowntree (1801–1859), *York Historian* Vol 23, pp. 40–63, 2006.

Jackson, P., How did Quakers Conquer the British Sweet Shop? *BBC News Magazine*, 20 January 2010.

Johnson, B. P., 'The Gilds of York' in Stacpoole pp. 447–610.

Joseph Rowntree Reform Trust., 'Trusting in Change – A Story of Reform', York 2004.

Joseph Rowntree Trust., 'The Joseph Rowntree Inheritance', York 2004.

Knapp, A. W., *Cocoa and Chocolate*, London 1920.

Knight, C. B., *M. A. Craven & Son Ltd: A History of the Company*, York 1948.

Kotey, R. A., (ed), 'Economics of Cocoa Production and Marketing', University of Ghana, Legon, 1974.

Lang, W. R., 'Terry's – Two Centuries of Chocolates', *Yorkshire Life*, May 1967.

Leak, A., *The Liberty of St Peter of York 1800–1838*, York 1990.

Lee, A. J., *The Growth of the Popular Press in England, 1855–1914*, London 1976.

Liptrot, K., 'Campaign for statue of Joseph Rowntree', *The Press*, 21 August 2012.

Martin, G. C., *The Adult School Movement: its Origin and Development*, National Adult School Union, 1924.

Mason, L., 'Poverty and Policy, The Rowntree Study of 1899' in White, E., *Feeding a City*, York, pp. 203–212, 2000.

Mason, L., *Sugar-plums and Sherbert: The Prehistory of Sweets*, Totnes 1998.

Masters, C. W., *The Respectability of Late Victorian Workers: A Case Study of York, 1867–1914*, Newcastle 2010.

Matthew, J., 'Science and Technology 1831–1981' in Feinstein, pp. 30–52.

Mayhew, H., *London Labour and the London Poor*, London 1851.

Meakin, B., *Model Factories and Villages: Ideal Conditions of Labour and Housing*, New York 1905.

Miller, M., *English Garden Cities – An Introduction*, Swindon 2010.

Milligan, E. H., *Biographical Dictionary of British Quakers in Commerce and Industry 1775–1920*, York 2007.

Morton, M. & F., *Chocolate – An Illustrated History*, New York 1986.

Moss, S., *Chocolate – A Global History*, London 2009.

Murphy, J., *New Earswick – A Pictorial History*, York 1987.

Needler, R., *The Needlers of Hull*, Beverley 1993.

Nuttgens, P., (ed), *The History of York*, Pickering 2001.

Nuttgens, P., 'Twentieth Century York' in Nuttgens, pp. 302–358.

Oddy, D., (ed), *The Making of the Modern British Diet*, London 1976.

Opie, R., *Sweet Memories*, London 2008.

Othick, J., 'The Cocoa and Chocolate Industry in the Nineteenth Century' in Oddy, pp. 77–90.

Packer, I., 'Religion and the New Liberalism – The Rowntree Family, Quakerism, and Social Reform', *Journal of British Studies* Vol 42, Issue 2, pp. 236–257, 2003.

Peacock, A. J., *York 1900–1914*, York 1992.

Peacock, A. J., *York in the Great War*, York 1993.

Pearce, W. T., (ed), *Fry's Works Magazine, 1728–1928*, Somerdale 1959.

Pickwell, W., *The Temperance Movement in the City of York: its Origins, Basis and Progress*, York 1886.

Pollard, F. E., *Bootham School, 1823 – 1923*, London 1926.

Raistrick, A., *Quakers in Science and Industry*, York 1950.

Robbins, K., *The Abolition of War: The 'Peace Movement' in Britain 1914–1919*, Cardiff 1976.

Roberts, H. E., 'Researching Yorkshire Quaker History: A Guide to Resources', Yorkshire Quaker Heritage Project, Hull 2007.

Richardson, P., *Indulgence*, London 2003.

Richardson, T., *Sweets: A History of Temptation*, London 2002.

Rogers, T., *A Century of Progress 1831–1931*, Bournville 1931.

Rowntree, B. S., *Poverty: A Study of Town Life*, London 1901.

Rowntree, B. S., *Poverty and the Welfare State*, London 1951.

Rowntree, B. S., *English Life and Leisure: A Social Study*, London 1951.

Rowntree, C. B., (ed), *The Rowntrees of Riseborough*, York 1940; rev'd E. M. Sessions 1979; rev'd 1982, 1986, 1996.

Rowntree, G., *The Reminiscences of George Rowntree*, privately published, 1936.

Rowntree, J., *Pauperism in England and Wales*, 1865.

Rowntree, J., *The Temperance Problem and Social Reform*, London 1899; facs. 2010.

Rowntree, J. S., *Friends' Boys' School, York: A Sketch of its History 1829–1878*, privately published, 1879.

Rowntree, J. W., *A History of the Adult School Movement*, Headley 1903.

Rowntree & Co., *Industrial Betterment at the Cocoa Works*, York 1905.

Rowntree & Co., 'The German Visit to New Earswick', *Cocoa Works Magazine*, Issue 89, pp. 721–724, 1914.

Rowntree & Co., *Works Rules 7th Edition*, York 1953.

Rowntree & Co., 'The Cocoa Works in War-time', *Cocoa Works Magazine*, York 1947.

Royle, E., 'Nineteenth Century York' in Nuttgens, pp. 244–301.

Rubinstein, D., *York Friends and the Great War*, York 1999.

Rubinstein, H., *The Chocolate Book*, Harmondsworth 1982.

Ryan, O., *Chocolate Nations – Living and Dying for Cocoa in West Africa*, London 2011.

Sheils, S., *Among Friends – The Story of the Mount School, York*, London 2007.

Simmons, J., (ed), *Cocoa Production*, New York 1976.

Sinclair, A., 'Eighteenth Century York', in Nuttgens pp. 215–243.

Smith, L., *Pacifists in Action: Experience of the Friends Ambulance Unit in the Second World War*, York 1998.

Smith, S., '"The City Itself is But Poor": Evidence for the Depressed State of York's Economy during the 1720s', *York Historian* Vol 21, pp. 21–25.

Spender, B., *Education, Learning and Community in New Earswick – An Enduring Rowntree Legacy*, York 2011.

Stacpoole, A., (ed)., *The Noble City of York*, York 1972.

Stapledon, O., 'Experiences in the Friends' Ambulance Unit' in Bell, J., (ed), *We Did Not Fight 1914 – 18: Experiences of War Resisters*, London 1935.

Strong, L. A. G., *The story of Rowntree*, unpublished manuscript, 1948.

Swann, A., 'Quakers and education: a study of Quakers and education in York 19th and 20th centuries', unpublished University of York thesis, 1967.

Tatham, M., (ed), *The Friends' Ambulance Unit 1914–1919 – A Record*, London 1919.

Taylor, W. B., 'The Emergence of a Confectionery Industry in York' in White, E., *Feeding a City – York: The Provision of Food from Roman Times to the Beginning of the Twentieth Century*, pp. 213–30, Totnes 2000.

Taylor, W. B., 'The Workshops and Manufactories of York in the Second Half of the Eighteenth Century', *York Historian* Vol 10, pp. 18–3, 1992.

Terry, J., *Terry's of York 1767–1967*, York 1967.

Tillot, P. M., (ed), *A History of the County of York – The City of York*, London 1961.

Vernon, A., *A Quaker Businessman – The Life of Joseph Rowntree 1836–1925*, York 1987.

Vipont, E., *Arnold Rowntree: A Life*, London 1955.

Waddilove, L. E., *One Man's Vision – The Story of the Joseph Rowntree Village Trust*, London 1954.

Wagner, G., *The Chocolate Conscience*, London 1987.

Walvin, J., *The Quakers – Money & Morals*, London 1997.

Ward, H., 'The Freemen of York' in Stacpoole, pp. 737–756.

Wheeler, E., 'The Early Days of Caleys', *Mackintosh Caley Magazine*, Vol 6, pp. 8ff, 1935.

Wheeler, H., *Half a Pound of Tuppenny Rice: Life in a Yorkshire Village Shop*, Stroud 1993.

White, E., *Feeding a City – York: The Provision of Food from Roman Times to the Beginning of the Twentieth Century*, Totnes 2000.

Whitworth, A., (ed), *Aspects of York*, Barnsley 2000.

Wild, A., *The East India Company Book of Chocolate*, London 1995.

Willis, R., *Portrait of York*, London 1972.

Wilson, V., *The Story of Terry's*, York 2009.

Wilson V., *The Best Years of Our Lives? Secondary Education in York 1900–1985*, York 2010.

Windsor, D., *The Quaker Enterprise: Friends in Business*, London 1980.

York Times: 'One Woman's Courage: The Story of Mary Ann Craven and the Progress of Cravens of York', Vol 1, Issue 3, pp. 26–29, 1961.

Websites

www.cocoareworks.co.uk – dedicated to the experiences of women who worked at the Rowntree's factory.

www.guise.plus.com – for the history and genealogy of the early Rowntree family.

https://www.hull.ac.uk/oldlib/archives – researching Yorkshire Quaker history.

www.jrf.org.uk – Joseph Rowntree Foundation.

jrtheatre.co.uk – Joseph Rowntree Theatre.

www.nationalarchives.gov.uk – The National Archives.

www. paulchrystal.com – Paul Chrystal.

www.quakersinyorkshire.org.uk – Quakers in Yorkshire.

www.quaker.org.uk – Quakers in Britain.

www.rowntreesociety.org.uk – The Rowntree Society.

www.theretreatyork.org.uk – The Retreat, York.

www.visityork.org – Visit York.

www.york.ac.uk/library/borthwick/ – Borthwick Institute of Archives, University of York.

www.yorkandthegreatwar.com/York-Casualty-Roll-of-Honour – York and the Great War.

www.york.gov.uk/leisure/Libraries/archives/ – York in the First World War

www.yorkquakers.org.uk – York Quakers.

Index

VILLAGES
AROUND
YORK
THROUGH TIME
Paul Chrystal

AMBERLEY

Acknowledgements

Thanks go to the following for their help and advice, and for being so generous with their photographs and postcards; the book would be much diminished without them. Any errors that remain are all mine.

Elaine Armstrong, *Joseph Rowntree School*; Jenny Bell, *Haxby Town Council*; Benjamin Brown; Chris Brown, *Brown's Nurseries*; Melvyn Browne; Carol Carr; Colin Carr; Betty Chapman; Anne Chrystal; Alan Clark; John and Dawn Gates; Julian Gladwin; Mark Harrison, *Huntington Methodist Church*; *Haxby Local History Group*; Chris Headley, *New Earswick Folk Hall*; David Ingham; Mr and Mrs Lockwood; Richard Ludlow, *Robert Wilkinson VC Primary School*; Ian Mason; Benjamin Mould; *Northern Scientific (York)*; John Pearson, *York Golf Club*; Carol Prangnell, *Headlands Community Primary School*; Foxton Ronald (Bill) Pulleyn; Nancy Pulleyn; Richard Pulleyn; Philip Roe; *Joseph Rowntree School*.

For Anne, Rachael, Michael and Rebecca

Front cover illustrations: Old Haxby in the late 19th century; the beautiful floral decoration which greets everyone entering the village from Wigginton. We have Jacob Verhoef, formerly of nearby Dutch Nurseries, to thank for this. Back Cover illustrations: Strensall army camp in the early 20th century; Strensall war memorial. Page 5 illustrations: Haxby Carnival parades in the 1960s and, in Briergate, with Minnie the Minx in the mid-1990s.

First published 2010, 2015

Amberley Publishing
The Hill, Stroud Gloucestershire, GL5 4EP
www.amberley-books.com

Copyright © Paul Chrystal, 2010, 2015

The right of Paul Chrystal to be identified as the Author of this work has been asserted in accordance with the Copyrights, Designs and Patents Act 1988.

ISBN 978 14456 5067 8 (print)
ISBN 978 14456 5068 5 (ebook)

All rights reserved. No part of this book may be reprinted or reproduced or utilised in any form or by any electronic, mechanical or other means, now known or hereafter invented, including photocopying and recording, or in any information storage or retrieval system, without the permission in writing from the Publishers.

British Library Cataloguing in Publication Data.
A catalogue record for this book is available from the British Library.

Typesetting by Amberley Publishing.
Printed in the UK.

Introduction

This is a revised edition of the bestselling *Villages Around York Through Time* with half of the photographs completely new and a revised and updated text.

With a highly photogenic and historical city like York on the doorstep it is easy to overlook the many picturesque villages surrounding the city – each of which has their own individual heritage and historical significance. This book tells the story of five of those villages in pictures and in words and demonstrates how their heritage lives on today, how it has changed or how it has disappeared. It does this by juxtaposing contemporary photographs with older ones so that each page gives a fascinating 'then and now' picture of the villages and the villagers. Informative captions complement the pictures and, in so doing, provide what is effectively a brief history of each village from earliest times up to today.

The five villages here to the north of York have a number of things in common: they are each close to or on the River Foss; they were all until fairly recently agricultural communities and they are now all pleasant and rewarding places to live in – largely but by no means exclusively for workers in York and further afield. They also have characteristics which are unique to themselves.

Haxby – politically a town but still very much a village at heart – is the largest of the five. *The York Herald* put it very well in 1911 when it said: 'Haxby is a peaceful spot and one can understand that the office workers of the city of York who live here find rest and refreshment in the sight of field and garden at the close of day'; the same can still be said today in 2015.

Likewise Wigginton – smaller than Haxby and often unfairly overlooked as a result – it has its own history and character which are well worth experiencing and exploring.

Strensall will always be associated with the military and the Army has certainly exerted a strong influence on the village – but there is more to it than that, as shown here by the intriguing histories of schools and churches. York Golf Club on the edge of the village provides another fascinating story.

Huntington too has a fine church, a fine Hall and some wonderful stories from down the ages involving royal pardons, cavalry officer chivalry, Zeppelin raids and bomber crashes.

New Earswick, much younger, is world famous for Sir Joseph Rowntree's innovative and visionary garden village, putting it at the forefront of early twentieth century social reform in Britain. Many of us pass through the village every day forgetting, I'm sure, just how important it is in the history of social welfare.

So, a book to be dipped into or read straight through as a glimpse of aspects of English history through five villages from the Norman Conquest to the early twenty-first century. It will interest, entertain and inform local resident and visitor alike and indeed anyone who has moved away from the area and needs a nostalgic reminder of what they remember and how far it has changed. If it inspires the reader to pursue their local history further then it will have achieved its aim.

A book like this is, of course, only as good as the photographs it contains. The majority have been provided by the individuals and institutions acknowledged above; their generosity ensures that the history of these villages lives on a little longer and can be enjoyed and researched by future generations.

So, a book to be dipped into or read straight through, giving a glimpse of aspects of English history reflected in and by these five fascinating York villages.

Paul Chrystal, June 2015

CHAPTER 1

Haxby & Wigginton

The Village Looking West

Looking down The Village in the 1970s with the Red Lion on the right. Up until the second half of the twentieth century the 2000 acres of the parish were almost totally devoted to agriculture with 1100 acres under cultivation and 800 as pasture at the time of enclosure in 1769. Parish registers from around 1850 show that of the 218 men recorded 144 were farmers or farm labourers and a further forty-six were in trades supporting farming such as blacksmiths and carpenters. The 1941 Farm Survey shows there to be no fewer than thirty-eight farms in and around Haxby including many, like the 107-acre Church Farm at what is now No. 44 The Village, in the centre of the village itself.

The Red Lion

The Red Lion appears on Ordnance Survey maps from the mid-nineteenth century. Bicycles and a horse and cart feature in this Edwardian photograph. Apart from its function as a hostelry the Red Lion also served as an eighteenth-century business centre: the meeting to finalise the construction of the two miles of the Foss Navigation north of Haxby was held here in May 1795 with a cost of £460 being agreed with contactors John Harrison & Co. The other old village tavern was, and still is, the Tiger Inn, first mentioned in records in 1840 when two cottages and a blacksmiths were converted to make it into a public house.

The Village Looking East Toward the Memorial Hall

Haxby's entry in Domesday: '6 carucates [the amount of land you could plough in one season], 1 bovate taxable, 4 ploughs possible. St Peter had it and has it. There are 7 villagers and 3 ploughs. Value pre 1066, 20 shillings, now 10 shillings.' The devaluation was a result of the destruction caused by William I's Harrying of the North – his scorched earth campaign to subdue revolting northerners. Brick and tile making was the other main industry here with five different brick makers recorded in 1881, all exploiting the rich clay seam under Haxby's topsoil. They were concentrated in North Lane and on Usher Lane and behind York Road (Nos 103 and 105 where the brick ponds, now fishing lakes, can still be seen). The 1881 census shows us eighteen people in Haxby in the brick and tile business, the most prominent of which was the Driffield family.

The Old Haxby Co-op

This gabled corrugated iron building in The Village opened in 1904 as the Haxby branch of the York Equitable Industrial Society selling groceries, drapery and boots. Celebrations for the opening included tea and a concert attended by 200 people. Further down at No. 50 was another idiosyncratic building: the left-hand section was the rate office where the Parish Clerk collected rates, doubling as a fish shop in the evening. The right-hand side of the building housed the village fire pump which was wheeled out once a year for a good polish.

The New Haxby Co-op

The second Co-op was in the building now occupied by the St Leonard's Hospice charity shop further down The Village from the earlier Co-op building. The older photograph shows the opening in 1920 of the new shop which was in turn replaced by the present supermarket in Ryedale Court in 1986. The Co-op grew out of The Rochdale Society of Equitable Pioneers – a group of twenty-eight weavers and other Rochdale workers – in 1844. At the time, increasing mechanisation was causing growing unemployment and poverty, so they opened their own shop selling food they could not otherwise afford. Over four months scraped together £1 each to raise £28 capital and on 21 December 1844, they opened their shop with a meagre stock of butter, sugar, flour, oatmeal and candles. After three months, tea and tobacco were added and they soon won a reputation for high quality provisions. By 1854, the co-operative movement had nearly 1,000 shops.

Wyre Pond

Little has changed in this pleasant corner of The Village since the original 1960s photograph. The scene of perennial flooding, partly due to all the rubbish that had been tipped into it over the years, it was filled in in the 1940s and re-excavated in 1977, flooding problems largely resolved as a result. Wyre is Anglo Saxon for pond thus indicating the pond's antiquity. Some of the cottages nearby date from around 1820.

The Green and Haxby Dames' School

Some of the houses here are early eighteenth century. Prominent among them are Prospect House, originally the farmhouse for Prospect Farm until the 1950s. The copper beech was planted to commemorate George V's Coronation in 1911. In the nineteenth century the Dames' School classroom and accommodation for the teachers were at Nos 65 and 67; fees were 3d per week. Dames' Schools were small private schools set up to provide working class children with a basic education before they were old enough to go to work. They were usually run by women who taught the children to read and write and other useful skills such as sewing. The quality of education varied enormously: some provided a good education, whereas others were little more than crèches.

The Haxby Cobbler

Thomas Johnson – the Haxby cobbler from 1922–40 – lived in Pear Tree Cottage – in the middle here on the right, now No. 31 The Village; before that he had lived at No. 57 The Village and at No. 4 West View Terrace. The business was run from premises next to the Primitive Chapel, demolished in 1930. This description from Alan Clark's book on Johnson gives some idea of living conditions around 1908: 'A single living room with a cupboard under the stairs for coal, a pantry with shelves off the living room with a tiny alcove housing a tap and sink. The toilet was outside at the end of the garden. Stairs off the living room gave access to the two bedrooms. With no gas or electricity the coal fire was needed to boil the kettle and make toast. An oil lamp provided lighting when required.'

Wortley House

Wortley House at No. 70 The Village, now Dr W. Inness' dental practice, on the far left, then Miss Jefferson's sweet shop at No. 64 The Village, now Paddyfields Cantonese restaurant (Grant's restaurant before that). Today's picture shows the fine building that is Wortley House: it has the distinction of being the only building in the village not to have surrendered its railings for the war effort – they were concealed behind thick hedging at the time of collection. The house has long had a public health connection: before becoming a dental practice it was the home and surgery of Dr A. W. Riddolls between 1932 and 1960; pre-NHS consultation charge was 1s 6d (7½p).

Bentley's

Village grocer's shop, taken around 1905 with North Villa next door. It later became Asquith's and in the Second World War it was W. M. Thompson, grocers of York. It eventually became Foxton Bell's Central Garage and Showroom before demolition to make way for Clark House and the £1m Haxby Shopping Centre. The garage was a Ford and Austin main dealer; contemporary advertisements tell us they offered: 'engine reconditioning using modern equipment, high pressure washing and lubrication, recellulosing and body repairs.' Abel's Farm was also sold to make way for the arcade; nearby Abelton Grove is named after Mr Abel. The new photograph shows Haxby's other shopping arcade: Ryedale Court further down The Village.

Fish and Blitz
Walker's Fisheries 1938; now
55 The Village. The children
are (l-r) Mavis, Jack and Joyce
Walker. Walker's offered: 'All
kinds of Wet Fish, Kippers,
Finnan Haddocks etc; Fresh
supplies daily – all orders
promptly attended to'. In 1945
Walker's had an unfortunate
visit from the Luftwaffe
when a lone fighter strafed
The Village with cannon fire,
narrowly missing a bus and
shattering the shop window
– no one was hurt. It is now
a pizza takeaway next door
to the current fish and chip
shop, Miller's.

North Lane

North Lane and South Lane were back lanes designed to give access to the farms along The Village. Entries in the Liberty of St Peter petty court sessions court book give some idea of just how dominant agriculture was in the village:

> Thomas Plowman of Haxby, farmer and John Whitwell of Tadcaster, grocer v John Halton of Haxby, husbandman. Rent in arrears, property neglected and deserted, so Plowman given possession 3 Oct 1835.
>
> Thomas Plowman of Haxby, gentleman, Thomas Hodgson of Towthorpe, gentleman, and Samuel Wilkes-Wand v William Wailes of Skeldergate, York, innkeeper. Trespassing in pursuit of game 28 Nov 1835.

St Mary's Church

The new photograph shows St Mary's church; this was built in 1878 in Gothic style at a cost of £1800 on the site of the chapel of Our Lady which had burned down and is pictured here in a very early photograph. St Mary's has a single bell on which *'fili dei miserere mei 1621'* is inscribed. Initially the original church had no burial licence and there are stories of corpses being 'casually lost', as happened to a certain Thomas Westeby whose body, on the way to being buried at Strensall Church, 'by reason of the great distance and the badness of the ways' fell into the River Foss. The earlier chapel owned a number of properties for which the rent was payable in hens and eggs.

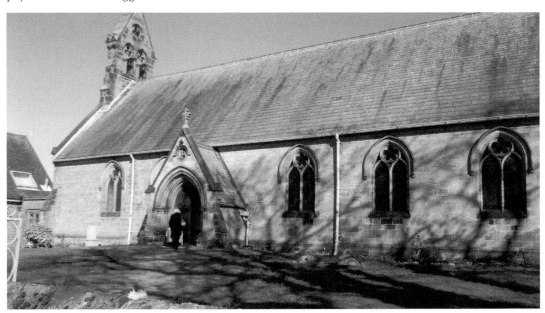

The Roundabout

Widd's Farm was near to where Westow House is now. Westow was originally a private residence; Harrowells solicitors occupied it in 1985 at the time the adjacent Ryedale Court shopping centre was built and opened. Harrowells was established, in York, in 1908 and now has around 130 staff still based mainly in York with the subsidiary offices in Clifton Moor and Haxby. A tree was planted at the roundabout for the coronation of Edward VII in 1903. The farm on the corner of York Road and The Village was imaginatively called York Road Corner Farm, demolished in 1929 to make way for Norbryte House which accommodated the Post Office.

The Post Office

The Post Office on the corner was very much a general store selling, amongst other things, hardware and crockery, fancy drapery, fresh fruit, drugs and patent medicines, corn, offals, etc. Adverts from the 1950s boast: 'We sell all the best makes of chocolate and sweets' and exhort us to 'Just give us a trial; we can satisfy you' and 'Remember the resident traders first' – a sentiment that deserves to be echoed more than ever today.

Haxby Board School

The first school in Haxby was where the Tiger is now; this was superseded by the 1851 school: The Church of England School 'for the children of the labouring poor of Haxby' – sixty boys and eight girls; staff comprised the head, a sewing mistress and a pupil teacher; this is now St Mary's Hall in North Lane. The Board school opened in 1876; it cost £2,200 and had fifty-three pupils on roll. The Revd Hodgkinson, vicar of Haxby around 1851, was one of the early fundraisers. Early school governors though, seem to have missed the point completely; this from the day book for 8 November 1878: 'The registers have not been marked since Monday for the following reason, viz on Tuesday members of the board ... came to the school and with sticks violently drove the children, some out of the school, and others from getting in.' The school is now the Memorial Hall dedicated to the memory of the Haxby fallen in the World Wars: twenty-seven in the First World War (3 per cent of the population) and nine in the Second World War.

Haxby ARP and First Aid Post 1941
Nurses and first-aiders outside Haxby Hall. Mavis, Jack and Joyce Walker make another appearance here on the back row while Dr Riddols can be seen on the front row in the centre. The modern picture shows a mid-90s photograph of girls at the Barbara Taylor School of Dancing in the Memorial Hall.

Tiller Girls in Haxby

Women's Land Army girls on the binder on the Lazenby farms (The Grange House and Grange Farm on Crossmoor Lane). The Grange comprised 102.5 acres split roughly 50/50 between arable and pasture. The main crop was wheat; 180 chickens, 8 horses, 24 cattle, 3 pigs and 6 sheep comprised the livestock. The farms were also home to a wartime searchlight battery manned by the Haxby and Wigginton Home Guard commanded by Tom Pulleyn, local builder. Their HQ was in the then First World War Memorial Hall in South Lane and training was at Strensall Camp. Between 14 February 1941 and 23 September 1943 there were eighteen air raid warnings in Haxby and six major incidents in the area.

Hurricane Hits Haxby

Salute the Soldier Week (a national war effort fundraising effort) May 1944 with personnel from 60 Maintenance Unit RAF and a repaired Hawker Hurricane on the village green. This crashed aircraft recovery unit was stationed at Shipton and repaired mainly Halifax bombers; some of the personnel were billeted in Haxby. They also requisitioned Wigginton Recreation Hall (a wooden building on the site of the current hall built in 1984) and held Friday night dances which were very popular with locals and servicemen and women from Strensall and York; French troops from Elvington and Canadian airmen stationed at Eastmoor near Sutton. RAF film shows were shown on Wednesday nights.

The modern shot shows a contemporary, albeit fictional, threat to world peace. This entry from the Scarecrow Festival is Darth Vader, the terrifying cyborg commander of the brutal Galactic Empire in *Star Wars*.

Haxby Hall Vandalised

A good example of 1960s planning vandalism where a perfectly fine building was replaced with the dullest construction imaginable, in this instance to serve as a home for fifty-two elderly people and ambulance station in 1965. The original Grade II listed building situated in 22 acres was built in 1790; an unusual, striking feature was the glass cupola over the stairwell. Notwithstanding, it was demolished in 1963 despite local protests. It had started life as a private residence and was used up to 1853 as the Revd John Heslop's Classical and Mathematical Academy for 'Sons of Gentlemen of High Respectability; £50 pa including washing.' In the Second World War it was requisitioned to accommodate evacuees from Hull and Middlesbrough as well as being the local First Aid centre and HQ for the ARP (see page 22).

Ralph Butterfield County Primary School 1954 and 1964

The school was named after and honours Ralph Butterfield OBE, a prominent North Yorkshire educationalist who also distinguished himself at Passchendaele where he won the Military Cross. The staff are (*l-r*) Mr Basil Hurdus (Head); Miss Smith; Miss Curry; Miss Francis; Mrs Hollinrake; Mr Jack Fall (later Head at Headlands). Basil Hurdus was a Headmaster in Haxby for twenty-six years until his retirement in 1964. At its opening the school accommodated 200 children in five classrooms at a cost of £30,684 with a further £2,650 for furniture. In 1965 pupil numbers were 242, 7 of whom passed the eleven plus that year. In 1970 a growing population led to the building of the Usher Lane annexe (which in 1974 became Oaken Grove School, closed in 2002). The lower photograph shows the opening of the school's swimming pool in July 1964 by international swimmer Pauline Clarkson from Haxby.

Whiteland Cottages, Usher Lane

Named after one of the four pre-enclosure arable fields in the village (the others were Lund, Mill and York). These Tarran prefabs went up after the Second World War; they were finally defabricated in the 1990s and replaced with the sheltered housing seen below. Over four million homes were needed at the end of the war to replace bombed stock and to house the record two million or so couples who had married during the war. £150m was voted to build prefabs such as these and by July 1948 160,000 had been snapped together at a cost of £216m. There were a number of different designs, the most common being the Arcon Mark V; the Airoh was made from left over aircraft materials. All had two bedrooms, fitted fridge, heated handrail, coal fire with back boiler, inside toilet, fitted wardrobes.

Swarthdale 1977

In 1977 Swarthdale, in what used to be known as Usher Park, ended at No. 30 (on the right here). Beyond was open countryside which was only later developed into the long loop road it is now, merging into Usher Park Road. The older photograph shows Alan Chapman of number 28; his widow, Betty, still lives there. Goland Cottages are opposite on the other side of Usher Lane – named after nearby Goland Dike, a tributary of the River Foss. During the Second World War a Nellie Howes lived in a railway carriage parked in Usher Lane. The lane was named after the Usher family who lived near the junction with Station Road; Windmill Lane got its name from the brickwork's windmill which stood where the junction is now with Usher Lane; it was demolished in 1950. Swarthdale may be named after the village of Swarthdale on Swarth Beck near Over Kellet, Carnforth in Lancashire, or after Swarthdale Springs south of Hovingham. Then again, it may just have been made up...

Swarthdale in Snow

The only real differences today are the trees and mature gardens you would expect after 30 years. Usher Park is symptomatic of the house building boom in Haxby and Wigginton in the 1970s and 1980s to accommodate the increasing population. In Haxby alone it grew from 3,783 in 1971 to 9,064 in 1981 (it had been 711 in 1901) – a 240 per cent increase in 10 years. Apart from housing, the growth led to two new schools – Oaken Grove and Headlands – an extension at St Mary's, a Roman Catholic church (St Margaret Clitherow) and other essential shops and services.

Park Estate

Built in 1922 this is now The Avenue; the new photograph shows the range of architectural styles of the houses on the development. In the inset we can see builders from Pulleyn's at work. They are (*l-r*) Francis John Pulleyn, Mr Copley, Stanley Pulleyn and Verdun Pulleyn. John Pulleyn started the building business; his son, Francis John, set up the family brickworks. Nearby on York Road is The Old House where Tom Holtby lived after his retirement from stagecoach driving, forced due to the advent of the railways. He had a horse breaking business in Minster Yard, York and then invested in a brickyard in Haxby. This, like his other ventures in banking (lost over £800) and newspaper ownership (lost £600), was financially disastrous for him although he still managed to leave £3,000 to the village on his death in 1863.

Haxby Gates Crash

British Railways Riddles 'Standard' 9F 2-10-0 locomotive No. 92220 *Evening Star* rushing past Haxby Road signal box (demolished 1988) as the 08:23 Scarborough Spa Express, Sunday 14 August 1983. Haxby's station, where Pulleyn's garage now is on Station Road, opened in 1845; it was closed to passengers in 1930 but remained open for freight and coal for some years after. Goods included boxes of fish, Lyon's cakes, calves, animal feedstuffs, straw, grain and soldiers on the way to Strensall. *The York Herald* of 12 December 1864 carried a report of a fatal accident enquiry. Thomas Hawcroft, stationmaster at Haxby, was run over by a wagon while trying to help his porter and later died after his foot had been amputated. The lower image shows the aftermath of a rail accident when, on October 28th 1968, a DMU from York to Scarborough collided with a car on the crossing. The train driver, George Craven, was trapped in his cab for forty minutes. There were no other injuries, just lots of glass and shock.

Wigginton's Mill and the Parish Bull

This is looking down The Village from Wigginton pond with Manor Farm on the right, about 1910. Mill Lane is named after the mill that stood on Sutton Road opposite the Shipton Road junction, now the site of Windmill House and the Windmill Trading Estate. It features on the 1769 enclosure map. The Windmill public house was next door, demolished in 1930. In 1906 revenues from the land in Wigginton amounted to £11.00; 6s 8d of which was paid for tithe, 30s to 10 deserving poor and the rest for the services of the parish bull who performed in the Bull Field, now Mill Lane playing field. In 1791 the fee per cow was 1s; the last bull came and went in 1952.

Wigginton and the Harrying of the North

Further down the road about 1895. Wigginton's entry in Domesday reads as follows: 'In Wigginton there is one curucate, taxable, which one plough can plough, Saex Frith the Deacon (from which Saxford Way) held this, now St Peter has it. It was and is waste; there is underwood here.' The 'waste' was due to the devastation caused by William I's soldiers in the Harrying of the North (see page 8). The reference to St Peter indicates that the church owned the land. Around 1777 local church fees included: burial inside the church 10s (50p), 10d for burial in the churchyard with a coffin, 5d without; wedding licence 10s, banns half a crown [12½p]. The population in 1801 was 260, 340 in 1901 and 3,714 in 2001.

F. R. Pulleyn Wigginton Garage

Foxton Ronald (Bill) Pulleyn went into the motor trade at age fourteen and by the time he retired he had three garages: one in Haxby which is still thriving under Richard Pulleyn, one in Wigginton and one on Wigginton Road. He set up the first of these in 1958. The photographs show an impressive display of Morris motorcars in 1960 and some early Minis. The children posing for the photograph are Barbara and Richard Pulleyn with next door neighbour, Margaret Cass. Behind the garage was a blacksmith's worked by Victor Pulleyn who previously drove mule trains in the army in Mesopotamia (modern-day Iraq) during the First World War; a corn mill and steam engine also operated there.

Wigginton School and the Relief of Mafeking

One of the finest buildings in Wigginton. Boys entered through the kitchen, girls at the other end of the building; a wall down the middle of the yard segregated girls and boys at playtime. This is the second school in the village, the first having been opened in 1835 by Miss Anne Dealtry in Rectory Cottage, close to Rosevale nursing home. Attendance was a chronic problem, described in 1876 as 'sadly irregular and neglected' due largely to 'potatoeing and haymaking' and, on one occasion in May 1900, the Relief of Mafeking. Poor attendance resulted in poor academic standards. The second school, pictured here today, was opened in 1904 and was eventually replaced by the present school in Westfield Lane in the late 1960s. The older pictures show a rather poignant circular distributed to local schools recommending prayers suitable during the First World War years.

NORTH RIDING COUNTY COUNCIL EDUCATION COMMITTEE.

Prayers for use in Schools in time of War.

I.

ALMIGHTY FATHER, we Thy children pray Thee to help our country in this time of war. Defend our sailors, soldiers and airmen, and those of our Allies, in all dangers and grant them victory and good success. Comfort the wounded, the sorrowful, and the sick. Teach us to be loving and unselfish at home, and grant us the blessing of peace in Thy good time, through Jesus Christ our Saviour. Amen.

II.

O LORD God of Hosts, stretch forth, we pray Thee, Thine Almighty Arm to strengthen and protect the sailors, soldiers and airmen of our King, and those of our Allies, in every peril, both of land and sea and air, especially our own fathers, brothers and friends, and others who have gone forth from this place. Shelter them in the day of battle, let Thy Holy Angels watch about them, and grant that in all things they may serve as seeing Thee Who art invisible, through Jesus Christ our Lord. Amen.

III.

LOOK, we beseech Thee, O Lord, upon the people of this land; and grant that in this time of trouble they may walk worthy of their Christian profession. Give to us Thy children grace to fulfil our daily duties with a sober diligence, and keep us from all unkindness in thought, word and deed; through Jesus Christ our Lord. Amen.

IV.

For Evening Prayers.

O GOD, Who never sleepest, and art never weary have mercy upon those who watch to-night; on the sentry, that he may be alert; on those who command, that they may be strengthened with counsel; on the sick, that they may obtain sleep; on the wounded, that they may find ease; on the faint-hearted, that they may hope again; on the light-hearted, lest they forget Thee; on the dying, that they may find peace; on the sinful that they may turn again—and save us, O good Lord. Amen.

NOTE.

One or more of Nos. I., II., III. may be used each morning and evening No. IV. is for evening use only.

Wigginton Carnival and a Zeppelin Raid

An annual May Day event, this shows maypole dancing just before the Second World War; the May Queen was Betty Donald, the daughter of the then rector. Wigginton, like Haxby, had a thankfully quiet time during the World Wars, with the exception of two notable occasions. The first war saw a zeppelin bomb the B1363 nearby and the second brought refugees, including a group of children fortunate enough to have escaped the Channel Islands shortly before the German invasion, chaperoned to Wigginton by a Madame de Routon. A Halifax bomber crashed into a field where Windsor Drive now is and an RAF lorry ran over and killed a local tramp, Richard Dickinson, nicknamed Dick Dick, famous for his bad temper and wooden leg.

Brown's Nursery

The Browns run the Nursery in Corban Lane; they are the fourth generation of nurserymen in the Brown family in the village, their original premises being in Mill Lane, close to where the Sunnyside Farm Shop is today. The old photograph shows Chris Brown's great grandfather setting off for market in 1911 with a cartload of cauliflowers and rhubarb. The new photograph shows their extensive nursery on Corban Lane today.

Jack Gates, Butcher

The inset photograph, taken around 1930, shows Jack Gates' butchers and house on Mill Lane with the white-roofed pig sties top left; the other buildings housed the pigs and cattle before slaughter and then sale in the shop. Brown's original nurseries were to the left of the sties; around that time Mr and Mrs Brown lived in a railway carriage on the site of their future house. The cottages on the other side of the road to the right were demolished in the '60s to make way for the elderly peoples' bungalows there today; the land in the foreground is now Westfield Grove. The new photograph shows nearby Moorlands, resplendent with rhododendrons in the early 2000s.

CHAPTER 2

Strensall

Approach to Village, Strensall

Coming in to Strensall

Taken at the end of the nineteenth century, this photograph shows that the horse and cart leaving the village was already in open country on the way to Haxby or Wigginton. Today, there are houses to the right and Robert Wilkinson Primary School on the left. Early records tell us that of the 2,908 acres 804 were at one point given over to arable land (mainly for corn and potatoes), that many of the inhabitants worked at the tannery and that in the nineteenth century the other industry was pottery, there being two potteries in the village (Strensall and Britannia). *Baines's Directory* of 1823 has eleven farmers or yeomen out of a listing of twenty-six gentry, tradesmen, retailers and farmers while *Bulmer's 1890 Directory* has twenty-three farmers out of a total listing of fifty-nine tradesmen and professionals. The new picture shows the way into the village today from Sheriff Hutton, by foot and by road.

Strensall.

Looking Down The Village in the 1920s

Looking towards the Sheriff Hutton junction with The Ship Inn (built 1819) on the right. There's a blacksmith on the immediate right with some of his repairs parked outside the forge. Creaser's – one of the three village stores – is visible beyond The Ship. The small house on the left was one of the five Poor Houses – now demolished and replaced by the ubiquitous Tesco in the new photograph. The Ship was a popular watering hole for travellers on the Foss Navigation and workers at the tannery behind. Another grocer's, Hodgson's, was over the road from where the newer photograph was taken.

Doctor in a Trap

Dr Haslam and a lady around 1910 in their pony and trap on their way out somewhere. Soon after this photograph was taken Dr Haslam swapped the trap for a car – one of the first in Strensall. His surgery was on Station Road and he practiced under the title of Physician, Surgeon and Public Vaccinator. Today the modern picture shows the village has a twelve-doctor practice in Southlands with six practice, eight community nurses and other health professionals serving 17,000 patients from Strensall, Huntington, Dunnington and Stamford Bridge. The practice has evolved out of a single-handed practice which opened in the 1930 and now covers an area of about 200 sq. miles.

Creaser's

Three of the staff posing with the delivery horse and cart around 1880. Today, the site is occupied by Strensall Library. York Cooperative Society later took over the premises after Creaser's. As in Haxby, the petty court session reports illustrate the dependence on agriculture:

> William Carr of Strensall, woodman v Henry Dowker, gentleman. Illegally shooting over Towthorpe Common 1 Apr 1837.

> John Blanchard, gentleman v William Bosomworth, cabinet maker, both of Strensall. Trespassing in pursuit of game 3 Jun 1837.

Playing in the Street

Taken at the turn of the century when the main road was still relatively safe to play in. The boys are wearing the sailor suits very fashionable at the time. The Ship Inn and Creaser's are clearly visible; the pub named through its association with the Foss Navigation nearby. James Green was the landlord in 1890. The Navigation brought much trade to the immediate area and fostered local business; this in turn had a marked effect on the population in the years after it opened in 1797. In 1801 the population was 297; in 1811 494; in 1901, 581; in 2001, 3,815.

Sheriff Hutton Junction

Taken about 1910 this shows Leek's, the other village store and more children wandering around nonchalantly in the road. Note the Cadbury Cocoa advert in the window. Today the building is occupied by a branch of Boots as the new picture clearly shows. On the left of the Sheriff Hutton road around 1850 were Poor Houses at Goldsmith Closes owned by the Trustees of the Poor while further on near the road junction leading to Sutton on the Forest was a tile and brickworks; we know that pancheons (earthenware bowls) were shipped down the Foss Navigation to York in 1846.

The Post Office

In the 1930s at what is now No. 155 The Village and occupying part of an eighteenth-century house. The modern picture (*inset*) shows the left-hand doorway to have been bricked up – surplus to requirements when it became a private house again. Today's Post Office is over the road from here (see page 39), moving there in the 1940s into a building which had been a grocer's since 1891. The Croft family were the last to run the post office in the old building, staying on there to run a stationery shop for some years. The girls with the skipping ropes (page 39) were Edie Palister, Jessie Frost and Minnie Belt. Below, bikers revving up outside the barracks in the lower picture.

St Mary's Church

The first church here was Norman, completed in 1150. Made from Tadcaster stone it was unflatteringly described as 'rude and massive' with oak pews. Rebuilt in 1801 it failed to impress the then vicar, the Revd John Hodgkinson who found it 'entirely wanting in architectural or ecclesiastical style'. He got his chance to remedy when he was heavily involved in another rebuilding in 1863. Sir Gilbert Scott designed what is the present church in the Early Decorated style costing £1523 12s 6d raised by subscription. A new vestry and floor were added in 1974.

On the March, Strensall Camp.

Blowing Up Your Trumpet

Strensall's association with the Army began in 1876 when parts of Common and Lord's Moor were bought for military training for £300,000. Initially it was a camp for about 8,000 men living under canvas until the present permanent buildings were erected in 1880. A number of soldiers died from bronchitis and pneumonia as a result of the cold and damp conditions. The rifle ranges (part of which can be seen in the contemporary shot) were set up at a cost of £3,800. The commandant in 1890 was Major General N. Stevenson. Today 160,00–170,000 thousand troops pass through the barracks and the adjacent firing ranges every year on various training activites. The IRA detonated a bomb under a barrack hut here in the 1970s; fortunately it was unoccupied at the time and the terrorists succeeded in only blowing up the instruments of the army band.

STRENSALL CAMP, NEAR YORK,

The Impact of the Army

The impact of the camp on the village was obviously significant. *Bulmer's Directory of 1890* lists the following local professionals, tradesmen and companies directly associated with the military: Armstrong & Sons, Army contractors; George Bowles, camp coffee house; R. P. Culley & Co. Army contractors and messmen to camp stores; Rev. J.B. Draper, acting chaplain; William B. Cunliffe, photographic artist, Strensall Camp; William Taylor, camp livery stables; Richard Tinson, camp postman.

The Suez Canal Village Hall

Originally an army hut on the banks of the Suez Canal this amazingly resilient building was painstakingly taken to bits and shipped back to Strensall from Egypt in 1920; once rebuilt it provided the village with its popular social venue for the next sixty years. It was demolished in 1980 and replaced by a house at 9 York Road ('Woodhurst'). The new village hall is in Northfields as shown in today's photograph (*inset*)– highly functional, architecturally challenged, although it must be said that it does bear a vague resemblance to the old Egyptian hut. It was built in 1989 at a cost of £209,000. The new village hall is in Northfields. The war memorial is in the modern picture to the left.

Ma West's Cafe

This was set up as a kind of social centre for the soldiers from Queen Elizabeth Barracks opposite; it provided a change for anyone who may have wanted to escape from mess life and go somewhere to get a cup of tea, perhaps, in a more relaxed environment. It followed the tradition of a colonel's widow who set up a small cafe in a tent nearby in the 1880s for the troops. As its popularity grew the tent was replaced by a series of ever larger wooden huts. No alcohol was permitted and temperance type lectures were given in the evenings. A twenty-first century equivalent of sorts, a Chinese take-away, now occupies the site. The Half Moon Inn is in the new picture.

The Manor House, Strensall

Manor House

Also known as The Hall, this was lived in in 1851 by a seventy-year-old widowed farmer John Creser (ancestor of the grocer's?) with his two daughters, Mary and Maria, and two sons, Matthew and George. The house came with 61 acres of land, 23 of which were pasture and 37 arable. The original manor house was moated and dated from 1649, rebuilt in 1757. There was a smithy nearby in Coney Garths; other streets thereabouts included Hall Inge, Pudding Park, Palling, Butt Close and Long Wall Butt.

Strensall Military Occupation
Two more old photographs showing the military occupation of Strensall in the early days of the twentieth century.

The Old Clubhouse Opens

The original clubhouse was built in 1907; this splendid photograph shows the opening ceremony on 17 May with Sir Leslie Rundle doing the honours. York Golf Club had been founded in 1890 and was originally at the Knavesmire. The fact that it was public land caused problems as cows, horses and other livestock grazed on land that was also frequented by nursemaids with their perambulators. One of the early club rules was indicative of the hazards: 'Members are to refrain from striking while people or cattle are in the way'. To avoid accidents to man and beast the Club moved to what was army land in Strensall in 1904.

'Mak All t' Trains Cum t' York.'

The first train to pass through Strensall was on 7 July 1845 travelling from York to Scarborough via Haxby. George Hudson, Railway King, was on board – no doubt very proud as it was he who had urged Robert Stephenson to 'mak all t' trains cum t' York.' That famous day ended with dinner for 700 in York. Close to the station was the now demolished brick works (the Littlethorpe Brick and Tile Company) from which millions of bricks were shipped by rail. As with all change, the railways had its detractors, particularly at the Scarborough end where the concern was that 'a great influx of vagrants and those who had no money to spend' would ruin the resort. 'The novelty of not having a railway will be (Scarborough's) greatest recommendation.' This old photograph is from 1914; as in Haxby the station closed in 1930 but was re-opened for military use in the Second World War. Three trains a day passed through the village on the way to Scarborough and back to York in 1945. The fare from York to Strensall was 6d in 1884. The new photograph shows a somewhat less romantic modern train passing the other crossing at Breck's Lane.

St Mary's Hall

The old Methodist Chapel in Church Lane built in 1823. Scrubbed up and in Sunday best this Sunday school class look all look a bit glum. A new (the present) chapel was built in The Village in 1895 as the congregation had outgrown this one, although the old chapel was still in use until 1921 for special events. The railway continued to exert an influence on the village: there was a restaurant in the station by 1905 and mail was delivered twice daily at 6.00 a.m. and 3.50 p.m. There was a post office at the camp as well as the one in the village; soldiers also benefitted from a Money & Telegraph Savings Office and an Annuity and Insurance Office. The new photograph shows the somewhat dilapidated but brightly painted chapel today.

The Joiner's Shop and the Tannery

Carpenters posing during a job in the village, possibly connected with local agriculture or with construction. The modern photograph shows what remains of another Strensall's industries: tanning. Opened in 1806 as Hirst & Sons the tannery was able to benefit from the Foss Navigation which had opened as far as Strensall in 1797, with the extension to Sheriff Hutton Bridge begun in 1801. The Navigation passed conveniently nearby for the delivery of materials such as bark and lime and the despatch of finished goods. *Baines Directory 1890* lists three boot and shoemakers (including another Creaser) and a tanner, William Walker, at the tannery ('oak bark tanners of shaved and dressed hides'). Later owned by Leeds tanners Charles F. Stead & Co. it employed fifty or so people in the 1960s. By the time it closed in 2004 only nine workers remained; since then it has remained derelict and half-demolished until the new Tannery development in 2015.

Sunday School 1934

The Methodist Sunday School. William Warner was a preacher there and went on to become one of the first Methodist preachers to take the faith to the West Indies. The area's only Victoria Cross was a pupil at Stensall school around 1900: Lance Sgt Harry Wood served in the 2nd Battalion Scots Guards and won the Military Medal in 1914 for showing 'true grit' in Belgium; in October 1918 he demonstrated amazing bravery when his unit cleared the village of Saint-Python (Northern France) in the allies' final push of the war and was awarded the VC.

Strensall school pupils

Robert Wilkinson VC Primary School

The first school was a thatched cottage built in 1718 from an endowment left by local farmer Robert Wilkinson in his will. This paid the schoolmaster's wages; five pupils were on the roll. A larger school was built in 1807 then demolished in 1857 to enable a yet larger school to be built – the Endowed National School for ninety-three children. The older picture shows pupils at Strensall school in Edwardian days while the newer shows a recent visit to today's school by a truly versatile Victorian gentleman:

'Year 5 experienced a visit from a Victorian teacher called Mr Cade. We sat in rows and he taught us arithmetic using slates and slate pencils to write with. Some of us were lucky because we got to use inkwells and ink pens. Later he came back as a butler from Castle Howard. He showed us some rich children's toys. There was an egg and cup, a spinning top, a Diablo and many other toys we still use today. However, he told us the life of a servant was completely different because they never had time to play and just worked, ate and slept.' by Benjamin Mould and Benjamin Brown. Note the cane ready to be deployed.

Half Moon Inn

Looking toward The Village with the Half Moon on the left. Henry Nattriss was landlord in 1890. The pub's name may reflect the old tradition where large houses (including those owned by the church as here) were often open to travellers for food and drink; signs such as a half moon would have indicated that, as in this case, the (public) house was a place of refreshment. Alternatively it may be connected with the Earl of Northumberland whose badge was a half moon; the Earl was a friend of William Poteman, Prebendary of Strensall. The existing building was rebuilt in 1830 on the site of the earlier tavern. Messers Bellerby and Jackson owned the pub in 1849. The building projecting out into the street on the left was Bellerby Square, now demolished.

CHAPTER 3

Huntington

Broken Bell Ropes, Zeppelin Raids and Potato Pickers

Opened in 1877 the Board School was an extension of an earlier one classroom parish school. There were forty-nine pupils on the roll and parents had to pay until 1891 when education was made free for all. Fees were 2*d* for infants, 4*d* for juniors and 6*d* for seniors; a fourth child went free if the others were infants. The fine for non-payment was a crippling 5*s*. Entries from the school day book provide an interesting, sometimes poignant, commentary on the times:

8th December 1879: School closed on account of the Scarlet Fever for 5 weeks. 25 cases have occurred one of which terminated fatally. The child that died was aged 10 – one of the brightest and best behaved in the school.

8th May 1883: The bell rope broke this morning and we are unable to summon the children to school for a day or two.

28th November 1916: The absences this morning are chiefly due to the Zeppelin Raid last night.

8th November 1918: Nearly 50% of the children are absent, picking potatoes.

The Board School and the Memorial Hall

By the 1920s the growing number of pupils necessitated the use of the Memorial Hall (*see new photograph*) in Strensall Road (built in 1921) until the older pupils moved to Joseph Rowntree School in 1941. The Hall was built by local men back from the war who gave their services free. They used bricks from Wray's Brickyard, where Birch Park is now. There is a Roll of Honour in the entrance for the dead, injured and those taken prisoner. Huntington lost thirty men in the First World War war and twenty-six in the Second World War. Huntington's population in 1801 was 312, by 1901 it had doubled to 631; in 1961 it had grown to 5,681 thus necessitating a new junior school. This duly opened in 1962 in North Moor Road with 260 pupils on the roll.

Outside the Yorkshire Clubs Brewery, New Lane

The Loco Brewery moved from Chapmangate, Pocklington in 1934 into a purpose built factory in New Lane. Up to fifty workers were employed, some of whom were housed in Brewery Cottages, which survive to this day along with the iron railings which were in front of the brewery building. The brewery vehicles photographed here during the Second World War have had their headlamps masked (so that they could not be seen) and mudguards painted white (so that they could be seen) in the blackout. The brewery closed in 1968 and was demolished in 1973. Note the personalised license plate on the left-hand truck? The new photo depicts The Blacksmith's Arms in The Old Village.

Butter Cross in Church Lane

The butter cross is a type of market cross dating from medieval times. Its name tell us that they indicated the place in the market where people from the surrounding area would come to buy locally produced butter, milk and eggs. The dairy produce was displayed on the circular stepped bases of the cross.

The house on the right was badly damaged when a Wellington bomber crashed on the houses opposite the Blacksmith's Arms on the afternoon of 14 April 1943. The MK10 Wellington was from 429 Squadron, Royal Air Force based at Eastmoor and on a training flight when an engine fire caused it to crash. The pilot and four other crew were killed along with three ladies on the ground; the cottages were rebuilt with one of them appropriately named 'Phoenix'.

The church in the modern photograph is all but obscured by trees. Six of the eight bells were donated by the Mills family around 1881, one of whom had expressed a wish to be buried there; each member of the family provided a bell in payment. The church was restored in 1874; when the wooden steeple was replaced two stones of honey were found up there. Tether rings for worshippers' horses can still be seen by the entrance.

Clock Cottage

The cottage on the left was once the post office; it gets its name from the clock that was placed on the wall there in 1893 and which can be seen clearly on today's shot. It cost £8 10s, raised by public subscription. In 1953 an early seventeenth-century inglenook fireplace was discovered in the cottage by a builder carrying out alterations. It was subsequently restored to its original condition and left *in situ*.

'An Act of the Very Immoral Conduct'

These cottages were at the York end of Old Village. William Bowl and Francis Lonsdale lived there in 1843 when they were served notice to pay rent arrears within one month; in 1845 records tell us that an 'act of the very immoral conduct' was perpetrated in the house and led to the tenants' eviction. A bill for thatching in 1847 came to 13s 3d. In 1907 one of the cottages collapsed; Mrs Plowman and her two daughters were in at the time and had to escape through a window.

All Saints' Church and a Royal Pardon

'Nigel has a church and a priest' Domesday tells us. Nigel was Nigel Fossard who was Lord of the Manor in Huntington. The original church is thus dateable to before 1080. All Saints' was the setting for a royal pardon during the reign of Edward III: Cicely, wife of William Clere of Haxby was convicted with her husband of breaking and entering the church and of 'divers larcenies there and at Haxby'; but 'because Cicely was with child, her execution was deferred, and in 1345 the king, moved by pity and at the supplication of Queen Philippa, pardoned her'. As can be seen from the photo on page 66, the fine lych-gate from 1877 has now been removed.

West Huntington Hall

Sir Arthur Ingram had this built in 1629; it was restored in 1800 by Captain Sir Thomas Dowker. Other owners have included Dowager Lady Austin in 1909; Ethel Newton, local artist from 1914; the Army Kinema Corporation in 1948 (an organisation based in Croydon, responsible for providing the British Army wherever it was in the world with film entertainment); and Peter Gray, a dentist, in 1960. Dowker's daughter, Rosamund, married Lord Allan Spencer Churchill, third son of the Duke of Marlborough in July 1846. A true gallant, Churchill, stationed at York cavalry barracks, when visiting her once before they were married, couldn't get over the Foss as the bridge was broken, so he borrowed a washing trough from one of the cottages next to the Blacksmith's Arms and rowed across to his fiancée.

Dowker's Swing Bridge/Barge Passing Through Dowker's Mill
Named after Captain Dowker this swing bridge at the foot of Mill Hill was built around 1800 to allow barges to pass through on the Foss. The barges, crewed by one man and a boy, were pulled either by a horse or gangs of men called halers. See page 57. The painting is by Carol Carr. The new photograph shows the bridge over the Foss at Church Lane.

The Corn Mill

Situated at the highest point of the village, Hoggard's Hill (Mill Hill) ceased operations in 1900, thus bringing to an end 700 years of milling on the site. It was also called Etty's Mill after Charles Matthew Etty, miller there from 1890–97 and relative of William Etty the celebrated York painter. The bricks from the demolished mill were used to build Mill House nearby.

Home Guard

Recruited from Huntington and New Earswick their HQ was in West Huntington Hall's coach house. They wore the cap badge of the Green Howard's and their commanding officer was a Captain Palmer, a former Royal Engineer who rode on horseback, his rifle in a leather holder strapped to his saddle. This photograph was taken on the sports field in front of Joseph Rowntree School. As in Haxby, refugees from Hull and Middlesbrough were housed in Huntington. Today's picture shows the War Memorial in the grounds of All Saints Church which commemorates thirty men fallen in the First World War and twenty-six in the Second World War.

CHAPTER 4

New Earswick

Station Avenue

The objective of the Joseph Rowntree Trust when it developed the idea of the new garden village was to provide the worker with even the lowest means a new type of house that was clean, sanitary and efficient. Rowntree's deep concern for the welfare of his workers, the research findings of his son, Seebohm, into the plight of the urban poor, his Quaker beliefs and the pioneering work on garden cities by Ebenezer Howard all combined to drive Rowntree's New Earswick. This photograph shows Station Avenue from the Folk Hall complete with garden pumping station – now sunk underground as the new photograph shows. These houses were in groups of seven with an access tunnel between the third and fourth houses. They cost £318 7s 11d to build; rent was 6s 3d per week. The Second World War Morrison air raid shelter was in Station Avenue.

Western Terrace Water pump

In Western Terrace in 1908; the houses opposite are in Poplar Grove whose gardens run down to the River Foss. As can be seen, they were built in groups of four. The architect of the New Earswick houses and the Folk Hall was Raymond Unwin whose brief from the Trust was nothing if not challenging: to provide high quality housing at affordable rents with adequate living space within restricted floor space. The houses did not all front on to the street as the living room was always situated where it could get maximum sunlight. The building programme was as follows: 1902 – 123 houses; 1902–04 – 28; 1904–19 – 229; 1919–36 – 259. Total spend on land, houses and services was £450,000.

Western Terrace

Western Terrace about 1906. To meet his brief Unwin used some of the indoor floor space as a bicycle store and a coal store, obviating the need for outhouses and thus reducing costs and allowing upstairs space for a third bedroom. The toilet was downstairs and the bath was in the kitchen under a hinged table flap. A black range was in the living room with a pantry. The first houses had earth closets which were replaced in 1906 with a water system. In 1948 93 per cent of the 530 houses had three bedrooms; one had two and the rest four or five. Separate bathrooms came in thirty new houses built in 1954.

Hawthorne Terrace

Hawthorn Terrace – here the three bedroom houses cost £422 16s 0d to build and the weekly rent was 7s 9d. Floors in New Earswick were typically lino and red quarry tiles; taps and door knobs were all brass. The twelve bungalows for older residents featured a large room which could be used as a living room/bedroom or as two separate rooms (with obvious social and financial benefits on heating costs); in addition they were fitted with alarm bells for emergencies, connected to a qualified nurses' rent-free residence. All evidence that, socially and environmentally, New Earswick was years ahead of its time. The older picture shows a New Earswick kitchen in the 1920s with all mod cons – relatively speaking.

Hawthorne Terrace Shops

Note the ornate balconies, now removed, and the mansard gables on the flats above the shops; these allowed more internal headroom in the flats. Once a year on 1 June a barrier was lowered at Station Avenue to enforce the legal privacy of access as all the roads were private and a 1*d* toll was paid by vehicles passing through. Shops in the 1930s included Howard's haberdashery, Mrs Farrell's sweet shop, Ernie Wood's chemist, Fred Wiley the cobbler, the Co-op butchers, Burrell's bakers and Coning's wet fish shop.

York Equitable Industrial Society

This Edwardian photograph shows the Co-op in Station Avenue on the right (see page 10). It was the first shop to be built in the village in 1908, with the original post office next door. Provisions continued to be delivered by horse and cart though, despite the emergence of more and more shops: milk twice a day at 7.00 a.m. and 4.00 p.m. from Crompton farm and from Sorenson's (see page 82); vegetable and fish. Today the building houses a bakery as the new picture shows.

River Foss and the Foss Navigation

Mr Bewer, crossing keeper, takes a stroll along the banks of the River Foss in between trains; the houses are in Willow Bank and face out to give a pleasant river view. The Foss was canalised by the Foss Navigation Company as far as the bridge at Sheriff Hutton in 1806, a thriving town then. It cost £35,000; 1809 provided the best toll receipts: £1,384. The horses that hauled the barges could manage a weight of 27 tons given a favourable current; the same horse could cope with only 1 ton road cargo. The opening of the York to Scarborough railway through Haxby and Strensall in 1845 and the York to Hull line through Huntington in 1847 rendered the canal commercially redundant in 1852 – the first navigation to close as a result of the railways.

Chestnut Avenue

Built 1917/18 in blocks of four with a central passageway for access. Chestnut Avenue then and now epitomises the ethos of the village: tree lined, virtually car free avenues which were and are pleasant to live and play in. Cost to build was £309. 15s 7d and rent was 6s per week if the bath was in the scullery; if it was upstairs it was 6s 8d. Nurse Atkinson lived in nearby Rowan Avenue. She was the village District Nurse and midwife from 1944 until her retirement in 1969 during which time she estimates that she delivered about 1,000 babies. Dr Riddols (see page 14) was village doctor and President of the Nursing Association: one of his duties was to collect the 2d per week from residents to pay for Nurse Atkinson.

White Rose Dairy 1904

The inspiration of Seebohm Rowntree, author of the influential *Poverty: A Study of Town Life;* he established the dairy to ensure the provision of clean milk to village residents in the knowing that contaminated milk was a factor in the high infant mortality rate. To do this he brought in a Dane, Wilfred Sorensen (known locally and geographically inaccurately as Oslo), from the Manchester Pure Milk Co and bought some land for him to build a farm on and develop a herd. For the time unusually high levels of hygiene were adopted, the milk was filtered and cooled to destroy bacteria. The modern photograph shows the dairy cows and their calves of 2015.

Folk Hall

Built in 1907 at a cost of £2,278 15s 1½d. Rowntree actively encouraged women to get out of the home and use the many facilities offered there: 'In this country it seems to be the thought that women do not need recreation', he pondered, citing the example of Germany where it was and still is the norm for families to go out together as families, with the children. One of the functions of the Hall was as a place of worship – for all faiths. However, over time a separate Wesleyan Chapel and a place for Anglican worship were established while the Society of Friends and Roman Catholics continued to use the Hall. From 1945 it was home to the village nursery until its move to the primary school in 1997. At its opening there were thirty children between two and five each paying 1s per week, mornings only.

New Earswick Musical Society

The older photograph shows a NEMS production from the 30s. The society was founded in 1914 (out of the 1912 Choral Society) as the New Earswick Dramatic Society and ninety-six years later still performs two shows every year, now in the Joseph Rowntree Theatre in Haxby Road. In 1933 the Society had 260 active members and performed a staggering twenty-four productions – Gilbert and Sullivan plays and operas – one every two weeks. Recent repertoires are much more diverse and have included *The Railway Children*, *High Society*, *Oliver* and *Hello, Dolly!* The success of the society helped raise support for a new hall with seating for 450, a well lit stage and dressing rooms in 1935. The new picture shows a recent production in the Hall.

Folk Hall Snooker

Snooker was one of the many social activities held in the Folk Hall – one of the main purposes of which was to offer societies and clubs a place in which to run activities, reflective of the interests of the residents. The first football club was formed in 1912 soon followed by the cricket club; initially both played on the green opposite the shops in Hawthorne Terrace but Westfield Beck proved a hazard and the shop windows provided too tempting target practice for the batsmen. By 1923 both teams were able to play on pitches at the newly developed 16 acre sports fields. There were also tennis courts and a bowling green and a sports pavilion. The many adult education courses espoused by the Rowntrees took place at the Folk Hall.

German Garden Association Visits New Earswick 1909

In developing New Earswick, Joseph Rowntree was heavily influenced by Ebenezer Howard's (1850–1928) vision of a kind of utopian city where citizens lived in harmony with nature. This was described in his 1898 *Tomorrow: A Peaceful Path to Real Reform*, retitled *Garden Cities of Tomorrow* in 1902. Equal opportunity, good wages, entertainment, low rents, beauty, fresh air were the aim: factors we can recognise in Joseph Rowntree's New Earswick. Howard's humanism and progressive vision was influential in other countries too, not least in Germany where the German Garden City Association, '*unseren Deutschen Vettern*', flourished. The Association embraced Howard's vision, as evidenced by their visit here on July 7th 1909. There is, however, a sinister side to the story. Theodor Fritsch (1852–1933) claimed to be the originator of the garden city concept, anticipating Howard in his 1896 *Die Stadt der Zukunft (The City of the Future)*, the 1912 second edition of which was subtitled *Gartenstad (Garden City)*. Fritsch took a highly racist perspective – completely add odds with Howard's – that later contributed to Nazi ideology and made Fritsch something of a prophet of Nazism. His other work, largely published in his journal, *Hammer*, was anti-Semitic and supremacist. Despite the fact that in 1910 German eugenicists were sitting on the board of the GGCA and the long tradition of town planning and architecture being hijacked in the name of racial cleansing and eugenics, the Association rejected Fritsch. This did not, however, stop the establishment in Bremen of a *siedlung* under the Third Reich: part garden city, part half-open prison, part eugenicistic selection centre.

VJ Day

15 August 1945 – the day on which Japan surrendered and the Second World War was over. In Japan , the day usually is known as the 'memorial day for the end of the war' (終戦記念日) the official name for the day is 'the day for mourning of war dead and praying for peace' (戦歿者を追悼し平和を祈念する日). The official celebrations and victory parade in London took place, as here in New Earswick, on 8 June 1946. National pride and celebration takes many different forms: the new picture shows the English flags which adorned so many cars and houses during the 2010 World Cup in South Africa in June and July 2010.

Jack Alan, Stationmaster
The old York–Hull line ran through New Earswick and stopped at Earswick railway station until its closure in 1965. The aptly named The Flag and Whistle pub now stands on the site, built in 1982. Hall's tannery is in the background of the inset shot. Fred Potter was the last crossing keeper before the station's closure.

New Earswick Primary School and the Suffragettes

The first school was in the Folk Hall set up in 1909 for 25 infants. The permanent school here was built 1912 for 352 5–14 year olds to save them the trek to Haxby Road. This (the 'Open Air School') was another model of enlightenment: boys and girls were taught the same subjects (science teaching was usually the preserve of boys) and all the windows faced south, opened to an extent of 18 feet and were at head level to maximise natural daylight. Each child had a notional 15 sq. feet of floor area – 50 per cent more than was required by the Board of Education then. The old photograph shows pupils enjoying themselves at the pond, now filled in.

Gardening at the Primary School

Gardening was important at both schools even without the motivation inspired by digging for victory during the war years. This shows pupils gardening enthusiastically at the primary school. Two extracts from the Punishment Book:

'28th February 1927: L. Smith age ten – running home (twice warned) two strokes – hand; 12th December 1938: N. Peacock eleven – stealing three shillings – three strokes – hand at mother's request.'
The fine clock on the cupola was donated by Joseph Stephenson Rowntree, a Quaker teacher reading to pupils.

Joseph Rowntree School – Old and New
The first Joseph Rowntree Secondary
School was opened on 12 January 1942
by Rab Butler to cater for 480 children
(in classes of forty) from age eleven from
the village and surrounding area. As
with the primary school it was nothing
if not innovative for its time, taking
advice, for example, from the National
Institute of Industrial Psychology on
ergonomic matters such as ventilation,
heating and lighting. From the very start
practical skills were valued and taught
in equal measure to academic subjects,
as the older picture here demonstrates
taken from the 1946 prospectus. Adult
education was encouraged too, in line
with the Rowntree philosophy, with an
Evening Institute of 350 students. The
June 2010 Newsletter celebrating the new
school demonstrates vividly just how
much things have changed. The Costa
Coffee franchise is the first to open in a
UK school. The image below shows the
Hub with 2015 technology and art work.

ARTS & CRAFTS

Both the Art Room and the Craft Room are larger
than usual, and each has ample storage accommodation
extending along the full width of the room. The desks
in the Art Room are fitted with hinged lids to allow of
them being used as easels. This room has been provided
with special windows, the whole of the centres being
in one large piece of plate glass. These windows face
slightly north of east, so ensuring suitable lighting for
colour work.

The girls learn weaving, embroidery, soft toy, glove
and slipper making while the boys, in addition to ordinary
bookcrafts, have constructed their own potters' wheels
in the workshop. An electric kiln has been installed for
the firing of the ware. The Trust has also provided a
printing press, together with the associated equipment,
so that the boys may practise typography, while willow
cane basketry provides a useful outlet for those who
are less skilled in crafts. Both rooms are fitted with gas
and electric points, and each is also equipped with sinks.
The closest possible contact is maintained between the
teaching of pure art, design and craft, and also between
the teaching of these subjects and that of needlework
and handicraft.

The Hub

These contemporary photographs demonstrate perfectly the modernity of the new school, designed and constructed with the same careful attention paid to lighting, space, heating and acoustics which exercised the designers of the old school. The Hub is a communal dining area complete with wide screen television. Airy and spacious classrooms can be seen on the upper floors.

Gardening at the Secondary School

The cost of the first school was £30,395 (excluding extra costs arising from war conditions) giving a per pupil cost of £63. The staff comprised the Head and seven men and seven women – each qualified in a particular subject. Special needs pupils were catered for. The school was designed as an open-air building: innovations included south facing large windows low enough for pupils to see out of when at their desks, 'capable of any required degree of opening', depending on the weather or time of year to provide optimum ventilation and lighting; ceiling heating panels; and 'the long principal corridor (which) is slightly curved so as to minimise noise transmission by means of skin friction.' The modern photograph shows students transfixed by the methane bubbles experiment.

Physics, Design and Technology

Equipment included an electric kiln, a printing press and aquaria. Mechanical engineering included the conversion of an old car into a runabout truck. The new picture shows students learning the finer skills involved in drilling in a Design and Technology lesson. Today's students benefit from cutting edge laboratory facilities which are up to university and leading industry standard: nowadays these students need to be familiar and conversant with state of the art technology and equipment if they are to compete successfully in higher education and industry.

Domestic Science

Domestic science in the 1940s and 1950s included cooking by electricity, gas or coal, working in the domestic flat adjacent to the department and used by the Domestic Subjects Mistress, assisting in the village Nursery School, and feeding the animals. The gym had room for a full-sized boxing ring when required and had a radiogram and piano for use during folk dancing. The sports hall in the new school has a wooden sprung floor and can be set up for a wide range of sports including volleyball and tennis within its 595 sq meters. There is also a 57 sq. metre multi-gym with cardiovascular machines and free weights. These are complemented by six outdoor tennis or netball courts. The new photograph shows sixth-form art students at work.

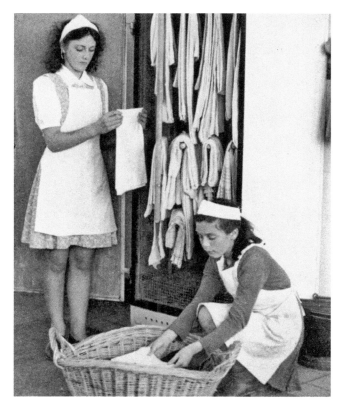

Joseph Rowntree School 1946

One hundred or so years later the new school is a fitting twenty-first century testament to Joseph Rowntree's turn of the twentieth century vision. It cost £29 million and opened for lessons in February 2010. Like its predecessors it is innovative: one of the key features is a centre for autistic children offering specialist teaching and care for all children on the autistic spectrum. In November 2009 a time capsule containing a school uniform, a prospectus and dried pasta was buried by Year 11 pupils under a paving slab at the entrance.